Peter Caton has travelled widely across the UK, by train and on foot. *Remote Stations* continues his theme of travel, railway and walking books, combining his love of interesting trains with remote places. It follows *The Next Station Stop* in which he travelled 10,000 miles around the UK comparing modern rail travel with that of his youth.

Information on all Peter Caton's books and a blog can be seen on his website *www.petercatonbooks.co.uk*.

The author is always pleased to hear from readers through his website, Facebook or Twitter.

Facebook
Peter Caton Books

Twitter
@petercatonbooks

REMOTE
STATIONS

PETER CATON

Matador
9 Priory Business Park,
Wistow Road, Kibworth Beauchamp,
Leicestershire. LE8 0RX
Tel: 0116 279 2299
Email: books@troubador.co.uk
Web: www.troubador.co.uk/matador
Twitter: @matadorbooks

ISBN 978 1789014 082

British Library Cataloguing in Publication Data.
A catalogue record for this book is available from the British Library.

Printed and bound in Malta by Gutenberg Press Ltd
Typeset in 11pt Adobe Garamond Pro by Troubador Publishing Ltd, Leicester, UK

Matador is an imprint of Troubador Publishing Ltd

To my father who introduced me to the pleasures of both railways and remote places and to my nephew Ben, a young volunteer at Didcot Railway Centre.

CONTENTS

INTRODUCTION

What better way is there to explore some of the wildest and most beautiful parts of our wonderful country than by being the only passenger to alight from a train at a deserted railway station? To watch the train depart into the distance, knowing that there won't be another for several hours, or maybe not until the next day or even the next week. To enjoy the solitude of a remote station and walk amongst mountains, hills, moors and marshes, marvelling at the engineering that brought the railway here and wondering why no one thought to close the station that hardly anyone uses.

There are 2,563 railway stations in Britain. Most are well used, serving cities, towns and villages, taking people to and from work, to shops and visit relatives. A few, but more than you might expect, serve nowhere in particular and see just a handful of passengers. They may seem insignificant but each little station has a story to tell and an importance to those who use it. Some exist simply as an accident of railway history and with no settlement to speak of attract few passengers. Others are a lifeline to isolated communities, whilst one or two really do seem to serve no purpose at all.

Combining my enjoyment of wild places and of train travel I set out to visit forty of our most remote stations, to find stories past and present and explore the countryside around them. To pick just forty wasn't easy, so a few guidelines helped. To start with I looked up a definition for remote – *'Situated away from main centres of population'* seemed adequate and suitably broad to encompass a wide range of stations.

I would choose no more than two stations on any line, include as much variation as possible and a geographical spread across the country.

Most would still be open but I'd walk to a few of our most interesting and remote stations that are long closed. Adding to the variety I would include a few stations on preserved railways.

The idea came to me as I travelled 10,000 miles around the UK comparing modern rail travel with journeys from my youth and writing *The Next Station Stop*. I'd even started making the list but then came across Dixe Wills' book *Tiny Stations*. It seemed that his *'eccentric look at lost Britain through its railway request stops'* had beaten me to it. I put the idea aside and went back to coastal walking. After a while I started to consider it again but then up popped Paul Merton with his *Secret Stations* television series based on Dixe's book.

It was a conversation with the owner of a bookshop in Abingdon that made me think again. *Tiny Stations* could be described as a travel book with a railway theme and Paul Merton didn't really talk much about trains at all. There was a place for a book written in my very different style and with the emphasis on railways. I went back to my list, edited it a bit to swap some of the stations Dixe had visited and started planning journeys.

I would start in the west of Scotland and make my way around the country in a roughly anticlockwise direction. There would be twenty one trips in total, with each railway line having its own chapter. The book would describe not only the stations themselves but anything I came across of interest on the line – people I met, idiosyncrasies of the railways and historical stories.

Not only would the stations be as varied as possible but the emphasis of the chapters would differ according to what I felt would most interest the reader. Some include stories from many years ago while others concentrate on the stations as they are now. Whilst I have described each of them this is by no means an architectural study, although as I travelled around the country I did however wonder if I was becoming an expert on railway station waiting shelters.

Information and stories came from many sources but we are fortunate to have an excellent independent bookshop in my home town of Upminster and I should thank Jeremy Scott of Swan Books (*www.swanbooks.co.uk*) for finding copies of some out of print and quite obscure publications which provided many snippets of interest.

I have illustrated my travels with 48 colour and 120 black & white photographs, both recent and historical. Unless stated these were taken by me in 2016 or 2017 but where the date or photographer differs I've noted accordingly. Many of the historical photos came from Tony and Nicky Harden (*http://stores.ebay.co.uk/railwaystationpictures/*) to whom I am grateful for permission to reproduce them.

Experience has shown that readers of railway books are often extremely knowledgeable and that some like to contact authors to point out errors. I have done my best to check facts but there is bound to be the odd mistake, so I apologise now – but please still do tell me so I can correct them in future reprints.

As I set out from Euston on the Highland Sleeper I had high expectations for my travels, but the beauty of the railway journeys, remoteness and solitude of some of the stations and the wondrous country in which they lie, surpassed them all. I had expected to uncover stories about each station, not to play a small part in one myself, but then I didn't think that someone would try to close one of my remote stations before I'd even finished the book. Nor did I expect to be making a visit to a Victorian castle and a remote hospital, or to find a station that had closed before it officially existed.

My adventures were to take me to some wonderful places – the top of a snowy mountain, remote hills, moors, marshes and fens, a station a mile out to sea and to two hotels that vie for the best locations I've ever stayed at. I left almost every station wishing to return one day. I hope I will but also that the tales of my travels might encourage a few others to seek out our most remote railway stations and the wonderful scenery amidst which many of them sit.

MAP I

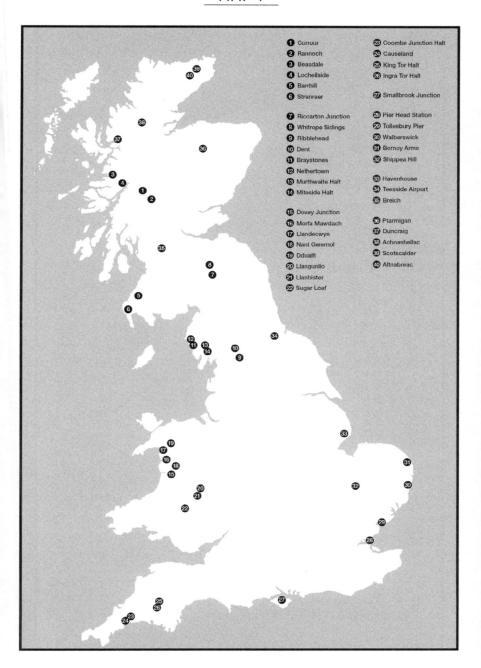

1. Corrour
2. Rannoch
3. Beasdale
4. Locheilside
5. Barrhill
6. Stranraer

7. Riccarton Junction
8. Whitrope Sidings
9. Ribblehead
10. Dent
11. Braystones
12. Nethertown
13. Murthwaite Halt
14. Miteside Halt

15. Dovey Junction
16. Morfa Mawddach
17. Llandecwyn
18. Nant Gwernol
19. Dduallt
20. Llangunllo
21. Llanbister
22. Sugar Loaf

23. Coombe Junction Halt
24. Causeland
25. King Tor Halt
26. Ingra Tor Halt

27. Smallbrook Junction

28. Pier Head Station
29. Tollesbury Pier
30. Walberswick
31. Berney Arms
32. Shippea Hill

33. Havenhouse
34. Teesside Airport
35. Breich

36. Ptarmigan
37. Duncraig
38. Achnashellac
39. Scotscalder
40. Altnabreac

MAP 2 – West Scotland

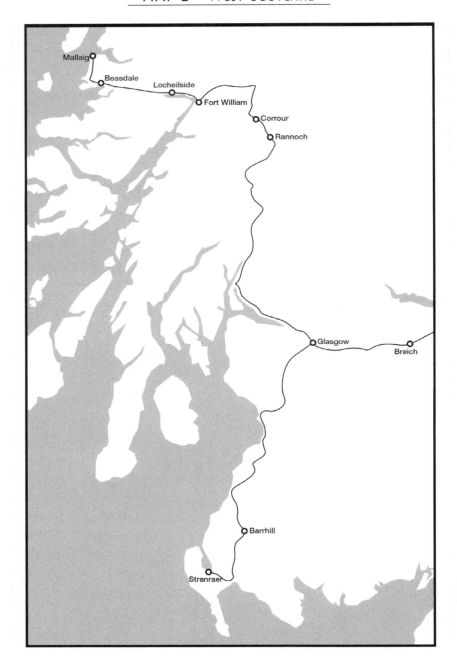

CHAPTER ONE

WEST HIGHLAND LINE: CORROUR & RANNOCH

Is there a better train journey than the Caledonian Highland Sleeper to Fort William? Board mid-evening at Euston, enjoy a civilised meal in the lounge car, sleep as the train travels to a different country, a different world, and wake as it trundles through the tranquillity of Scotland's West Highlands. And what's more, it calls at Corrour, arguably Britain's most remote station, which seemed an appropriate place to start my travels.

Euston was far from tranquil as I arrived on a cool spring evening. The concourse was packed – '*Emergency services dealing with an incident at Watford Junction*'. As commuters waited for their trains home an announcement that the sleeper was ready for boarding sent me to Platform 15, where my ticket was checked by a gentleman in what must be the smartest uniform on the railways. Coach G I was told required a long walk – a quarter of a mile. At sixteen coaches this is the longest train in Britain and I was at the very front. I'd be "*practically driving the train*". After walking 0.1% of the way to Scotland could I ask for a discount on the ticket?

Two sleepers run to Scotland, both dividing on the way, their thirty seven Scottish stops including some of our most remote railway stations. The Highland Sleeper splits at Edinburgh, with portions continuing to Inverness, Aberdeen and Fort William. Just two coaches leave London for the last of these, with two more added at Edinburgh. It's dubbed the

'*Deerstalker Express*', as amongst the walkers, tourists, travellers visiting relatives or attending to business, are a small number of well-to-do grouse shooting types. Scottish MPs use it to travel to London and the late Sir Charles Kennedy was a regular passenger. On the day of his funeral the southbound train carried a wreath in his honour. It was perhaps the influence of some of these passengers who helped reprieve the train when British Rail tried to axe it in 1995.

After checking in with the steward and ordering breakfast for the morning, I made my way to the lounge car, keen to get a seat. Fort William passengers share with those on the Aberdeen portion and it can be busy. One of the few trains to still offer a good choice of cooked food, travellers were soon tucking into plates of haggis, burgers, pasta and the like.

On this most British of trains, the majority of the passengers were couples of mature years. I chatted to two of the exceptions; a young lad Ben and his mum, who had travelled down from Leeds and were going to Fort William for an Easter treat. Ben liked trains. He jumped up and down with excitement as we pulled out of Euston. His fluffy rabbit sat on the table as they enjoyed dinner. The rest of us, excited or not, managed to stay in our seats and if anyone else had brought a soft toy it was safety tucked up in their cabin.

As we headed north, one by one (or more precisely two by two – I was the only single diner), passengers settled bills and retired to their berths. I said goodnight to Ben and his mum and headed down the narrow corridors, meeting another interesting lady. Passengers talk on the sleeper. She worked on Ardnamurchan, a wonderful part of Scotland – one that I'd visited for tidal islands but never had a railway. Her husband was in a London eye hospital and she was returning from a visit. The sleeper provides a real service for locals, it isn't just for tourists. She was glad of company as we negotiated the next coach – in almost total darkness. A power failure meant there was no light but such events seem par for the course on the slightly eccentric Caledonian Sleepers.

Not wanting to miss the best views I'd set my alarm for 7am. The

Highland Sleeper is a rare morning when I'll jump straight out of my bed, so I was soon dressed and heading for the lounge car. Meeting the steward who'd checked me in last night I was informed that we were approaching Arachar and Tarbet and that yes the train would definitely stop for me at Corrour. I should however see the guard to get instructions. It's a request stop and only calls if required. Little tags marked the reserved breakfast tables but still bleary eyed I checked them all and couldn't find my name anywhere. The steward solved the mystery. The tables were labelled with breakfast orders – mine was 'Bacon Roll'!

To the left was a spectacular view down a deep valley to Loch Long, then to the right Loch Lomond, the water dead still on a cool spring morning. Patches of snow still lay on the mountains opposite. It was a good time of year to travel, before leaves obscure many of the views. I chatted to a Peter and Fiona, a couple travelling from Kent to Fort William, as the locomotive pulled its little train of just four coaches beyond Loch Lomond to Crainlarich, junction for Oban and once for Callandar too. Surrounded by mountains, in most places this would count as a remote station, but with a population of 185 on the West Highland Line it's almost a metropolis.

Soon we traversed a horseshoe curve, built because there wasn't enough money for a viaduct, then ran along mountainside to Bridge of Orchy. From here the train climbs towards Rannoch Moor, passing Gorton, once a private station and one of the remotest on the line, but now just a loop used by engineers. There was once a school here, held in a railway carriage on the platform.

Of all the challenges facing the West Highland Railway's engineers, the greatest was negotiating the inhospitable peat bogs of Rannoch Moor, one of Europe's last wildernesses. No roads crossed this uninhabited plateau, standing a thousand feet above sea level and surrounded by mountains. Even today there is only one and that's near the edge. A railway built by traditional techniques would just disappear into the bogs, but by floating the track on a raft of brushwood and heather the line was taken across this most desolate yet beautiful of places. Beyond Rannoch station the railway crosses a viaduct and traverses the wildest part of the moors – a landscape that sees trains and deer but rarely people. A clump of trees ahead, planted to provide a little shelter, indicated that we were approaching Corrour, my first remote station.

My instructions were to make my way to the guards van as only that door would be opened. Here I found I wasn't the only passenger alighting. I'd come from Essex, the other had travelled a little further – from Japan. She'd flown into Heathrow last night, boarded the sleeper and was now meeting a friend who worked on the estate. Soon I was alone on the platform, with three hours to explore what is truly a remote spot. The highest mainline station in Britain, Corrour is ten miles from the nearest public road and has just one house.

*On a Wet Morning the Author Watches the Highland Sleeper Depart Corrour
and his Adventures Begin
(Peter Wilson)*

REMOTE STATIONS

The Highland Sleeper Departs Corrour

Before the railway came there was just moorland here and the station owes its existence to Sir John Stirling-Maxwell, the 10th Baronet of Pollock, who allowed the West Highland Railway Company to build the line across his land, on the condition that they provided a station serving his estate. Guests visiting for deer stalking and grouse shooting were conveyed from the station by horse drawn carriage to the head of Loch Ossian, from where a small steamer took them to his shooting lodge. Although a private station, Corrour was used by the general public almost from the outset but did not feature in the public timetable until 1934. The station still serves the estate and Loch Ossian Youth Hostel, but most people alighting onto the platform with moors and mountains on all sides are walkers. A surprising 12,000 passengers use it every year and on summer weekends the station can be packed with hikers.

With so few roads in the area the West Highland Railway found that additional traffic came from unexpected sources. Fifteen miles west of Corrour, at the head of the picturesque Loch Leven is the village of Kinlochleven. In the early years of the 20th century this was a haphazard settlement which had sprung up around the British Aluminium Company smelting works. Navies based here built the first large Highland hydroelectric scheme but it was a lawless place, resembling a Wild West frontier town, with gambling dens and saloons. There were no local policemen to keep order, just the two officers who came once a week to escort the postman on his round. With no roads to Kinlochleven the railway provided land access for navies, albeit by a fifteen mile walk across the moors from Corrour. It was a dangerous journey but some of those making it were escaping from justice, seeking anonymity amongst the rough navies of Kinlochleven. On one occasion police officers from Glasgow heard that a wanted man had been seen at Corrour station and set out to Kinlochleven to find him. There was no trace here but a search of the moors found not only his body but the skeletons of three other unfortunate souls who had perished on the hazardous walk.

As arguably the most remote of all our railway stations, Corrour has featured in several television programmes but its greatest exposure came in the 1996 film *Trainspotting*. Despite the title the film is about heroin addicts not trains but featured Corrour when four lads from Edinburgh came to sample the great Scottish outdoors.

Exploring the station doesn't take long – just a small shelter on an island platform, which with no door seemed somewhat inadequate for such an exposed location. The small signal box, redundant after radio electronic token block replaced traditional semaphore signals, was listed by Historic Scotland in 2014. When it was built in 1894 the design had to be modified on instruction of the estate owners who wanted it to match the waiting room. This was sadly destroyed by fire, hence the current rather rudimentary facilities. There was once a footbridge but this was moved one stop south to Rannoch and passengers now follow a path across the tracks.

In light drizzle I set out along the track to Loch Ossian, reaching the tiny youth hostel after a mile. Housed in what was once the waiting room for the steamer, the eco-hostel is an ideal base for climbing nearby Munros and provides reasonable facilities, albeit without a fridge. Guests are advised to keep perishables in the north facing wash room, or the loch! Continuing south of the loch for another mile or so, I sat on a rock

Corrour

Undated Photo Prior to Removal of Footbridge
(Tony & Nicky Harden)

for a while enjoying the beauty of the views to surrounding mountains and the solitude of remote Scotland – and getting gradually wetter!

Back at the station I was in time to see the next train north. Four couples with rucksacks alighted, along with a family, plus the obligatory one man and his dog. Within minutes all had dispersed into the hills. Crossing the tracks once more I followed the path north to Corrour Summit where a sign marks the highest point on the line, 1,350 feet above sea level.

Highest Point on the West Highland Line – Just North of Corrour

By now quite wet, I sought refuge from the rain in Corrour Station House, Corrour's only dwelling. Built to Swedish design in 2000, this has provided accommodation and refreshment for walkers, albeit with several gaps when ventures have failed. There were new owners again this year and the bar was open. They live here all year but open only from March to October, as few people get off the trains in winter. The thirteen off the train from Glasgow this morning I was told was unusual.

I was the only passenger to board the 12.30 to Glasgow but another nine got off. All carried the rucksacks which it seemed were compulsory for anyone leaving the train here and were soon setting off to explore Corrour's remarkable scenery. There's not much else to do here unless you enjoy killing animals. Alighting at Rannoch after a twelve minute run back across the moors, passing snow fences and deer, I was met by Scott from Moor of Rannoch Hotel. It wasn't a long walk – about 100 yards to the most distant of Rannoch's three houses.

When one thinks of railway towns the likes of Crewe, Swindon and Doncaster come to mind but Rannoch is a railway hamlet. Nothing existed here until the Victorian engineers brought the railway across the moor, the hotel being built to provide accommodation during its construction. Had an earlier plan succeeded to take the line to the coast down Glen Coe the settlement of Rannoch Station would never had existed.

The approved route was challenging to say the least, requiring ledges cut into mountainsides, numerous bridges, viaducts, and most difficult of all, crossing the hostile peat bogs of Rannoch Moor. Five thousand men worked for five years to build what at 101 miles was the longest stretch of British railway ever to be constructed at one time. The HS2 High Speed Line is expected to take double this to reach Birmingham from London, and this with modern machinery and through far easier terrain.

Returning to the station I enjoyed lunch in its busy tea room, catering for railway travellers, walkers and tourists who drive up the long road beside Loch Rannoch. For a settlement of six people Rannoch has a remarkably busy station. With just three trains each way per day, plus the sleepers, there are long gaps, although I never found the station deserted. A small exhibition in a waiting room illustrates the history of the railway and the old signal box, like that at Corrour redundant since the line went over to radio signalling in the 1980s, stands well preserved on the platform. It's open to visitors, few of whom can resist a tug on the levers.

Like most of the West Highland Line stations, Rannoch has a single island platform with distinctive Swiss chalet style buildings that were designed by Glasgow architect James Miller. It's an attractive building in a wonderful setting. At the north end of the platform is a bust of Mr J.H. Renton, one of the West Highland directors, who used some of his personal fortune to save the railway from bankruptcy when financial crisis threatened to thwart its completion. When the final length of rail was laid in September 1893 he was given the privilege of driving home the last spike. His bust was sculpted into a huge boulder by railway navies and has stood on the platform ever since.

With rain having given way to warm sunshine I set off for an afternoon's walk. Starting from such a remote moorland station one could walk in any direction. It's twenty miles to Glen Coe, or eleven to Corrour but I chose a less ambitious stroll to Loch Laidon and into the forest that covers much of its northern bank. It was a lovely walk with views across the water to snow-capped mountains. An unusual feature at the top of the loch is a sandy beach, through which a stream flows from Dubh Lochan, a small loch beneath the station.

As someone was kind enough to open a tea room on such a remote station I felt it was my duty to fully patronise it, so returned for cake, getting the last available seat, despite there being no train for another two hours. Rannoch station is one of the few on our network to be a destination in its own right. Nor are there many where wild deer can be seen within yards of the platforms but wandering back towards the hotel I met half a dozen, including a huge stag by the roadside. Every afternoon the couple in the cottage by the station feed them with vegetable scrapings from the hotel, supplemented by reduced price fruit from Morrison's in Fort William, to which the lady travels by train every fortnight. Not many wild deer get to enjoy juicy mangoes and pineapples.

It was deer that brought patronage to the new station when the line opened in 1894 (or more precisely those who like shooting them). In order to boost both passenger and freight traffic during the shooting season the West Highland constructed the lane across the moor from Loch Rannoch, the only road to touch the railway for thirty two miles

Local Wildlife at Moor of Rannoch Hotel

after it leaves the A82 at Loch Tulla. A venison slide was built at the station, down which deer carcasses were slid from the road directly into waiting trucks.

There was a wonderful south facing vista from my room at the Moor of Rannoch and a good view of the railway, which seemed to go through long periods of quiet punctuated by a few minutes of activity, especially when trains pass each other here. In such a place it didn't seem right to stay inside for long, so another wander took me back to the station where the third southbound train of the day was passed by a northbound freight on its way to the Fort William Alcan aluminium smelter. The station bridge provides views of all the railway comings and goings and is a good spot to gain an impression of the vastness of Rannoch Moor.

And so to dinner. I'm not used to staying in the sort of hotel where guests gather in the lounge, peruse a menu over drinks and are escorted to their table once the food is nearly ready to serve. I hope I behaved appropriately. It was all very friendly. Remote hotels, like railway restaurant cars, tend to attract interesting people and over an excellent dinner, then cheese and biscuits back in the lounge, we talked of travel, trains, books and football. All in all a very refined and enjoyable evening. I did have to excuse myself for a few minutes – the southbound sleeper was due. From my footbridge vantage point I watched the locomotive and coaches that had brought me to Corrour this morning cross the last northbound service, then the station go to bed for the night.

Trains Pass in the Night at Rannoch

Undated Photo of Rannoch
(Tony & Nicky Harden)

Breakfast next morning was enjoyed with the good company of other guests and of several deer who looked in through the dining room window, perhaps hopeful of some Fort William mangoes. One night hadn't been long enough but soon I was leaving Rannoch, heading north to Fort William. As we climbed over the moors it started to snow.

The Highland Sleeper Departs Rannoch for Fort William

From Corrour (which I'd now found is pronounced Kerr – Our) the line descends, passing snow shelters that were erected after blizzards blocked the tracks in its first winter. Soon the railway runs above the lonely 5½ mile long Loch Treig, which with no roads is so inaccessible that when a freight train derailed here in 2012 the driver had to be rescued by helicopter and the locomotive cut up on site, there being no way of retrieving it from the mountainside.

The remoteness of the railway has often caused problems in winter snow but there was one occasion when it led to a drama on the train. A doctor and his wife were travelling back to Dorset from a fortnight's walking when the guard came through the train in an agitated state asking if there was a nurse on board. Enquiring of the guard as to what may be wrong he was told that they were about to have another passenger. A lady was in labour and with the train approaching Tulloch there was nowhere suitable to put her off for many miles. She was moved to a first class compartment and the doctor attended, assisted by his wife and the Marchioness of Bute, who was travelling in the next compartment. The Marquess of Bute contributed by sharing some of his painkillers, while the ladies collected towels from the lavatories and boiling water from the dining car. By good fortune a nurse travelling back to Canada boarded at Crianlarich, just in time to assist with the birth which concluded with the arrival of a boy forty minutes out of Glasgow. An ambulance was waiting there for mother and baby, who was named Evan McLeod after the nurse and doctor.

The line bends sharply west at Tulloch, another station serving just a few houses, but also a bunkhouse hostel in the converted station building. Here the scenery changes, with moors and mountains replaced by spectacular gorges as the track runs beside the fast flowing River Spean.

Spean Bridge station was once the junction for Fort Augustus on Loch Ness, the railway a hopelessly optimistic venture that closed to passengers in 1933, just 30 years after opening. It was from Spean Bridge that on 29th January 1889 a party of seven men set off by horse-drawn coach on what was to become a legendry expedition to investigate the proposed route across Rannoch Moor. It is a story that merits retelling.

The group, comprising of civil engineers (including Robert McAlpine of whom we shall hear more later), estate managers and a solicitor, were hardly suitably attired for a forty mile journey, which at best could be described as intrepid and more probably as foolhardy. With no roads they walked the final 2½ miles to the north shore of Loch Treig, progress delayed as their guide had failed to show and again when the boatman who was to take them down the loch didn't appear until dusk was falling. As he rowed an ancient craft on the stormy loch with sleet falling, the vessel started taking in water and the travellers used their boots to bail. Had it not been for two gamekeepers who saw their plight and took them in their own boat, the journey may well have ended in the icy loch. Arriving at Lord Abinger's shooting lodge, cold, wet and hungry, they found that the messenger tasked to warn of their approach had not appeared and neither food nor beds were ready.

Next morning they climbed 1,300 feet to the edge of Rannoch Moor, where their guide pointed to the direction they should take then returned to the lodge. What a sight the men would have made as they squelched their way through the bogs, walking in single file, some carrying umbrellas and wearing felt hats as rain alternated with sleet. They had arranged to meet Sir Robert Menzies of Rannoch Lodge at a spot in the wilderness by the River Gauer but on reaching here met only his head keeper who invited them to stay the night at the lodge. Foolishly they declined and although the nearest cottage was 8 miles away and their ultimate destination 14 miles distant, trudged further into the moor. With dusk due in three hours they soon realised their error and in failing light struggled to distinguish footholds from bog, sometimes falling headlong into the peaty water.

Soon five of the party could go no further and the other two went for help. McAlpine, despite having no knowledge of the moor and little sense of direction, set off alone in the hope of reaching Inveroran. James Bulloch, the chief engineer, had limited experience of the moor from earlier surveying and set off for the cottage at Gorton. At this time of course there were no houses at either Corrour or Rannoch. After falling and lying unconscious for four hours, Bulloch groped his way along a fence, which led him to a track and eventually Gorton Cottage, where help was summoned.

Meanwhile back on the moor the remaining group had split into two. Jon Bett, the 60 year old manager of Breadalbane Estates, had lapsed into unconsciousness and the two men with him tried to keep warm by running round in circles. During the process they lost Bett, so on finding him tied a handkerchief to an umbrella that was providing a makeshift shelter. At 2.30am shepherds from Gorton reached the three men and soon found the other two not far away. Bett, still semiconscious had to be half carried, half dragged to a small hut that the rescuers knew of two miles away. Returning in the morning the shepherds brought food and soon the men were able to continue to Gorton, where they met Bulloch. News was received that McAlpine too was safe, having reached a cottage after 14 hours alone on the moor. During the following night, which was spent at Inveroran, a blizzard broke and the party had to climb over deep snowdrifts as they made their way to Tyndrum station on the Callander & Oban Railway. Had the snow come a day earlier it is doubtful that they would have survived that night on Rannoch Moor.

I was glad to be in the warmth of the ScotRail's train as we approached Fort William beneath the mass of Ben Nevis, an appropriate finale to a railway line remarkable for so many reasons, not least its remote stations. My journey however was not ending here. Seven years after reaching Fort William the West Highland Line Extension opened to Mallaig, and as the train reversed I stayed in my seat, heading north in search of more of Scotland's remotest stations.

CHAPTER TWO

WEST HIGHLAND EXTENSION: BEASDALE & LOCHEILSIDE

The large gathering of passengers on Fort William station just fitted into the four coach train heading north. Probably the most scenic line in Britain and definitely one of the world's great railway journeys, this is a popular run for tourists. Every day in summer two steam trains run to Mallaig, both packed with visitors enjoying the spectacular views. It was not however for tourists that the West Highland constructed the railway, but for fish and without this business the line had no prospect of paying its way.

Although they had reached the sea at Fort William, its position at the head of Loch Linnhe was far from the lucrative west coast fishing grounds and had no easy access to the Western Isles. The West Highland from Glasgow had been built through swathes of sparsely populated land but at least reached a town of significant size. The Extension was also to pass through remote areas with just a few isolated communities but for this line there was no obvious terminus. A harbour had to be built and Mallaig Bay, four miles south of Loch Nevis, was selected. As the West Highland constructed the forty mile railway, the tiny community of crofter-fishermen was developed into a port and the town of Mallaig soon became a major fishing centre. The railway's first sod was cut by Lady Margaret Cameron of Locheil on 21st January 1897 and the line opened just four years later.

With only three trains a day I'd worked out a complicated plan to visit Beasdale and Lochielside, but avoid spending six hours sitting by a loch. Giving the bonus of traversing most of the line and a night by the seaside, I travelled first to Arisaig, the most westerly station in Britain.

As we pulled out of Fort William the guard told us to "*listen very carefully, I will say this only once*", before explaining that passengers for all stations before Mallaig were to alight at the middle doors. This is another line with remote stations that don't merit a long platform. A trip to the toilet led to a rather awkward moment when I pressed the button to open it and found a lady on the throne. I understood that she wasn't happy but not why it was my fault that she hadn't locked the door, however it wasn't really appropriate to debate the matter.

Leaving the main line at Inverlochy, we crossed the River Lochy on an iron bridge with castellated piers, which was designed to be sympathetic with the adjacent Inverlochy Castle, then the Caledonian Canal with a good view of Neptune's Staircase. This series of eight locks is the longest staircase lock in Britain. After Corpach the line runs beside Loch Eil which is served by two remote stations; Loch Eil Outward Bound, which opened in 1985 to serve the adjacent Outward Bound centre, and Locheilside, which I would be visiting tomorrow. The train ran at a good pace along the rare stretch of straight track beside the loch, then into the valley towards Glenfinnan.

Here we slowed, not only for the curves but to allow passengers to take photos of the viaduct made famous by Harry Potter, who crossed it on the Hogwarts Express. To the left is Glenfinnan Monument to the highlanders who followed Bonnie Prince Charlie in the 1745 Jacobite rebellion. The attractive station building contains a museum and a coach in the siding provides refreshments.

The twenty one span viaduct, one of more than a hundred bridges on the route, was built by Robert McAlpine, head of the Glasgow contractors constructing the line – the same Robert McAlpine who had survived the walk across Rannoch Moor in 1889. He was known as 'Concrete Bob' for his enthusiasm to make use of what was a fairly new building material. His 28 year old son Robert was appointed to take full charge of the railway's construction with his younger son Malcolm as assistant.

It was Malcolm who solved the problem of slow progress in drilling into the hard rock for the line's many tunnels and cuttings resulting from insufficient air from steam compressors. The solution came to him while sitting in a dentist's chair in Helensburgh. He noticed the dentist activating the drill by pressing a knob on the floor with his foot and was told that this released a high pressure water flow onto a Pelton wheel, which powered the drill – a water turbine. Malcom had a special turbine built, which was attached to a compressor and powered by water falling 140 yards from Loch Dubh, where a 7 foot dam had been constructed.

Having left a few passengers to explore Glenfinnan we continued into the mountains, soon to reach Loch Eilt and one of the most beautiful stretches of the line. Here the railway runs on the opposite bank to the road, with superb views to the loch, its tree covered islets and the mountains beyond.

I had considered visiting Lochailort, the next station and one of the three request stops on the line, but decided that despite serving just a few houses, a hotel meant it wasn't the most remote. There's a lot of competition for remotest station on the West Highland lines. During the railway's construction a camp at Lochailort housed 2,000 of the 3,500 navies working on the line. The school house was converted into an eight-bed hospital staffed by two nurses and a doctor and was the first hospital to be set up on a construction site in Britain. One of its few serious casualties was young Malcolm McAlpine, who was badly wounded in a blast when supervising a rock cutting. The doctor found that he had a fractured pelvis, broken ribs and internal injuries from rock fragments, so a telegram was sent to his father Robert McAlpine (senior) in Glasgow, telling of the grave injuries and saying that he wasn't expected to live. There followed a most remarkable rescue operation.

Sir William Macewen, Glasgow's most distinguished surgeon, agreed to travel to Lochailort but the last Fort William train had already left. A special was arranged but on reaching Craigendoran found that the West Highland was closed. The driver had been instructed to proceed no further but was eventually persuaded to continue with McAlpine saying he would take full responsibility. After negotiating the closed line they arrived at Fort William at 5am. A coachman was roused and after seven hours over the terrible road they reached Lochailort where Malcolm was found to be still alive but very poorly. With few instruments Macewen performed a major operation then sat with his patient for four days and nights, before deciding that the only hope of saving Malcolm's life was to get him to Glasgow.

The jolting of a road journey would have killed him, so eight navies carried the patient by stretcher two miles to the shore of Loch Eilt where a boat was waiting. From the end of the loch it was a gruelling four mile trek to Glenfinnan where they spent the night, a window having to be removed from the hotel so that the stretcher could be taken in. At first light Malcolm was carried a further two miles to the closest point then reached by the railway, where a locomotive and van were waiting. To prevent the patient being jarred a long chain coupling was provided and navies sat facing each other in two rows, one on the wagon and one on the engine's buffer beam, their legs touching to absorb the shocks as the train proceeded slowly to Lochielhead. From here a steamer took the stretcher to Banavie where a special train was ready to take the party to Glasgow. On arrival the navies carried the stretcher through the city's streets to Professor Macewen's nursing home where Malcolm could receive the treatment he needed. His life was saved and the later to be Sir Malcom McAlpine lived until 1967.

Approaching Beasdale we were back by the sea at Loch nan Uamh. There was no stop at the request station and in nine minutes we were at Arisaig, a village which predated the coming of the railway. A mail coach ran three times a week, taking 7½ hours to reach Fort William. There was once a ferry to Skye and boats still run to the Small Isles of Eigg, Muck and Rhum. The pretty village standing on Loch nan Ceall is much improved since a new road bypassed the centre. When passing through Arisaig to walk to a tidal island I'd added it to my long list of places to come back to 'one day' and the West Highland's timetable provided an excellent opportunity. My carefully planned schedule included a sandwich from the only shop and checking in at the Arisaig Hotel, before starting the walk back to Beasdale.

The five mile walk took me through a herd of moody cows and alongside the fast flowing Brunery Burn, as I ascended a wooded valley towards Arisaig House, the reason for Beasdale station. Having ventured beyond private signs to seek shelter from a shower under a large oak tree, I decided against extending their unknowing hospitality by sneaking closer for a photo.

Now a high quality guest house, the current Arisaig House was built in 1939, after the original 1863 shooting lodge burnt down, but soon requisitioned by the military for top secret operations. The building's isolated position and single access road made it ideally situated to be sealed off as a Special Protected Area and the house was chosen as base for SOE Special Training School STYS21. It was here that some 3,000 allied agents were trained for work behind enemy lines, including the assassination in Prague of Reinhard Heydrich in 1942. Beasdale station provided easy access for the training school's staff and students.

The final section of the walk was along the main A830 road, the Road to the Isles. A hail storm raised two questions. Why do we get wet when the hailstones just bounce off clothes and why didn't I put on waterproof trousers until it had almost stopped? I was soaked when arriving at Beasdale and still quite damp boarding the train fifty minutes later. The wait gave me ample time to explore the tiny station, which although built for private use also catered for the public from its opening, with steady custom all year round.

It was a pleasant little station with plenty to investigate. A white wooden fence ran along the length of the platform and either side of the entrance. Across the single track a stream babbled as only streams can. Behind it was moorland with a scattering of trees. Shelter was provided by an attractive wooden hut, from which dangled three

Glasgow-bound Train Heads South from Beasdale

hanging baskets, their blooms not yet open. The station house, which is now a holiday home, was shuttered up. No one was at home. The single platform was covered in pinkish gravel, with not one piece of litter. Indeed Beasdale, as a plaque proudly proclaimed, is holder of a Bronze Tidy Station Standard. Behind the station on the exposed hillside grew some seriously old and twisted trees.

Travellers were well provided with information. A sign indicated the directions of travel for Mallaig and Fort William. Another advised of onward travel information. There is no taxi rank but buses stop at the roadside. A help point gave two options; one for unspecified 'help' and one for people needing urgent assistance – 'emergency'. Two signs, one slightly skew whiff, advised that smoking wasn't permitted.

I sat for a while on the station seat until a brief hailstorm sent me scurrying into the shelter. This stopped as suddenly as it had started and I resumed my inspection of Beasdale's fine little station. Two large and slightly mysterious grey electrical boxes had been manufactured by Samuel James Engineering of Leicester. I looked them up later and found they are *'one of the UK's leading suppliers of LV switchgear and control systems for the rail industry*', so now I know where to go should I ever have need for an automatic changeover panel. Square pots filled with flowering daffodils had been manufactured by Errington Reay & Co Ltd, the wording adding *'established 1878'* lest anyone think that ScotRail might have purchased them from some inexperienced pottery maker. Finally the track; jointed with wooden sleepers.

Tidy Station Plaque at Beasdale

The line curves away at both ends, giving the station a suitably remote feel, although cars passing on the road outside compromised its isolation. I counted nine in five minutes, so by extrapolation about a hundred per hour. Beasdale was like a number of remote stations I was to visit – very few or no houses nearby but regular traffic on an adjacent road. With the train due I fixed my gaze intently on the cutting to the left but then looking away for an instant heard the hoot of a horn and there it was. A hasty arm extended prompted application of the brakes and the 17.18 to Mallaig stopped just for me.

After a pleasant evening at the excellent Arisaig Hotel I was back at our most westerly railway station for the 10.26 to Glasgow. Purchase of a single to Lochielside ensured that the train would call there, as this is another request stop. We slowed at Beasdale but didn't stop. At Lochailort one man boarded, clearly a regular who knew some of the other passengers. In contrast to yesterday's train north the majority of

Undated Photo of Beasdale
(Tony & Nicky Harden)

travellers were locals not visitors. A family of tourists however provided some entertainment, their eldest daughter displaying the best of teenage stroppiness in refusing to get her dad's coat down from the rack with a hopelessly unconvincing attempt to show she couldn't reach. Still we've all been there, many of us in both the teenager and parent role.

A word to the guard confirmed that we would stop at Lochielside; just for me. The station serves a few scattered cottages but there is no village and it's not an obvious starting point for walkers, so usage is small. With 86 minutes until the next train (I was to travel back north or it would have been six hours) I had to decide between a walk beside the picturesque Loch Eil, or through woods onto the mountainside. Demonstrating typical indecision I started on the former, changed my mind and came back to the railway. A sign by a cottage south of the station said that the crossing was private and for use of authorised users only, so I duly authorised myself and climbed over the padlocked gate.

It was a lovely walk on sheep-cropped grass alongside the sea loch with superb views in all directions but having jumped across one stream I had to turn back at the next which was too wide for my leap. Instead I walked north to photograph the station from the loch side and found some interesting remains in the trees. Opposite the station platform

Locheilside

and outside the railway fence was the concrete base of a building with a deep pit in it. There has only ever been a single platform here so another explanation was required. Research found that they were remains of workshops dating from construction of the railway when there was a pier at Locheilside to bring in materials.

The station was basic and without much character – much less interesting than Beasdale. A modern bus stop type shelter (without hanging baskets), a blue seat, a radio aerial with associated equipment and a few signs, were about it. Even the gravel lacked the colour of most of the platforms on the West Highland. It was however neat and tidy and perfectly adequate for the 500 or so passengers that use it each year. I hope that the similar number who use Beasdale appreciate the efforts made to keep that station looking so attractive. My Locheilside car count was twelve in five minutes, so slightly busier than Beasdale but with neither serving anywhere in particular, both were definitely remote stations.

The northbound train was the same service I'd caught from Fort William yesterday and again was busy with tourists. It was the same guard too. She greeted me as *"Mr Arisaig"* and kindly worked out that I could save six pounds by booking a return from Fort William to Morar, my next destination. She'd started work before six in the morning, travelled down to Crainlarich and would finish for the day

Station Signage – Locheilside

when we got to Mallaig. There can't be many better jobs for railway guards. Approaching Glenfinnan she told passengers to have cameras and selfie sticks at the ready and photos were duly taken as people below waved to the train.

Morar had been on my 'one day' list for more than thirty years after seeing its silver sands from a steam train on my only visit to Mallaig. After a quick lunch at the Morar Hotel, which was built in 1902 as the Station Hotel, I walked across the sands to the sea with wonderful views to the island of Rhum and back across the bay to the mountains surrounding Loch Morar.

There was a bit of a crisis on the train back to Fort William when an elderly gentleman didn't get to the only door to be opened in time to get off at Morar so was carried on to Arisaig. Fortunately he seemed remarkably unconcerned at having to wait an hour for the next train north. The pace of life is slow in the Highlands. At Fort William, the first place I'd been to with more than a single shop for three days, I boarded the sleeper for a final run through remote Scotland. The train was busy but with no business at its remotest stations. We passed through Corrour without stopping and no one joined at Rannoch where the guard swaps with the last northbound service. In what I suspected would become a common thought, I left the West Highlands with a feeling that one day I'll come back and spend a little longer around its remote railway stations.

Highland Sleeper and Mallaig to Glasgow Trains Wait at a Wet Fort William

CHAPTER THREE

GLASGOW SOUTH WESTERN: BARRHILL & STRANRAER

Ask someone to name some scenic Scottish railways and they'll invariably say the West Highland or Kyle of Lochalsh lines, maybe adding the Far North and Highland Main Line, but few will mention the Glasgow and South Western route to Stranraer. It may not have the full splendour of lochs and mountains but its varied route provides excellent views of coast, islands, hills and valleys, then wild moorland as it runs into Scotland's little-known south westerly corner.

After arriving by sleeper and completing a morning's work, I returned to Glasgow Central for the 14.12 to Stranraer, one of the few trains to run the full length of the line. Most now start at Ayr or Kilmarnock and it was only campaigning by SAYLSA, a Community Rail Partnership that saved three through trains a day.

Soon leaving Glasgow behind, it was a pleasant run through countryside to Kilmarnock where we reversed and almost all the passengers got off. The well preserved station which dates from 1846, deserves mention as an example of what can be achieved with old railway buildings. Most of the station's many rooms had been unused for many years until a small group formed a trust to bring them into use as Kilmarnock Station Community Village, including office space and meeting rooms. The station now boasts a book shop, The Killie Browser, next to Storm in a Teacup coffee shop. Further down the platform are the office of the Community Rail Partnership and the G&SWRA Records Office.

A short run to Troon brought us to the coast and views across blue sea to the Isle of Arran. It was a warm day and with no air conditioning in our two coach '156' I took the opportunity of there being few passengers to open some windows, avoiding that awkwardness of having to ask the permission of fellow travellers, knowing their response may be dictated by politeness rather than preference.

From Ayr, where the train filled up again, we embarked on an almost sixty mile journey through one of Scotland's largely undiscovered areas. Heading inland, we crossed the River Doon, called at the village of Maybole, then descended once more to the sea at Girvan, where most of the passengers alighted at the art deco station. Just sixteen of us remained for the run through Barrhill to Stranraer.

As we climbed from the town there was a superb view over the sea to the unmistakeable granite rock of Ailsa Craig. Glendourne Bank to Pinmore Tunnel is one of the steepest on our railways and its maximum gradient of 1 in 54 made our little train work hard as we headed into the Carrick Hills. At one point the single track line was so hemmed in by trees that leaves came in through the windows as we brushed branches on either side. Twice we slowed to cross viaducts before halting at the remote Barrhill station, where I was the only person to alight.

Barrhill is just as one would imagine a country village station to be. Attractive buildings on one side, a small shelter on the other, well tended flowers blooming on the platform, semaphore signals by the track and a little signal box that looked to have come out of a museum. It was only closer inspection that showed that the booking office was closed, with the building not for public use and that there was no sign of the village.

After a word of greeting to the signalman who had exchanged tokens with our driver, I set off to find Barrhill village, the reason for the station's existence. It owes its continued presence not only to the village of 300 people but because it serves a wide area, all the other stops between Girvan and Stranraer having been closed.

Northbound Train at Barrhill

Undeterred by signs showing that road to the village was closed, I continued down the hill until reaching the roadworks. Prepared to climb over walls into fields if necessary, I found progress was far simpler. In a well-planned, if perhaps not often practiced operation, work stopped as I approached. Not a word was said but a man in a hard hat approached and gestured that I was to follow. Still in silence I was led past idling machinery and a deep trench, until it was deemed safe for me to continue my walk unaccompanied. My cheery word of thanks elicited just a tiny nod of recognition as the men returned to their digging duties.

Approaching the village a sign indicated Barrhill's greatest claim to fame – Martyrs' Tomb. I duly followed a path into woods, over a footbridge across the fast flowing Cross Water and found the tomb of John Murchie and Daniel Mieklewrick who in 1685 were shot by soldiers and buried here – for the crime of carrying bibles.

The village itself lies in the valley of the River Duisk and consists mainly of two low terraces of whitewashed cottages, a pub, shop and school, plus of course a mile up the hill, its own railway station. This I returned to without difficult, the roadworks being suspended for an

REMOTE STATIONS

hour to allow people to access the station for the 'busy' trains around 6pm.

On the platform I met a lady carefully cutting dead heads from yellow pansies hanging from the small signal box. She lives in the village and gives her time to help keep the station so attractive, no doubt contributing towards the Bronze Tidy Station Standard plaque on the platform. It didn't used to be this quiet she told me, especially on market day, which was held in the abandoned brick-built buildings that I'd passed outside the village. She thought that few tourists came this way because of the midges but told me that Michael Portillo and Dorothy L Sayers had both visited, the latter featuring the station in her detective novel *The Five Red Herrings*. It would have been a brave little midge who dared to bite Mr Portillo in his political days but I hope the now more mellow television presenter was left untroubled.

Signal Box – Barrhill Station

The diminutive signal box on the down platform is the third in Barrhill's history. The first was built in 1887 and removed in 1907, the second burnt down in 1935, to be replaced by the current wooden building that was transported from Portpatrick and dates from 1908. It is the sort of signal box one expects to see at a preserved railway or a museum. The frame inside came from the earlier destroyed 'box, but was substantially renovated in the 1940s. Levers operate semaphore signals and points for the passing loop and there's even a backing signal, which allows for wrong direction moves over the points, not an instruction to reverse as Percy thought in *Thomas the Tank Engine*.

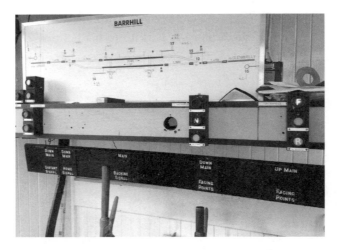

Interior Barrhill Signal Box

Barrhill is one of the last stations to possess a Tyer's Electric Tablet machine for the increasingly rare single block token system operated on the line. Tokens (or tablets) are exchanged with the driver at signal boxes along the route and ensure that only one train may enter each section of single track. Requiring manned signal boxes along the line, one suspects that this once widely used system may not survive here much longer and that one of the less romantic but more automated radio based methods will be installed.

After the 17.33 had left for Glasgow I crossed the tracks, exchanged a few more words with the pansy lady who was now watering flowers in the up station shelter and followed a path onto the hillside. From here the remoteness of Barrhill station was evident. It stands surrounded by countryside, with no houses nearby, the village out of site and the hills of Dumfries and Galloway in the background.

Unusually for a remote station Barrhill is staffed, but although the ticket office remains little changed for over 100 years, it has now closed, however the signalman is happy to assist passengers. The ringing of a bell he told me indicated that the train had left Girvan so would be here in 15 minutes. And so it was. Several passengers alighted but I was the only one to board for the spectacular run to Stranraer.

With the driver accepting a new token and the tall semaphore signal raised, we left a station that seems to belong to a bygone age and were soon in the pine trees of Arecleoch Forest, then on the open moors of south west Scotland. This is wild country as illustrated by the remains of snow fences that protected the line in years gone by when winters were harsher. There are many tales of trains becoming stuck in snow drifts, probably the most dramatic occurring in the winter of 1908.

The snow started at about midday on Monday 28th December. By early evening it was drifting on the seashore at Girvan where the 16.15 from Glasgow was waiting to depart with driver Willie McEwan and fireman Charlie Robison on the footplate. Conditions were far worse on the moors and as a northbound train approached through the blizzard its driver told his fireman to run and stop the Stranraer train departing. Officials dithered but with no precedent for halting a train, it was let go onto the steep climb to the hills. Men were digging snow from the tracks at Barrhill but again the train was sent on to battle with the storm. With no snow fences the cuttings were filling and soon the engine ran into a drift. McEwan backed out, charged at the snow and the locomotive fought through. For another mile they struggled on before the train became stuck fast in a cutting, unable to move forward or back.

Robison set out to walk to Barrhill, taking the engine headlamp with him but soon deciding it was more bother than it was worth as he floundered in the snow, he hung it on a telegraph pole cross-bar, so high had the drifts risen. An engine was despatched from Barrhill but reached only halfway before it too became stuck and abandoned in the snow. Meanwhile drifts were growing around the 16.15. There was no steam-heating and powdery snow seeped into compartments until it reached passengers' knees. It wasn't until 11 o'clock the next morning when a party from Barrhill reached the train on foot, by which time the only way to get food in was through lamp holes in the carriage roofs. With no water left in the tender McEwan and Robison abandoned the engine and retreated to a hut, an action for which they were castigated at the enquiry.

Rescue efforts continued, with a train leaving Ayr on Tuesday morning carrying a squad of Troon dockers. When this ran into a drift near Killochan the workers jumped out with the shovels. Unfortunately they left the doors open and by the time the locomotive was free and the route ahead cleared, the coaches were drifted up, outside and in! With the dockers' train stuck fast a trainload of unemployed men were gathered up in Kilmarnock and taken to Barrhill. Here, ill-clad and ill-shod, they took one look at the arctic wilderness and fled back into the train. The snow plough from Ayr was no match for the drifts so more and more engines were brought up to push. They huffed and they puffed until eventually seven of them got the plough moving but instead of rounding a curve they pushed it straight onto the moor!

On Wednesday they managed to clear the doors on one side of the 16.15 and finally release the passengers, who were walked to a relief train which took them back to Barrhill where they were lodged for the night. By Thursday morning the line round Dumfries was clear and Stranraer passengers were taken this way, arriving in the evening three days after they'd left Glasgow. For a long time there remained on the moors near Barrhill a reminder of the great drifts – an engine headlamp hanging from a telegraph pole high above the ground.

At Glenwhilly, where a seriously remote station closed in 1966, we slowed to exchange tokens. It all seemed very old fashioned. The signal box here controls a passing loop and must be one of the most isolated on the whole network. In 1947 a train was stuck here in snow for three days.

At Luce, another station which closed in 1966, there was once a siding alongside the goods shed with no buffers on it. So many wagons were shunted over the end that two firm grooves formed in the earth. This extension to the siding worked fine until one night a driver pulled off too quickly, the wheels failed to engage with the rails and the trucks took the side out of the goods shed.

Soon we turned sharp right, heading back to the sea but slowing again for the token at the charmingly named Dunragit. After 35 miles with barely a house we entered Stranraer, passed Stair Park, home of the town's football club, then suddenly emerged onto the pier beside Loch Ryan.

When I'd arrived at Stranraer in 2010 to pick up a hire car for visiting Galloway tidal islands, it was a bustling port. Sadly for the town and for the railway, a year later the ferry service to Northern Ireland was transferred to Cairnryan on the northern side of the loch. Where once foot passengers walked a few yards from train to ship, now most join a coach link at Ayr. Thirty years ago this might have brought about the railway's demise but in more enlightened times it would be politically unacceptable to sever the link to such an isolated town of 13,000 people.

It is Stranraer's isolation that qualified the station for my remote list. It's nearer to Belfast than Glasgow and 20 miles from Newton Stewart, the closest neighbouring town. As the crow flies the station is the second furthest from any other in Britain, beaten only by Berwick-on-Tweed, and in terms of railway miles it's also the second most isolated, the 25 miles to Barrhill exceeded only by Lockerbie to Carlisle. Finally, not only is the town miles from anywhere but reached by an exposed 500 yard walk beside the derelict port and its abandoned car parks, the station stands remote on a disused jetty.

Stranraer is not the most exciting place to spend a wet evening.

It attracts passing trade on the way to the ferry but not that many tourists. Even in June I was the only person on the train who seemed to be in the 'visitor' category. It reminded me of Campletown, another isolated Scottish town. That the small hotel I'd selected was slightly odd seemed fitting and with its advertised restaurant closed I dined in a chip shop, where the menu emphasised in capitals that all day breakfast was served with EITHER tea or coffee, and a sign indicated a one pound charge for non customers to use the toilet – payable in advance. Clearly Stranraer is not a place for frivolous consumption of hot drinks or reckless use of bathroom facilities.

How different it was next morning with blue sky and sunshine. I took a pleasant walk along the loch, watching ferries come and go at Cairnryan across the water, then made my way beside the fenced off port to Stranraer station. And what a contrast its ugly corrugated metal canopy makes to the pretty Barrhill. The train arrived just as I did. Three passengers ambling to a taxi were told to hurry by its driver as check in at Cairnryan closed in ten minutes. It was good to see that a few people still use the railway to link with the ferry and there is an electric bus meeting most trains, but sad to look at the old dock, now abandoned by ships, its machinery rusting. A lone seal looked up at me from the water, his doleful eyes seeming to concur.

Dating from 1862 when the line opened, Stranraer is the oldest harbour station in Scotland. Under the canopy it is much more attractive, with wooden-clad buildings housing a waiting room, booking office and toilets. A plaque tells that the station was opened after reconstruction on 2nd October 1984 by Mr J.B. Sherwood, Chairman of British Ferries Ltd. Only one of the two platforms is still in use but this is of a good length and still receives occasional steam excursions. Once up to seventeen coaches, hauled by two steam locomotives formed the Northern Irishman sleeper service which left Stranraer for London at 10pm six nights a week. Through trains ran via Dumfries until this was closed by Beeching's axe in 1965, after which the sleeper was diverted through Ayrshire until its demise in 1990.

The loss of 60,000 annual ferry passengers has affected the

Stranraer

Harbour Pier Station   Stranraer

Undated Postcard of Harbour Pier Station
One of the most changed remote stations
(Tony & Nicky Harden)

Stranraer line, to the point where some have doubted its future. Whilst in the current climate closure seems unlikely, the harbour station itself may not survive, with opinions divided as to whether it should be replaced by a new one closer to the town. Local community groups favour regeneration of the station and would like to see it as the heart of a much needed waterfront development. A £50 million scheme for housing, retail and leisure facilities on the abandoned ferry port has been agreed, so it seems that the station will remain, but hopefully that unsightly corrugated canopy can go.

As my return train slowed to collect the token on the moors at Glenwhilly I thought again what a shame it is that more people don't use the line. It's a lovely run by sea, valley and moors and perhaps regeneration of Stranraer's waterside may make it a more appealing destination. In the meantime I can recommend it for anyone who enjoys the remote country, isolated stations and the old fashioned signalling systems of our childhoods.

MAP 3 – North West England

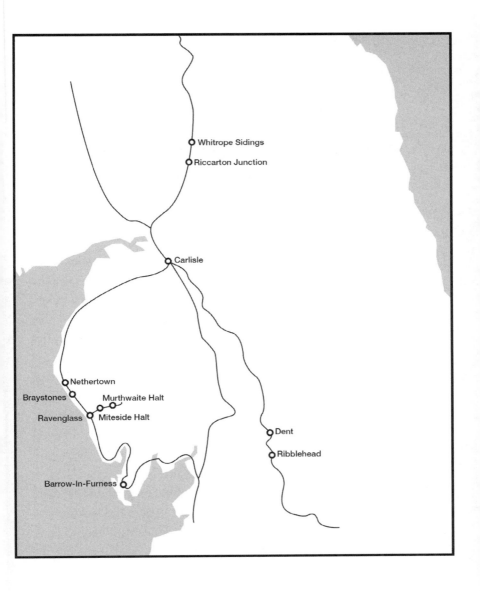

CHAPTER FOUR

WAVERLEY ROUTE: RICCARTON JUNCTION & WHITROPE SIDINGS

So I travelled north on the *Flying Scotsman*, walked 2½ miles to an abandoned railway station, the subject of an extraordinary dispute between railway enthusiasts, visited another station that closed before it existed, drove across beautiful moorland that no one seems to know about and caught a train on a railway that had been reopened after lying dormant for 46 years. My day, which also included cutting my leg on a rusty nail while sneaking into one of our most remote heritage railways, finished with watching a comedian in a Donald Trump mask, then bumping into a friend 400 miles from both of our homes, before falling asleep at Edinburgh Waverley. I was awoken by an over-enthusiastic shunter at Carstairs and then next morning by the station announcer at Euston. Perhaps I should explain.

On deciding to include a few closed stations in my remote list there was no doubt that Riccarton Junction had to feature. A station and small village that were built in the Southern Uplands purely to serve a remote railway junction, was too good to miss. That it was on the famous Waverley Route to Edinburgh, which was so controversially closed almost fifty years ago, added to the attraction, as did the tale of railway preservations feuding over its restoration.

But how to get there? Buses were few and far between and it was too far to walk. Reluctantly I hired a car in Carlisle. I could have caught one of Richard Branson's tilting Pendolinos from Euston but took a far better offer. My sister, brother-in-law and their son Ben (who anyone that has read *The Next Station Stop* may recall is very fond of trains) had a spare seat on the *Flying Scotsman* charter train from York.

The platform was packed. Orange bibbed stewards kept us behind the yellow line while a couple of British Transport Police officers maintained order. Passengers were distinctly middle class, a few families but mostly older rather than young, and here for a sedate day out on a steam train. All very British and perfectly behaved but of course there's no telling what havoc might have incurred without the restraining police presence.

A distant whistle elicited a ripple of excitement along the platform, then round the corner came the *Flying Scotsman*, backing onto its train with a multitude of cameras clicking. The locomotive provided romance but being able to remember just one journey on a service train hauled by a steam locomotive, for me it was the coaches that provided nostalgia. The Mark 1 stock, maroon in colour, with a mix of compartments and seats around tables, were just as I recalled from early childhood journeys. The toilets and buffet were as basic as I remembered but the moving metal plates between coaches no longer scared me.

Flying Scotsman at Carlisle

Being used to pootling along at 25mph on heritage railways, it was strange to be travelling at speed behind a steam locomotive as we made good time up the East Coast Main Line. Public interest in the *Flying Scotsman* far exceeds any other locomotive and at every bridge and viewpoint people waved or took photographs of our celebrity train. Soon after passing above picturesque Durham we stopped for water, then headed west, following the river along the very pleasant Tyne Valley Line. Cows and sheep, used to seeing small trains, turned and ran as our fiery monster stormed by. Mobile phones were kept in pockets as passengers chatted and looked out of the window – travel as it used to be before airline seats, headphones and laptops.

And so to Riccarton Junction. Perhaps the most controversial of Beeching's closures, the Waverley Route from Carlisle to Edinburgh saw its last through train in 1969. Completed by North British Railways in 1862, the line ran through the remote and scenic Scottish Borders, serving Galashiels, Melrose and Hawick, as well as many smaller settlements along the sparsely populated route. Most isolated of all was Riccarton Junction – thirty seven houses, two miles from the nearest road and built solely to serve the railway at its junction with the Border Counties Line to Hexham.

I parked my little grey car near Steele Road, where once a tiny wayside station served scattered houses. A signpost adorned with a small steam engine indicated 17 miles to Hawick and 2½ miles to Riccarton Junction. Cloud hung over Arnton Fell and the weather looking that it could go either way I set out equipped for sun or rain, with both waterproofs and shorts in my rucksack. A short climb along a forest track took me to the railway. This too is now a forestry track and I soon had to move aside to allow a huge articulated timber lorry to pass. If 1960s transport policy had been less short sighted it could have been on the railway, keeping lorries off the road and minimising environmental impact. I imagined a cold January night when the last passenger train travelled this way.

Dr Beeching's recommendations had been received with dismay in the Borders. It would leave Hawick (population 16,000) and Galashiels

(13,000) further from the rail network than any towns of their size in Britain. Managers in London said that there would be no disruption for passengers between Carlisle and Edinburgh as trains would be diverted via Carstairs but ignored arguments from the people of the Borders who would be hardest hit.

Support for the line was a major factor in the 26 year old Liberal David Steel (now Lord Steel of Aikwood) winning a by-election, overturning the large majority of the former Conservative who'd voted for Beeching's report. British Rail were lobbied to keep the northern end open as a branch linking Border towns with Edinburgh, but five years of arguments ended in July 1968 when Minister for Transport Richard Marsh formally announced full closure in the House of Commons.

British Rail organised farewell specials on the line's last weekend but incensed at such insensitivity, locals and railway enthusiasts protested. Saturday's train was delayed by 400 protesters carrying a mock coffin, then a bomb hoax. Sunday's was hauled by a Deltic, British Rail's most powerful diesel locomotive, but struggled to pull away on the gradient from Riccarton Junction, its wheels slipping furiously on the 200 yards of track that had been thoroughly greased by enthusiasts.

At 9.56pm on Sunday 5th January 1969 the overnight sleeper left Edinburgh for St Pancras. It was to be the final passenger train along the Waverley Route. British Rail feared trouble and sent a pilot locomotive ahead to check the line. Arriving at Galashiels the sleeper was met by huge demonstrations but continued on its way, passengers joined by Lord Steel who was travelling to London. Further protests greeted the train at Melrose and at Hawick, where the British Rail's plan to arrive ten minutes late, leaving just a very short stop, failed to thwart demonstrators. With police in attendance and 200 people on the platform, a replica coffin addressed to the Transport Minister was paraded accompanied by a piper, then ceremoniously loaded into the guard's van. The press, who had expected some demonstrations, then went on their way and Lord Steel retired to his bed, unaware that more protesters were waiting down the line.

As the train descended from the moors at Newcastleton the route ahead was blocked. Villagers had chained the crossing gates closed and were standing across the track. Led by Church of Scotland minister the Reverend Brydon Maben, they would not be budged. The minister squared up to railway officials who tried to move him and later admitted that he'd come close to punching a traffic inspector who was "*an idiot*". How good it was to see the church getting involved in the community.

Police were called but couldn't clear the line. The traffic inspector told the driver of the pilot engine to "*put pressure on the gates*", to which his response was "*If you want to drive the bloody engine, you can drive it yourself*". With seemingly no prospect of ending the impasse help was needed. The railway turned to the young David Steel MP, who summoned from his bed, in the freezing cold reluctantly addressed the demonstrators from the footbridge. Reverend Maben's response was unequivocal – "*I suggest we stay here 'til we are forcibly removed*", to which the police's response was to do just that.

The minister's arrest served only to increase the villagers' resolution. Still the police couldn't force the gates and the train could not pass. But where brute force failed diplomacy succeeded. After further discussion Lord Steel made an agreement with the crowd that if he could get the Reverend Maben released from the police station without charges, they would disperse. As the last Waverley Line train finally proceeded towards Carlisle, Lord Steel returned to his bed and the battle was lost – but perhaps not forever?

Whilst now mainly used by forestry vehicles, the track to Riccarton Junction is clearly of railway origin. A gentle gradient for walkers, although not so easy for the steam locomotives that worked the line up to a couple of years before closure, it runs on embankments, through cuttings and over bridges, all so characteristic of a double-track main railway line. Strawberries grew wild by the track, perhaps descended from seeds that once passed through railway passengers? Soon the cloud lifted and milky sunshine lit the valley where Riccarton Farm nestles by Liddel Water, a tributary of the River Esk. It was the farm that gave its name to the station, almost two miles to the north.

As the track emerged from a cutting, ahead was a large clearing

– Riccarton Junction. A track leaving to the right was the Border Counties Railway, which ran through Kielder to Hexham, but closed to passengers in 1956, the sparse local population having produced very little traffic. It had been built with hopes of exploiting mineral reserves and developed as an alternative route from Newcastle to Edinburgh, but through expresses never ran this way and with little freight traffic closure became inevitable.

Such is the growth of vegetation that one could easily pass by without realising there was ever a station here. It's hard to believe that there was once a maze of sidings, an engine shed with room for six locomotives, carriage sheds, coal depot, extensive smithy and a gas plant which powered the railway's three hundred lights until electricity arrived in 1955. There was even a boiler house to provide hot water for foot warmers, which would be filled by porters and issued to Victorian passengers when their trains halted at Riccarton Junction. The signal boxes which stood at each end of the station and the single storey platform buildings have all gone and just one station building still stands, a red-brick generator building at the west end of the platform.

Restored Sign Riccarton Junction

Little remains of the village of 37 houses that was connected by a footbridge and stood north east of the station, although the old school building and school master's house have been restored and are inhabited once more. At its peak 118 people lived in the village, someone from each house working on the railway. Whilst most houses were terraced, social hierarchy ensured that the station master and school master were afforded much grander three-bedroomed properties. Despite being a railway settlement, the teacher had greater standing, allowing him an indoor lavatory, while the station master and his family had to make do with outdoor facilities.

Station Master's House Riccarton Junction

Riccarton Junction

Undated Photo of Riccarton Junction
(Tony & Nicky Harden)

With no road access the community was totally dependent on the railway, which brought in all goods and even took away coffins of the deceased (for which they kindly did not charge carriage). When a doctor was needed he'd travel by passenger train from Newcastleton or Hawick and an engine was always kept in steam to get him there in emergencies. Church services were initially held in the engine shed, then the waiting room. The minister walked along the Hexham branch from Saughtree. The station buildings contained a post office and branch of the Hawick Co-op, its stock of course arriving by train. When it closed in 1963 or 1964 villagers used the telephone box on the station to place their orders. The station buffet also served as the village pub but in later years people also travelled to larger towns, a train making a special stop on three nights a week for those returning from the cinema. It seems hard to believe that it was as late as 1963 when this enclosed railway world finally received another link to the outside world, the Forestry Commission building an unmetalled track to the village.

With the sun now shining brightly I sat by the southbound trackbed to eat my lunch, looking to the hills that rivalled views from the Settle to Carlisle line. The Waverley Route wasn't the quickest to Scotland but made up for lack of speed with scenery and comfort. Before exploring further I changed into shorts, a decision instantly regretted as I climbed the steep bank to the station master's cottage, hopped over the fence and fought my way through a mass of nettles and brambles. Scratched and stung I reached the cottage but decided it was unsafe to enter or to search for the 'outdoor sanitation'. The roof had fallen in and nettles filled the rooms where once railway families lived in this prime spot overlooking the station.

Back by the platform, my legs a little more scratched and a little more stung, I set out to explore, first descending east of the station where a tall chimney still stands, although with no building around it and no clue as to its origin. That is because it's not a chimney but a drain. To provide a reasonably flat base for the railway thousands of tonnes of ash were spread, up to 60 feet deep in places. In the 1980s it was realised that this had value for the manufacture of breeze blocks and a company dug it out but left the drain standing proud like a chimney.

The 280 yard long island platform, which once had bays at either end, is overgrown although a restored station sign stands amongst the weeds. Some edges of the island platform can however still be seen and the ballast alongside still shows indentations of sleepers. This was not from the original line but a more recent restoration by the Friends of Riccarton Junction (FRJ) that was lifted after a great deal of acrimony in 2011.

Set up in 1997, the Friends aimed to bring Riccarton Junction back to life. A newly painted sign was erected and the generator building restored to act as their headquarters. A red telephone box was purchased to replace the one that had stood on the platform and a short length of track laid by the Carlisle-bound platform. An article in *The Scotsman* on 11th July 2003 reported that a brake van had been delivered, the first of a collection of railway vehicles to be purchased as funds could be raised. Four days later the paper reported how things had started to go wrong.

Two miles down the line at Whitrope another preservation society, the Waverley Route Heritage Association (WRHA), was restoring two elderly carriages to be used as a visitor centre and had plans to re-lay a stretch of track. The WRHA was led by Len Ashton who lived at the signal box at Whitrope and had been set up by a breakaway group of FRJ members, who had left amidst disputes and divisions. With expulsions, claims of membership poaching and allegations of territory being annexed, there was no love lost between the two groups. Matters came to a head at the FRJ annual general meeting, chaired by former railway guard Geoffrey Evison, who the previous year had been expelled from WRHA for ungentlemanly conduct after allegedly verbally attacking another rail enthusiast during a telephone conversation.

It was an eventful AGM. According to Evison a sizable group of WRHA members turned up at the meeting only hours after taking out membership of the FRJ and *"were hell-bent on voting me and my committee out of office so that they could take over the whole show"*. Evison admitted losing his temper and indulging *"in a lot of shouting and swearing"*. Mr Ashton was allowed to address the meeting but Evison commented that he *"spoke like an extreme left-wing trade unionist"*, although perhaps telling him that he should go back to Liverpool where he belongs didn't help matters. Ashton told *The Scotsman* that many of those present had been sickened by Evison's *"performance"* and that *"WRHA is a professionally run organisation which has been successful in having a number of structures on the line listed and protected"*.

The feud continued and *The Herald* reported how Mr Evison ended up in court charged with breach of the peace after an expelled FRJ member managed to get the society's bank account frozen. Evison, who the paper described as 30 stone and nicknamed the Fat Controller, had marched into the Melrose branch of the Bank of Scotland and after demanding that the staff call the manager of the Newcastleton branch who had closed the account, told him that he should be *"put up against a wall and shot"*. His sentence was deferred for six months for good behaviour but just six days after this period expired he was back in trouble.

FRJ expelled Mr Evison after the bank incident, but he didn't seem very keen to go. As soon as locks were changed he drilled them out and replaced them with his own. It all made good copy for the newspapers and Evison told *The Southern, "I will continue to cause mayhem. I have received a letter and sent one back to the secretary telling him he can wipe his backside with it".* Evison found out about a meeting in Newcastleton Village Hall and called the police to demand they stop it. They were unable to do so but attended fearing there may be trouble, so were present to arrest Mr Evison when he demanded entry and pushed an FRJ member against a wall. Fining Evison £125 after he pleaded guilty to assault, Sherriff Kevin Drummond said that whatever the rights and wrongs of the dispute between members of the Friends of Riccarton Junction, he had a duty to protect public order.

The FRJ website explains the organisation's sad demise:

> *'Unfortunately, at the Annual General Meeting of the Friends of Riccarton Junction, a number of members, who later proved themselves to be nothing more than FIENDS of Riccarton Junction, were elected as either officers or committee members and as a result of their actions, the whole restoration project quickly ground to a halt. Regretfully, since then, no progress has been made and at an Extraordinary General Meeting of the "Friends", held on 11 April 2008, in accordance with the Constitution it was unanimously decided to wind up the organisation.'*

Leaving Riccarton Junction behind I headed back up the track, pausing to view replica milepost 66 and grazing on wild Waverley Route strawberries. With the morning's mist gone I was able to appreciate the fine views that were enjoyed by more than a century of railway passengers until Dr Beeching's cruel axe fell.

Next stop was Whitrope Sidings, home of the Waverley Route Heritage Association, a circuitous drive through magnificent scenery passing barely a house or car. Rounding a bend a diesel locomotive suddenly appeared on the bank ahead and in half a mile I was at WRHA, which must be one of our most remote railway heritage centres. It only opens on Sunday afternoons so I parked on the lane outside and walked back down to the level crossing. It hadn't crossed my mind to open the car park gate so I reached the station along the track, walking alongside a line of railway coaches of assorted age and colour. This not being the authorised mode of entry it probably doesn't matter that the platform gate was hanging off its hinges and that a protruding nail might snare the unwary trespasser. In this matter it was entirely successful and with blood dripping down my leg I set out to explore.

Whitrope Siding is probably a unique railway station. Until it was due for closure it never officially existed. The siding was used to stable banking engines used on the ascents to Whitrope Summit, at 1,006 feet the highest point on the line, and two railway cottages were built for staff. It became an unofficial stopping point for staff and their families, although there was no platform and access was by means of a stepladder kept in the guard's brake van. With rules somewhat more relaxed than on our modern railway, until 1964 members of the public were also unofficially allowed to board and alight from trains here but the stop ceased after the siding was taken out of use and the signal box closed in 1967. Whitrope was however listed in the closure notice issued in 1968, so the station that never existed closed on 6th January 1969.

WRHA was formed in 2001 from a chance encounter at Riccarton Junction. Two brothers, Andy and Matt Stotton were wandering round the derelict site when they met Len Ashton who was already living at Whitrope. All three hailed from Liverpool (to where you may recall 'The Fat Controller' Geoffrey Evison wanted Ashton to return) and soon struck up a firm friendship, with common interests in Liverpool FC and in forming a new organisation for the Waverley Route, not just one station.

Initially small acts of conservation work were carried out, replacing mile posts, painting bridges and picking up loose remnants that had survived on the moors. Key structures were listed by Historic Scotland and a short length of track laid at Whitrope. In September 2002 a South West Trains buffet car arrived, the first piece of rolling stock to move on the Waverley Route for more than thirty years. More coaches were acquired along with 120 panels of used track, each 60 feet in length, which Network Rail provided free of charge from the Settle & Carlisle Line. At Riccarton Junction WRHA volunteers cleared the garden of the station master's house, removing trees and shrubs so it could once again be seen from the platforms.

I wandered along the platform, constructed and well tended by the association's volunteers and peered into the exhibition coach which houses displays telling of the railway's history. A couple of hours ago I'd been at a deserted station which had few signs of the railway it had once served. Now I was at an equally deserted station, but surrounded by rolling stock and with rails heading in both directions. Volunteers have laid track as far as Whitrope Tunnel but rock falls meant that it has had to be blocked off and much work would be needed to take the line further. Just in sight was the diesel locomotive that I'd seen from the road. The Class 26 had recently returned home, coming here from Methil in Fife and having hauled trains on 2nd January 1969, was one of the last passenger locomotives to work the Waverley Route.

Whitrope Siding

REMOTE STATIONS

Exit proved less painful than entry, as I found the path back to the car park and simply opened the gate to reach my car on the lane. Feeling slightly guilty to have been wandering around a closed heritage centre and particularly so to have walked along its track, I vowed to join the association who have built a station where previously one only existed in its closure notice.

Gradually descending from the hills, views remained spectacular as the road followed close to the railway's route. It was tempting to stop at the magnificent fifteen span Shankend Viaduct, perhaps the Waverley Route's defining structure, but I carried on, passing through Hawick and Selkirk, both sadly bereft of their railway and soon reaching Galashiels. Here too it seemed that the last passenger train had called and few present on that cold January night in 1969 could have foreseen the remarkable day 46 years later, when on the day she became our longest serving monarch, Her Majesty the Queen rode behind A4 Pacific *Union of South Africa* to officially reopen the Borders Railway.

Re-awakening the northern part of the Waverley Route had been a long process – even longer than its closure. Just thirty years after the last passenger train ran, the Scottish Executive commissioned a feasibility study into reopening of the whole route from Edinburgh to Carlisle and after much debate it was decided to go ahead as far as Tweedbank, just south of Galashiels. Royal ascent was granted to the Waverley Railway Scotland Act (2006) and the Borders Railway project began. With 30 miles of new track, the longest railway rebuilding in Britain was a huge job. Bridges and stations were constructed, remedial work undertaken to alleviate mining damage, 1.5 million tonnes of spoil excavated and 93,000 sleepers laid. Work progressed in all weathers and on 15th February 2015 Cabinet Secretary Keith Brown secured the final rail with a golden clip at Tweedbank station. A railway had been reborn.

ScotRail's cheerful blue and white three coach diesel unit may not have the romance of the huge steam and diesel locomotives that hauled trains to Carlisle and beyond, but it was functional and busy. As with my previous journey on the line soon after it reopened, trains in both direction were well filled, with passengers travelling in and out of the Scottish capital and between the seven intermediate stations. Unlike my ride to Carlisle the day before, while I enjoyed the Border's scenery, most passengers fiddled with phones or read newspapers.

700,000 people used the Borders Railway in its first six months of operation, 22% above forecast. Patronage at Tweedbank was ten times the forecast and at Galashiels five times. The people of the Scottish Borders needed their railway back. Lord Steel was right and not for the first time Beeching was wrong!

So will the Waverley Route ever open through to Carlisle? The cost to restore a double-track railway along the entire 98 miles has been estimated at £1 – £1.5 billion, but as well as reconnecting communities cut off in 1969, it could take freight and diversionary traffic from the busy West Coast Main Line, timber from the Borders and Kielder Forest off the roads and bring tourists to this beautiful but little visited part of the country. The success of the Borders Railway has given a huge boost to campaigners who have always hoped that the Waverley Route could be reopened and it is perhaps no longer just a fanciful dream that one day trains will once again be running through Whitrope and Riccarton.

Edinburgh was packed. It was Festival season. I spent an hour wandering down the Royal Mile watching street entertainers. An American comedian in a Donald Trump wig kept a large crowd entertained. When I returned walking back up towards the castle he was starting the act again. The jokes were the same but with much audience participation, the show quite different.

On a whim I turned down a side road and suddenly became aware of someone walking right beside me. *"Peter"* he said. Somewhat startled I turned my head to see that it was my friend Jon from Essex. I'd no idea he was working at the Festival and he had no reason to know that I'd be visiting the Scottish capital after a day exploring remote railway stations. We went for a drink, put the world to rights for a couple of hours, before I returned to the station for the sleeper to London.

The Borders air must be tiring. I was asleep before we left

Edinburgh. At Carstairs the Glasgow portion is attached. There's always a bit of a bump but tonight's shunter was in a hurry. In the 'old days' when locomotives backed onto their trains it could barely be felt in the coaches but maybe the art has been lost as the sleeper shunting always seems rougher. I woke with the jolt but was soon back in the land of nod, sleeping through the night until stirred by a station announcement for the 6.55 from Euston to Manchester. Still half asleep I made my way home against the tide of London commuters heading for another dull day at the office. Could they have got away with a lie in and told the boss they'd been delayed by a signal failure at Riccarton Junction?

Tweedbank Station on the Recently Reopened Borders Line

CHAPTER FIVE

SETTLE & CARLISLE LINE: RIBBLEHEAD & DENT

I started with a complaint. My email to Northern Rail –

*'I travelled on the 12.49 train from Leeds to Carlisle last Monday.
Please can you tell me why on what is England's most scenic railway
line, Northern Rail choose to cover almost half the windows with
advertising vinyls, so restricting passengers' views of the wonderful
Pennine scenery. Thank you.'*

Three weeks later Northern Rail sent a reply saying that they had *'passed
your comments onto the relevant personnel with the aim of tailoring any
future developments to the needs of our customers which is reflected through
your feedback'*.

I wrote again –

*'Thank you for your email. Is this the extent of the reply or will I
hear more? I'd really like an answer to my question. And better still
to know that action is being taken to resolve the issue. Thank you.'*

Northern Rail replied –

*'Thank you for contacting Northern. This is the extent of the reply
we can provide for now. The marketing team have been made
aware and your feedback will be taken into consideration when*

Northern trains get their new livery. I am sorry I can't provide you with a response of what action is being taken. However, I can assure you that your feedback has been noted and is valued.'

On a busy train I was one of the fortunate passengers to find a seat adjacent to a window that fully served its purpose of allowing passengers to see out. Doubly fortunate in fact as above the main window was another small one which the guard opened. It was a hot day and the air conditioning had failed.

The Settle to Carlisle Line is a route I've travelled on several times, but on each occasion with seasons and weather varying, it is a different experience. Sun and fluffy clouds at Leeds promised a pleasant run to Ribblehead, one of several remote stations on the line. Scenery became progressively more rural as we travelled north west, stopping at a succession of attractive stations.

Hellifield, well preserved and in private hands, was once a major junction and seems far too large for the little trains that call here. Only freight, occasional diversions and the Sunday-only 'DalesRail' walkers' trains travel up the Ribble Valley Line through Clitheroe from Blackburn, although there is pressure to reopen it to regular passenger traffic.

It was the DalesRail trains that led to reopening of the smaller stations along the line. From the early 1960s on one or two weekends each year British Rail ran Ramblers Excursion trains, stopping at all stations on the line. Initially steam hauled, but diesel units by the mid-1960s, these were very popular with walkers, many joining walks led from stations by members of the Ramblers Association. An attempt to close the small stations in 1964 failed, largely because the roads around Dent and Garsdale were considered too narrow for buses, but despite putting forward dubious costs, six years later British Rail succeeded in stopping the local service and closing all stations to Carlisle, bar Settle and Appleby. No longer could walkers get off trains to explore the most scenic part of the line.

For the next part of the story I am grateful to FoSCL for allowing me to quote from a talk given by Colin Speakman in 2014 as part of the celebrations marking 25 years since the line was saved.

'But some of us hadn't quite given up walking from railways. During an Easter 1973 hike with the West Riding Ramblers over Rapes Highway, between Littleborough and Marsden, sitting behind a drystone wall in the rain having lunch, two or three of us discussed the idea of the Ramblers actually chartering their own excursion train service from British Rail, just as the RA was now doing with its coaches.

It seemed a good idea, so we approached British Rail and received the quotation of £300 for a three coach train to call at three of the disused stations – Dent, Garsdale and Kirkby Stephen, before running on to Appleby. The West Riding Ramblers Association Executive Committee, but only on the casting vote of the Chairman, agreed to run a train and risk £300. We needed 200 passengers to cover our costs. Within days every ticket was sold and we had to go back to BR and ask for more coaches until eventually with 500 tickets sold and 9 coaches filled we had to call a halt and turn people away. The Ramblers made a clear profit of £300 on the day. It seemed that at very least Ramblers Specials could become an annual or even twice annual event.'

Just as it seemed that Ramblers Specials could become a regular event British Rail decided that the closed stations should have their platform edges removed, lest a stone should come loose and damage one of the new Mark 3 coaches on a diverted West Coast Main Line train. The stations would become unusable but thanks to a helpful BR engineer and financial contributions from the Yorkshire Dales National Park Committee, it was agreed to make the platforms safe for use.

In 1975 permission was obtained to run trains on up to twelve days a year, in daylight hours only. In three weekends 3,370 passengers were carried, including on one occasion 199 cramming into an already busy four coach train at Kirkby Stephen. A small profit was made and

DalesRail was born. Buses linked with trains and on Saturdays a return service allowed locals to make a shopping trip to Leeds. By the next year the rules had been stretched, with any pretence at running for just twelve days dropped and oil lamps rigged up to provide station lighting for Christmas shopping trains.

DalesRail thrived into the 1980s but then came the biggest threat as British Rail announced plans for the line's closure. Even so, in spring 1986 a new service commenced, running in partnership with Cumbria County Council and stopping at all the DalesRail stations. Closed in 1969, these stations with their small communities and wonderful walking scenery were officially reopened in 1986. No longer needed, the DalesRail trains were cancelled, but later the new service introduced with direct trains from Lancashire using the link from Clitheroe to Hellifield that otherwise has no regular passenger service. These DalesRail trains still run every Sunday in the summer, bringing people to what is said to be the best railway line for serious hill walking in Britain.

I should leave the last word to Colin Speakman, whose efforts along with so many others made my journey today possible.

'I have to say, almost 40 years later, it gives me immense pleasure when waiting for a train in Leeds to hear the platform announcer read out the list of stations that I was responsible for reopening, originally for our DalesRail trains, all those years ago.'

Continuing into the Yorkshire Dales we stopped at the market town of Settle. Its beautifully preserved station, with restored buildings, well tended gardens, flower displays and signal box, is a tourist attraction in its own right. FoSCL, Friends of the Settle Carlisle Line, still very active after successfully saving the line from closure in the 1980s, have a shop here. I joined the Friends after being given a leaflet through the train window at Appleby station in 1982, the time of the line's lowest ebb, when just two trains a day ran each way and it seemingly being deliberately run down for 'closure by stealth' – reduce the service until few travel, then say there's no demand. How different it is now.

Climbing into the Pennines as the FoSCL refreshment trolley did steady business on board (even selling ice creams), the scenery changed from fields to moorland. There's no doubt that this is one of our most scenic railways, although those passengers behind Northern Rail's vinyls didn't get the best view.

Ribblehead station is one of our more unusual, the Carlisle-bound platform being some way south of the Leeds one. The former was removed after closure in 1970, to provide space for sidings to a quarry, and when it reopened in 1986 only southbound trains could stop. A big achievement for FoSCL was to get a new platform built, which opened in 1993 and is accessed by a barrow crossing from the end of the main platform.

Ribblehead

Undated Photo of Ribblehead with Original Southbound Platform
(Tony & Nicky Harden)

With 20,000 annual users, Ribblehead was the only one of my forty stations where people questioned its remoteness, however I'm happy that it qualifies. Although many people park nearby to walk or view the viaduct, the settlement consists of just the station, the old station master's house which is now let as holiday accommodation and a pub with bunkhouse. The Station Inn was to be my home for the night. I was glad to see a sign outside welcoming Grumpy Old Men and slightly relieved that they were expecting me, having booked by phone three months ago and received no reply to an email to confirm. What a view from my bedroom window – the railway to the left, Ribblehead Viaduct ahead and Pennine Hills beyond. I wasted no time before setting off to explore.

A path runs beneath the famous viaduct and it's only from here that the size of the 24 arch curved limestone structure becomes clear. A quarter of a mile in length, it is the longest on the line, although at just over 100 feet high is not the highest. It is the viaduct's location and history which have made it one of the most famous in England. Starting just north of the station, it crosses the head of Chapel-le-Dale, a wide valley where wind, rain and snow have buffeted the viaduct since opening in 1876.

The first party of engineers who arrived here in 1869 lived in caravans, as they made experimental borings looking for rock. Bedrock was found up to 25 feet deep, so a great deal of clay and peat would need to be removed for each pillar. It took three years to even plan the viaduct's dimensions. Had more navvies been available the embankments would have been extended and a less spectacular 18 arches required, but with sufficient stone masons found it was decided to go for 24.

Construction of such a structure would be a huge logistical operation in the 21st century, but in the 1870s and with no easy access to this remote spot, it was a mammoth undertaking. Of the 6,000 men who built the line, up to 1,500 worked on this section of the railway, the viaduct and Blea Moor tunnel a mile to the north, living with their families in 'shanty towns'. A workyard with blacksmith, carpenter, stables and stores was laid out and arrangements made for supply of food and drink. Bakers, greengrocers, milkmen, butchers and brewers brought carts to what was then known as Batty Green. A hospital with 20 beds was established by the road junction and in 1871 dealt with 35 cases of smallpox, all but 3 of whom survived. About 200 men, women and children died during construction here and were buried at St Leonard's Church, where the churchyard had to be extended.

W.R. Michell's book *Ribblehead Re-born* gives most interesting accounts of the viaduct's construction and the work undertaken to restore the structure so that trains can still run. When giving notice of its intention to close the line in 1984 British Rail cited heavy financial loss and crucially the cost of maintaining the tunnels and viaducts, notably Ribblehead Viaduct which the government said would require £6 million to repair.

It was not just the weather, but also stresses from heavy trains, plus some deficiencies in the Victorian workmanship, that caused problems with the viaduct. Repairs had been ongoing for decades, going back to the early 1900s when eight arches had to be re-bricked, with workers operating from timber scaffolding as trains rumbled overhead. By the early 1980s it was an ailing giant. Several piers were strapped with old rails and limestone blocks cracked so that water jetted out after heavy rain. Replacement with an embankment was considered but not possible as the viaduct is a listed structure. Trains or not, it had to remain.

Ribblehead Viaduct

Trials on two piers found that repairs could be carried out for £3 million, half the sum put forward as part of the justification for the line's closure. When in 1989 the government announced its reprieve, plans to repair the viaduct were put in place. First job was to lay a waterproof membrane to prevent water ingress into the stone, which was carried out during a two week shutdown of the line. In often stormy weather forty men worked day and night in three shifts to lay a rubberised membrane that lies beneath the ballast and waterproofs the structure.

The main repair work started in July 1990 with fifty men working in all weathers, but having to halt if winds exceeded 50mph when it was considered unsafe to use the scaffolding. Covering the entire structure in scaffolding had cost more than £400,000, the biggest single expense of the whole job. It was considered to be neither practical nor economic to replace damaged hand-dressed limestone blocks with traditional dressed stone, so concrete was used, however in extended periods of freezing temperatures this couldn't be mixed. In order to retain the aesthetics of the historic structure fibreglass moulds were employed to shape the concrete to match existing masonry and dye added to the mix so that it would weather to a limestony hue. By completion in December 1991 the famous viaduct was as good as new.

From the viaduct I followed the railway line north, passing the famous Blea Moor signal box, half a mile from a road and one of the most remote in Britain. This is excellent walking country and I was soon climbing onto Blea Moor, following a track that runs directly above Blea Moor Tunnel. Building the 1½ mile long tunnel was another mammoth undertaking for the Victorian engineers. Construction took more than four years as hundreds of navvies dug the tunnel by hand, using steam engines at the top of shafts to haul out the spoil. Terrible weather took its toll and one summer several men drowned in the cuttings during a rainstorm. Brick to line the tunnel was produced at a brickworks near to Ribblehead Viaduct. The tramway that transported spoil up to six huge heaps is still visible, as are three shafts which were left to ventilate the tunnel. With thoughts of dinner at the Station Inn I terminated my walk at the second of these, a round brick structure standing high on the hillside, although being now halfway to Dent, wished I'd looked up train times and walked back from there. The Settle Carlisle Line's most remote station would have to wait until tomorrow.

Dinner was worth returning for, both for the food and the view from the bar. Internet reviews for the Station Inn are decidedly mixed but I had no complaints at all. Not many pubs have train times helpfully written on a blackboard above the bar and a toilet labelled '*Loo with a View*' from which one can watch trains crossing Ribblehead Viaduct. The door to the inn having a screwdriver in place of its lost handle simply added to the Yorkshire charm.

View from the Loo – Station Inn Ribblehead

One advantage of midsummer travels, especially in the north of the country, is light evenings and the opportunity for an after dinner walk. The day visitors had gone and sheep were my only company as I wandered back to the viaduct, then to the station to watch the final train of the day depart. With the last link to the outside world gone, Ribblehead felt truly remote. It's a feeling I enjoy but a party of students who'd recently stayed at the bunkhouse found it more difficult to cope with. Already shocked to find that there isn't a convenience store round the corner, one girl was distraught at being told there's no wi-fi. How would she survive without posting her status on Facebook? After being stirred from my sleep by the rumbling of a passing train I went for another walk before breakfast. It's not a place to stay if you don't want to walk. With a couple of hours until the train to Dent I went first to the station and chatted to the volunteers running the small refreshment room. They'd come up on the train from Hellifield to spend the day making tea for passengers and walkers. An exhibition in the station buildings tells of the history of this part of the railway and like Settle, the station is becoming a destination it its own right.

The Settle Carlisle Railway Trust, which cares for historic buildings along the line, acquired the station buildings in 1999 and completed restoration within six months. They also restored the adjacent station master's house, which became a private house after the station was made unstaffed in 1967. Following a period as a centre for outdoor activities for pupils from a school in Lancashire it was bought by the Trust and after much work restored to its original exterior condition, with luxury self-catering accommodation inside. The whole station is a credit to the Trust who have done so much to retain both the history of the line's buildings but also to ensure they are used in a meaningful and sustainable way.

There was time for just one more walk, this time on the eastern side of the railway on the slopes of Park Fell. What a brilliant walk it was, passing through the old quarry where limestone was extracted, mostly for use in the iron industry in Durham. Long closed, it is now a nature reserve run by English Nature. A sign asked people to stay on paths to avoid disturbing nesting oystercatchers and lapwings. With still pools, interesting plant life and superb views in all directions, it is a wonderful place. Above the quarry is a limestone pavement, so typical of the Dales and so photogenic with the viaduct in the background. Once again I wished I was staying longer but the next remote station beckoned.

The 12.02 to Carlisle was busy. A guide in the front coach was giving a commentary on the line as a FoSCL refreshment trolley made its way down the train. With a journey of only ten minutes I sought out the guard to buy a ticket to Dent. She was busily engaged with a group of four who'd also boarded at Ribblehead but couldn't decide whether they would walk back or take the train. By the time they'd opted for the former I was just able to purchase my ticket before we halted at the highest main line station in England.

Carlisle-bound Train Departs Dent (1989)

Carlisle-bound Train Departs Dent (2012)
(Note the new waiting shelter)

Carlisle-bound Train Departs Dent (2016)

Standing on a steep hillside, 1,150 feet above sea level and five miles from the village of Dent, there can be no question that this is a remote station. It too is beautifully preserved, with the main building and snow huts just down the line now in private ownership and let out as upmarket holiday accommodation. Before telling the story of how this came to fruition I must just clarify the snow huts, in case like my wife you might have thought they were for storing snow. The stone building was actually built in the 1880s for railwaymen as a refuge while working on the track or digging trains out of the snow, not an uncommon occurrence on this exposed stretch of line. The winters of 1947 and 1963 witnessed many blockages along the route and snow so deep that it reached the roofline of the platform waiting shelter.

One day in 2005 Robin Hughes was driving from Dumfries to Bradford. As he crossed the Yorkshire Dales in low cloud he came across a sign to a railway station – the renowned Dent station. He stopped to take a look. Leaving the warmth of his Range Rover to shrill wind and horizontal rain, it was every bit as isolated as he'd imagined. The fenced off station building looked pretty sorry for itself, a green

Martian looking out a downstairs window. A note on the gate warned *'No Entry – Private Property'*. Another flapping on the fence said *'For Sale'*. Robin wondered fleetingly what it would be like to live in such a remote place and in such climate, then quickly dismissed the idea. Buying a railway station was not on his agenda.

The following year he came to Yorkshire with his mother. Again they stopped at Dent station. The green Martian was still in the window and the *'For Sale'* sign still up. Robin was curious. Why hadn't the station been sold? What was the price? He drove a mile up the hill to get a mobile signal and called the agent. *"It's sold"* she said. Further questions elicited that it was under offer for the asking price of £270,000 but it was agreed that Robin would be called if the sale fell through. His mother thought it was a mad idea.

Having received the property details Robin's interest was sparked. With a delay in the sale he arranged to talk to the seller. Neil Ambrose had owned the station since the 1990s and said there was no shortage of potential buyers but that some had been put off by strict restrictions on altering a Grade 2 listed building in a National Park. When Neil phoned to say the sale had stalled they agreed to meet and that Robin could spend a night at the station. He wanted to experience for himself what it was like to have a freight train pass ten yards from his bed!

Robin's plan was to renovate the house as luxury holiday accommodation. Not everyone would want to own the station but many would like to stay at this historic building in superb scenery and right next to one of our most famous railway lines. He shared his bedroom with the green Martian. He explored the house, the snow huts and the acre of land included in the sale. He discovered the overgrown siding where produce was once brought to Dent, but found no sign of the signal box that managed the sixty trains a day that once passed by. He estimated it would take £100,000 to refurbish the house but by the time he left Robin and Neil had the outline of a deal.

In November 2006 Robin completed purchase of Dent station. He had already had the exterior painted but there followed a winter of hard work. Conscious of the climate, oil fired central heating was installed, plus a coal fire in the lounge and a Rayburn in the kitchen. Contractors arrived by train from Appleby. Walls were plastered, furnishings sourced with a Midland Railway theme, appliances installed and the green Martian returned to its owner – Neil's son. Dent station had been transformed and the first guests arrived in April.

With the accommodation proving popular, in 2008 Robin turned his attention to the snow huts, 150 yards down the line. Despite a number of disputes with the Yorkshire Dales National Park (Robin mentions a planning officer with a reputation for diplomacy second only to Colonel Gadaffi), the building was renovated to a very high standard and is now available to rent as luxury self-catering accommodation. The station building and snow huts have featured on several television programmes, with guests including Michael Portillo, who when Minister for Transport was the man who turned down British Rail's closure application and rates saving the Settle Carlisle railway as his greatest achievement in politics.

A stay at Dent station is definitely another to add to my 'one day' list. Reviews are excellent and the website address is simple – *www. dentstation.co.uk*. The full story of how Robin purchased the station and turned it into holiday accommodation is told in his book *Ticket to Dent*.

Having decided that on this trip I'd do my walking at Ribblehead there was time for only a short wander up the steep lane from the station that heads onto the hillside. A wooden finger signpost pointed down the hill to Dent village, 600 feet below in the valley. There are no flat walks here! I'd visited twice before and walked on the Dales both times, the first being with my wife when we arrived on a locomotive hauled train and the second when writing *The Next Station Stop*. It's a superb base for walking and another reason to stay at the station.

Other than the station buildings there is just one house nearby, the station house on the lane which is privately owned and still lived in. The volunteers in Ribblehead café told me that the owners help look after the station. And what a wonderful station it is.

Windows in the main building on the northbound platform still have '*Ticket Office*' and '*Ladies Room*' etched into the glass. With the original waiting rooms in private hands a new stone shelter has been built on this platform, suitably in keeping with the rest of the station as one would imagine. Access to the Leeds-bound platform is by an old fashioned barrow crossing, which necessitates a 30mph speed limit for non-stopping trains.

Southbound Train Arrives Dent (1989)

Southbound Train Arrives Dent (2012)
(Note the new 'highest station' sign and gas lamps)

REMOTE STATIONS

The original shelter is still in use on this platform but I was disappointed to find that the notice advising passengers of what to do if they miss the last train has gone since my last visit. The notice '*in the interest of public safety*' advised of a pub a mile away that offers basic bed & breakfast, otherwise a 4½ mile walk. On that day my train had failed to arrive and I'd used the phone to seek information. This put me through to the signalman at Blea Moor who was able to tell me it would be here soon.

Undated Photo of Dent
(Tony & Nicky Arden)

As I waited for my train to Leeds other passengers began to arrive; thirteen of us in all. I wasn't the only one to take a photo of the famous 'highest station' sign with preserved gas lamp adjacent and old snow fence behind. As I travel I often scribble notes, which when decipherable aid my writing. I shall end this chapter by quoting directly from them: '*Dent, a station that is perfect in setting and preservation*'.

POST SCRIPT

Soon after my visit a small piece of news appeared on FoSCL's website. Northern Rail's interim Managing Director Alan Chaplin had responded to many complaints – the vinyls were to be removed '*immediately*'.

CHAPTER SIX

CUMBRIAN COAST: BRAYSTONES & NETHERTOWN

Just four railways remain from the network which once served the Lake District; two National Rail and two heritage. This trip was to take me on half of them; the Cumbrian Coast, one of the most scenic routes in England and the Ravenglass and Eskdale, a miniature railway from coast to hills. It was to be a trip of spectacular scenery, taking me to four remote stations and on a varied selection of rolling stock.

I started from Euston on a Virgin Pendolino, the tilting trains which have revolutionised the West Coast Main Line, increasing speed and capacity but for standard class passengers, at the expense of comfort. With an advance first class fare only £15 more than standard on the slower train via Birmingham, I took the opportunity of a more comfortable seat and less cramped coach interior, plus the bonus of a free breakfast. An excellent full English was served as we approached Milton Keynes, then after perambulation around the West Midlands, Virgin's ever helpful catering staff came round again just before Crewe. A mid-morning 'breakfast' was now available and would I like a bacon roll? Whilst rare for me to refuse, particularly when free, still quite full from the first breakfast I opted for an almost healthy selection of fresh fruit salad and chocolate biscuits.

The connection at Lancaster was only nine minutes and arriving a little late it was a rush over the bridge for the many passengers joining Northern Railway's train to Barrow. A 185 unit on loan from TransPennine Express, this was more comfortable than the Pendolino and in a few minutes its large windows allowed my first glimpse of the sea. Carnforth, our first stop, is an interesting station. Best known as the setting for famous scenes in the 1945 film *Brief Encounter*, its mainline platforms were removed when the West Coast Main Line was electrified in 1974, effectively making it a branch line station. Alongside the station is the headquarters of the charter company West Coast Railways, with coaches and locomotives stored in various states of preservation.

Leaving the main line we headed north west and were soon back alongside the salt marshes of Morecambe Bay, then the bogs of Leighton Moss, an RSPB reserve over which the railway had to be floated in a similar manner to that used on Rannoch Moor. Scenic rail routes seem to elicit more passenger interaction, perhaps as for once we look up from our phones and notice there are other people travelling too, and I chatted to a friendly couple on the opposite table who were returning home to Ulverston after seeing grandchildren in Sevenoaks.

At Arnside we crossed the River Kent on a spectacular fifty pier viaduct that dates from 1915 and replaced the original structure from the opening of the Ulverston and Lancaster Railway in 1857. It's four miles to the next station, Grange-over-Sands, but twenty by road and there has been a longstanding campaign to get a walk and cycle way on the Arnside viaduct. A local tradition of walking across on Christmas Day ceased after numbers grew to more than 800 and officials stopped people going onto the viaduct for obvious health and safety reasons.

Just before Ulverston we crossed the wrought iron Leven Viaduct, which was strengthened in the First World War to carry Welsh coal round the coastal line en-route to our fleet in Scapa Flow. I looked across the huge expanse of sands to the tiny Chapel Island which I'd visited on a guided walk for *No Boat Required* – a wonderful experience which I hope to repeat one day.

This little island nearly became a railway station. In 1837 George Stephenson was considering alternatives to the hilly route over Shap Fell, which the main West Coast Main Line now takes. His idea was to take the railway from Lancaster to Morecambe (then known as Poulton), before proceeding across the sands to Humphrey Head on the Cartmell Peninsular and then over the Leven Estuary to Furness. The line would have passed through Chapel Island, which he proposed as a station.

Both Grange-over-Sands and Ulverston stations merit mention for architectural interest and restoration to a high standard. The latter was the junction for Lakeside where passengers transferred to steamers on Lake Windermere. With mainly tourist traffic, from 1938 it ran only in summer but became another of Beeching's victims in 1965, although the northern end from Haverthwaite reopened as a heritage railway eight years later.

Beyond Ulverston the line passes Lindal, scene of one of the more bizarre incidents in railway history. Around 7am on 22nd September 1892 Furness Railway locomotive No. 115 drew out of Barrow, under the charge of driver Thomas Postlethwaite and his fireman, with a local goods train to Carnforth. East of Lindal station the two main lines and two goods lines ran along an embankment, with five sidings to the north. The train paused here to marshal trucks and the fireman went off to get breakfast. As he shunted, Postlethwaite suddenly saw cracks opening up in the ground below and felt his locomotive tremor. Knocking off steam and putting the locomotive into reverse, he jumped for his life as a 30 foot hole opened up, swallowing the track, locomotive and most of its tender. Severely shaken, but lucky to be alive, Postlethwaite was taken to North Lonsdale Hospital and recovery efforts began.

Breakdown gangs soon arrived with a crane and the tender was pulled clear, however to rescue the 35 tonne locomotive, its fire still alight and its funnel embedded into the wall of the hole, would be a massive task. Meanwhile passengers needed to get through. It was Ulverston market day and the 8.55 from Whitehaven and 10.05 from

Barrow were very full. Both were halted west of the subsidence and passengers instructed to walk to the other side, while their trains were slowly taken over the dubious track. Officials had to hurry people along as curious passengers paused to peer at the locomotive in its crater, but soon they reboarded their coaches and continued on to the market.

A large gang of permanent way men worked all morning, making good progress in sloping one side of the chasm with the plan to lay rails and drag the locomotive out, but as they took a much needed refreshment break the ground started to move once more. Men who a few minutes earlier had been working by the hole, stood in awe as it grew in size and depth, suddenly deepening to about 60 feet and taking the locomotive further into the earth. Movement continued and as the earth gradually closed over it, No. 115, now out of sight, could be heard falling still further into the chasm. The depth of its final resting place is unknown, but somewhere between 90 and 500 feet beneath the railway, Furness Railway No. 115 still lies preserved forever in Cumbrian mud.

The second collapse had taken with it more tracks and those which remained on the surface were twisted and impassable. For some time passengers had to alight at Lindal station and walk ¾ mile to join another train, while their luggage was carried by horse and cart. Trains of ballast were sent to fill the hole and after around 300 wagon loads had been swallowed up a solid foundation was established so tracks could be re-laid. The cause of the collapse was subsidence into an iron ore mine beneath the track, an accident that had apparently been foreseen by miners who claimed they could hear trains passing over their heads. There is a local story that once the line reopened an elderly lady was found standing on one leg as her train passed over the site, her explanation being that she wanted to ease the weight as much as possible.

A further change at Barrow was to take me north up the Cumbrian Coast. It was here that in 1966, returning from a family holiday at Seascale we'd changed into a train to Crewe which was hauled by a steam locomotive, the last time I'd travelled behind steam on a standard gauge service train. Today I was changing to a train hauled by a locomotive that was almost certainly older than the steam engine had been, a Class 37 that was built in 1965 and had achieved more than fifty years work on the railways. I don't normally take much interest in engine numbers but on this occasion it seems appropriate to record it; *37425*, with nameplates celebrating the engineer '*Sir Robert McAlpine*', '*Concrete Bob*', whose viaducts on the Mallaig line were quite different but equally majestic to those I'd crossed today.

A welcome bonus from Northern Railway's shortage of multiple units is the commendable decision to hire in ex British Rail Mark 2 coaches from the early 1970s, hauled by diesel locomotives from the 1960s. Capacity was mainly required on the Cumbrian Coast route to accommodate the many Sellafield workers who use the railway to commute, with the welcome bonus for all of quieter and more comfortable trains.

I say quieter, but that's only for those on the train who don't have to endure the under-floor engines of units. From outside the roar of locomotives can be heard from miles away as they pull their four coaches round this beautiful coastline. For someone brought up with 1960s train travel this was a nostalgic journey with a locomotive, seats round tables, jointed track and the characteristic braking noise from the Mark 2 coaches.

We headed inland round the Duddon Estuary, pausing at Foxfield, once the junction for Coniston, and passing a Pacer, Britain's least popular train. At Green Lane, one of the line's many remote stations, a lone red rose bloomed in the overgrown station garden. No one alighted or boarded. Millom was busier, mainly with school children returning home, their lively banter filling the carriage. Torrents of rain fell as we called at Silecroft and Bootle, both request stops with just a scattering of houses. No one got on or off but we stopped anyway. With the view masked by a sea of rain droplets I could just make out mist topped mountains as we crossed the Esk viaduct and approached Ravenglass, my base for the next two nights.

The Victorian Rosegarth Guest House, once the local doctor's practice, provided a comfortable room with superb views across the estuary (and served the most enormous breakfasts). With rain still falling I took a wander back to the station and around the headquarters of the Ravenglass & Eskdale Railway, meeting a particularly friendly ginger cat on the platform. A ride on this 15 inch gauge miniature railway would follow tomorrow (and in the next chapter) but for now I'd stay by the coast.

With the weather improving and the tide down I took a walk along the shore to the Eskdale viaduct, then splashed through reed beds alongside the Esk. My shoes were to stay damp for the rest of the trip but the sun showed its face as I turned left, climbing to Newtown Knott. Once the sky was clear the Lake District was suddenly quite different, with views across the Irish Sea to the Isle of Man and inland to mountain tops. The circular route took me past Ravenglass Roman Bath House, one of the tallest Roman buildings standing in northern England and part of the fort which protected the port.

I dined well at the *Ratty Arms*, once the station house. Its name comes from the miniature railway which is known locally as 'La'al Ratty', but requires knowledge of the Cumbrian dialect to consider its origin. 'La'al' is widely used by Lake District folks to mean 'little' or 'small' but 'Ratty' is less easy to explain. An origin suggested by dialect experts, which you may or may not choose to accept, is that the word 'ratoon' means 'narrow' and 'trod' is used to describe a track or pathway. Put the two words together and 'Ratty' emerges – apparently.

A roar from the southbound platform told of the arrival of the 19.30 to Barrow. '*Sir Robert McAlpine*' had returned from Carlisle. On my way out I said hello to one of a group of locals chatting at the bar, who I thought was the guest house owner. His blank look suggested I may have been wrong, which was confirmed next morning at breakfast when I realised the drinker had a longer beard.

It was a fifteen minute journey to Braystones, the first of my two remote stations on this isolated coastline. The two car 156 unit called first at Drigg, where rolls of barbed wire atop a security fence for the low level nuclear storage facility, glinted in the sunshine. Double gates, similarly topped, guarded the siding along which locomotives haul flasks of waste. Seascale, the next stop, was once a holiday resort, but despite a superb sandy beach, its proximity to Sellafield a mile up the coast wasn't good for trade. The huge nuclear processing and decommissioning site however provides both goods and passenger traffic for the railway, which would probably have closed without it. Security is tight, as I'd found when a machine gun carrying policeman objected to me taking photographs, a tale told in *The Next Station Stop*.

Braystones

Predictably I was the only passenger alighting at Braystones, a tiny station built on a ledge where the railway runs between beach and cliffs. Like many of the stations on the line, the single platform is low and it's a long drop down from the train doorway. Here though, this problem which makes using the station impossible for less mobile passengers, has been alleviated by installation of a 'Harrington Hump'. This simple idea, comprising of two ramps with a short flat top, is so named as one was first installed in 2008 at Harrington, six stops up the line. Easily installed and costing about a tenth of raising the whole platform, the humps are appearing at more and more stations around the country. With Braystones' few passengers using the hump, grass up to six inches high grew on much of the platform, as well as between the tracks and to add to the flora a large clump of thrift bloomed contentedly against one rail.

As they wait for trains and look out across the beach passengers may use a bus shelter waiting area, unusually constructed with doors on the opposite side to the track to give protection against winds coming off the Irish Sea. Even so it would be a bleak place to wait on a winter's day. The station house still stands, now in private hands, but empty and sporting a For Sale sign that I was told had been there for some time.

Although there is a small village half a mile from the station, it also serves a caravan park and a small beach dwelling community in chalets and bungalows at the foot of the cliff. A crossing leads from the station and has been the subject of debate for some years. Beach residents, some of whom live in their exposed homes all year but others who stay only in summer, have frequently raised concerns about the state and safety of the crossing. With no barriers or warning lights it is less safe now than when Braystones was looked after by a station master who would open the gates for vehicles and lock them when a train was approaching. Those on foot now simply open the white wooden gate and look to see whether a train is coming, whilst vehicle drivers are instructed to phone the signaller at Sellafield for clearance to cross. The signal box is closed in evenings and on Sundays, although occasional nuclear flask and maintenance trains still run, so drivers have to make their own decision as to whether it's safe.

This stretch of railway is susceptible to erosion, both from the sea and from water running down the cliff, the latter leading to a narrowly averted accident a few years ago. After residents had failed to get Network Rail to improve the crossing the matter was taken to the Office of the Rail Regulator, who eventually agreed to send an inspector to view the site. His arrival on 31st May 2010 coincided with a torrential storm which washed material down from fields behind the station, blocking the line at the crossing. The seaward side of the ramp plus its supporting rock and superstructure dropped 20 feet to the beach, leaving a hole beside the track. The crossing phone was used to call the Sellafield signaller who said he would stop all traffic, however a southbound train had already left St Bees and was thus beyond his control.

A few minutes later the train appeared under the bridge at Nethertown. In true *'Railway Children'* manner the residents ran to the end of the platform waving coats and fortunately the driver stopped in time. Asked by the inspector whether he'd been informed of the blockage the driver responded that he had received a garbled message over the radio but hadn't been able to make sense of it, so decided to wait until they got to Sellafield and ask the signaller there. With regular nuclear traffic the driver's comment that *"radio communication is useless here"* might have been expected to have gained the inspector's concern, but six months later correspondence revealed that he had no recollection of the comment – despite it being heard by three residents, two of whom were a bit deaf!

Landslips and storm damage are a regular occurrence on the exposed Cambrian Coast Line. In January 2014 north of Workington the tide destroyed a 25 metre wave barrier of rock armour and a 70 metre length of concrete sea wall, leaving the tracks suspended in mid-air. It is a constant battle to keep the route open but it was a less likely cause that led to a serious derailment in 1977.

Early in the evening on 4th July a train set out from Marchon chemical works near Whitehaven, bound for Essex. The diesel locomotive hauling ten 100 tonne wagons filled with sodium tripolysuphate (for use in detergent manufacture) was crossing a bridge just south of Braystones station, when it gave way under the enormous load. One wagon derailed and slid down the embankment, crushing a beach bungalow which had been occupied by a family until the previous evening. Half a dozen more wagons came off the rails, one of which demolished most of another bungalow, which again was only empty by good fortune, its owners having gone to visit a sick relative in hospital. Ambulances and fire engines rushed to the scene but fortunately there were no serious injuries, however with the track ripped up it was nine days before the line reopened. The bridge was never rebuilt and the public right of way which ran under it diverted to use the station crossing.

It is just a three minute journey to Nethertown, 1½ miles up the line, but with only four trains a day stopping (on request) I could get there much sooner by walking along the almost deserted beach. The sun shone, waves roared, gulls squawked and oyster catchers tweeted, but progress was slow with soft sand or shingle underfoot. I met a chap carrying a long pole with a gauge on top who stopped every few yards to write something down. Curious, I enquired and found he was working for the council, monitoring the height of the beach to assess the risk of erosion. The bungalows were a factor but the main concern was the railway. This was safe at the moment but would be at risk if the shingle recedes.

As I stomped through soft sand a chap approached asking if I was walking the coast path as the map showed it running along the beach. I explained that I'd walked Suffolk and Essex, but wasn't going all the way round and it was only after we parted that it dawned on me he'd only wanted confirmation he was going the right way.

From the beach Nethertown station is reached through a short tunnel under the railway which leads to the unused southbound platform. Access to the small village is by either a path or gravel track leading up the cliff, although there is no parking and barely room to turn a car at the bottom. A passing loop was removed in the 1970s and passengers now have to walk across the single track to reach trains. Hemmed in by cliffs on one side and with a sheer drop to the rocky beach below the platform, Nethertown feels even more remote than Braystones and on a stormy day one wouldn't want to wait long in its little shelter.

Generations of spiders had made good use of a payphone in the shelter but beneath a mass of webs it looked to have been many years since anyone made a call. Usage instructions were headed 'First North Western', the train operator who had lost the franchise twelve years earlier. Grass and wild flowers grew through gravel on the platform surface and if it wasn't for the plethora of signs one might be forgiven

Carlisle-bound Train Powers Through Nethertown

for thinking the station was closed. A Class 37 roared through with its four coaches, Nethertown not worthy of a stop for a 'big train'. As it disappeared under the bridge towards Braystones all was quiet again, save for the roaring sea and incessant gulls.

A quiet and sometimes desolate station, Nethertown was far busier in the 1940s and 50s when it served a large contractors' camp for workers building the Sellafield nuclear plant. The waiting room, ticket office and signal box are long gone but the station house, just above the beach and exposed to the waves of Irish Sea storms, remains occupied. With no Harrington Hump here, a set of wooden steps assist passengers to board, their position marked by yellow lines sprayed onto the gravel. I only just resisted the temptation to rearrange the coloured stones.

Signs on the fence with a little train on them indicate direction of travel to Barrow and Carlisle. On the former someone had used a red marker pen to fill in the train's light, given it eyebrows and written '*beep beep*'. There's not much to do here other than lean over the fence watching the sea.

A fair stretch of line can be seen to the north and in due course my two coach train could be spotted approaching along the cliff side.

It was going at quite a rate, almost as if the driver didn't expect to stop, but brakes were applied in response to my outstretched arm and it came to a halt alongside the platform, although with none of the doors lined up with the single set of steps. A less mobile person would have struggled to make the two foot step up to the train door.

There was no need to stop at Braystones but almost a hundred people were waiting on the platform at Sellafield. Every seat in the two coach train was taken. This is why the locomotive hauled trains are needed. I hope the commuters appreciate how fortunate they are to enjoy such views as they return home.

Once again I dined well at the Ratty Arms. A bearded man at the bar gave me the sort of look that suggested that in his opinion someone who approaches total strangers in a pub and warmly greets them, is perhaps a little odd.

I'd planned another walk before catching a mid-morning train to Barrow but instead nearly ended up staying in Ravenglass. All was well until emerging from the shower I turned to pick up a towel and felt a sudden pain in my back. A couple of minutes later I could barely move. The TV remote was lying in the middle of the bed and I couldn't reach over to get it from any position. There seemed no way I was going to be able to carry a rucksack on five trains to get home. This had happened once before and then it had got worse through the day to the point I couldn't walk more than a few yards. I visualised being stuck in a Pendolino, paramedics easing me out of my seat at Euston.

Very gingerly I descended the stairs for breakfast but with every movement sending a pain shooting through my back, reluctantly declined the huge full English. I couldn't even reach to pick up the marmalade. It seemed I might be spending the day watching the tide rise and fall through my bedroom window.

The magic of ibuprofen eased things slightly and whilst bending wasn't possible, by sitting on the bed and picking up clothes with my feet I very slowly filled the rucksack. Somehow I got it onto my back and paying the bill, made my farewells at the Rosegarth, although not entirely sure that I might not be back in a few minutes to rebook the room.

Ravenglass is a strange place. My wife and I came here on our honeymoon in 1982 and still laugh about the tourist leaflet that promised much to do, but other than the steam train that took you away, nothing was in the village. It is little more than a single street ending at a quay. Not much seems to have changed since our visit, or indeed for many years before that and few would visit without the railway, but I liked it. What Ravenglass thought of the man in wet boots who greets stranger in pubs, confuses coastal walkers, stops trains at lonely stations and hobbles down the road with a rucksack on his back, I'll never know (I hope!).

Barrow 2016 (or is it in 1960s?)

Whether it was the tablets or the effect of moving, after a very slow walk to the station I was slightly more mobile and able to board the locomotive hauled train. The test would be could I get up after sitting for an hour, or would I spend the day shuttling between Barrow and Carlisle. The answer was positive and my journey could continue but with a pause to photograph what could have been a scene from the 1960s – two trains headed by Class 37 diesel locomotives, with a semaphore signal at the end of the platform.

CHAPTER SEVEN

RAVENGLASS & ESKDALE: MURTHWAITE HALT & MITESIDE HALT

My afternoon by the sea under sunny skies at Braystones and Nethertown had been preceded by a damp morning heading into the Lake District hills, behind a steam locomotive more than twice as old as the diesel that had brought me to Ravenglass. *River Irt*, the oldest locomotive on the Ravenglass & Eskdale Railway, was to take me in search of two remote and very small stations.

The miniature railway is an unlikely survivor from the Victorians' insatiable demand for iron and the need for efficient transport to bring ore to the coast. The Whitehaven Iron Mines Company required a more practical way than carts and pack horses to move ore from its mines in the hills above Boot village and in 1875 opened the railway to Ravenglass, linking with the small port and what we now call the Cumbrian Coast Line but was then the Whitehaven and Furness Junction Railway. To keep costs down and allow sharper curves through the difficult terrain, the line was built to narrow gauge. The selection of three feet was unusual and in England only the Southwold Railway used the same gauge.

It was however not a success and after only two years the railway company was declared bankrupt but saved by the receiver at the insistence of Whitehaven Iron Mines, who relied on it to carry their ore. Five years later the mines themselves failed after a rapid fall in the price of iron ore but again the receiver stepped in to keep the railway running, its income now mainly from summer passenger traffic. It struggled on despite being deemed unsafe to carry passengers in 1908, but the final straw came four years later when Nab Gill Mines were flooded out and in April 1913 the three foot gauge railway closed. For many lines this would have been the end and perhaps I'd have been walking up the valley in search of long closed stations rather than riding behind an ancient steam locomotive.

In 1915, whilst war raged in Europe, the model railway engineer Wenman Joseph Bassett-Lowke came to hear of the line's demise. Accompanied by his friend and fellow 15 inch gauge enthusiast Robert Proctor Mitchell, Bassett-Lowke visited the Lake District and within a fortnight of viewing the line had not only acquired a lease but started converting it to the narrower gauge. Having previously supplied locomotives for parks and pleasure grounds, they saw the Ravenglass & Eskdale as an opportunity to test them over a much longer line. Remarkably, within two months the line was carrying passengers to Muncaster Mill, a mile from Ravenglass, and despite the war by 1917 it once again reached Boot. Bassett-Lowke's small locomotives proved inadequate for the very steep climb to the terminus so a decision was made to cut the line back to Beckfoot, although it was soon extended once more, this time over part of an old mineral branch, first to Dalegarth Cottages, then to the current terminus by the valley road.

For some time the line flourished, carrying both passengers and freight – coal, cattle-food and fertiliser up the line, timber, wood and wool to the coast. Even Royal Mail was carried but the biggest boost came from opening of the Beckfoot Granite Quarry half a mile from the terminus.

The Railway changed ownership in 1925 and again in 1948 when it was bought by the Keswick Granite Company, who after five years decided that the industrial side of the operation was unviable. The line had to survive on passenger business alone but 40,000 summer visitors were insufficient to cover costs and it was no surprise that the company put it up for sale. After two years the only offer came from a scrap merchant who wanted to purchase the track and it was announced that the 1960 summer season would be the last. The entire railway was to be put up for sale by public auction on 7th September 1960 and if no reasonable bid was received its assets, including station buildings, land, track and rolling stock, would be divided into sixty lots and sold off piecemeal. It seemed that The Ravenglass & Eskdale was to be no more.

This however was a railway that had already come back from the brink several times and much loved by locals and enthusiasts who did not wish to see it die. An advertisement appeared in *The Times* and a preservation society was formed. Donations were collected but despite much publicity their funds fell far short of the anticipated £14,000 selling price.

Just as it seemed that despite everyone's efforts the railway would be closing forever, on the day of the auction two interested parties came forward. Colin Gilbert, a Midlands stockbroker and Sir Wavell Wakefield MP, a local landowner, had been impressed by the enthusiasm of the Preservation Society. Wakefield had stepped in to save Ullswater steamers from bankruptcy in 1954 and the two men undertook not only to pay the considerable shortfall to purchase the railway but to inject a similar sum as working capital. Purchased for £12,000, the railway had once again been saved at the eleventh hour and proceeded to thrive under the chairmanship of Colin Gilbert. On his death in 1968, Wakefield (by then Lord Wakefield of Kendal) acquired his shares. His family still own the railway and have invested in many improvements to maintain its place as a major Lake District visitor attraction.

On a wet September morning just a handful of passengers waited on the platform, few wanting to board the little train until the locomotive had backed onto the front. With a shrill whistle *River Irt* emerged from the shed, reversing slowly to collect her eight carriages. Photographs were taken before we climbed into the tiny coaches, all selecting the closed ones, this not being a morning for travel open to the elements.

The oldest working 15 inch gauge locomotive in the world, *River Irt* was built in 1894 by Sir Arthur Heywood in Derbyshire. Originally named *Muriel*, she operated on estate railways until being requisitioned by the military in 1916, probably working at the Gretna Munitions Factory. On moving to Ravenglass in 1917 it was found that the locomotive could not produce enough steam for a continuous run up the valley, so a new boiler was fitted. She was renamed *River Irt* after the river that flows from Wastwater, England's deepest lake, to its confluence with the Rivers Esk and Mite at Ravenglass, and with various modifications has worked the line ever since.

The seven mile run along the estuary, through hills and woods to Dalegarth at the foot of the Scafell mountain range, was not seen at its best through rain splattered windows. At each of the seven request halts the guard waved the driver on, our only stop being to pass a coast-bound diesel hauled train at Irton Road. At Dalegarth there was time to watch the locomotive being turned on the hand operated turntable, take a walk to the fast flowing River Esk and purchase a selection of food to take for my lunch from the excellent Fellbites café.

River Irt Waits at Dalesgarth

Before departing I had important business with the guard. I needed the train to stop at Murthwaite Halt. He was quite excited. It would only be the third time he had stopped there this year and he'd speak to the driver. Hopefully the driver would remember as once he forgot and the guard had to apply his own brake at the last minute. Stopping on the Ravenglass-bound train would be no problem but he was concerned about my return and relieved that I would be walking to Miteside. Situated on a steep gradient, it's hard for locomotives to pull away and worse with today's wet rails, so the guard would need to put sand under the wheels. The railway prefers passengers to only alight from trains heading down the valley, although I was told that one of the drivers will always stop, maintaining that it is his duty to do so as the railway is an advertised public service.

The rain having at last ceased I chose an open sided coach for the four mile run to Murthwaite. The track soon turns sharp left as it joins the original line to Boot, before passing Beckfoot Halt and quarry, then entering Gilbert's Cutting. At the instigation of Colin Gilbert, over the winter of 1963/64 3,000 tonnes of earth and rock were removed and 700 feet of track laid to construct the cutting that replaced a series of severe reverse curves. At Irton Road we paused to pick up seven walkers with rucksacks and poles, then at Murthwaite Halt stopped just for me.

Named after a ruined farm and consisting of a cleared but not raised platform area, a seat and a name board, this tiny station is a relatively recent addition to the line. As the train disappeared round a sharp left bend I felt almost abandoned at this remote spot beneath Muncaster Fell. I had an hour to walk to Miteside Halt and pick up the next train if I was to get to Braystones and Nethertown this afternoon.

There is a clear path, however not always on the same alignment as indicated on the Ordnance Survey map, and in several places it would have been more accurately denoted as a stream. Starting north of the railway, it took me through fields, than back to the track by the remains of Murthwaite Crushing Plant. Granite from Beckfoot Quarry was brought here to be ground and sorted, primarily for use as railway ballast or road stone. In 1929 the quarry business was so important to

Murthwaite Halt

the railway that a standard gauge line was considered necessary. With insufficient room to lay parallel tracks on the bending route, it was achieved by straddling the standard gauge tracks either side of the 15 inch ones.

The damp atmosphere seemed apt for the derelict stone buildings, as they slowly succumb to greenery of moss, shrubs and trees. Soon the path crossed the railway, then headed up into ancient woodland, forming a perfect conduit for rain water to flow down to the River Mite. Feet that had started damp were now soaked. Unseen through the trees, a diesel-hauled train headed up to Dalegarth, its rumble echoing round the valley.

Reaching Miteside Halt with fifteen minutes to spare, there was time to walk the few yards down to the River Mite and look across to the few scattered houses that the railway has served for more than a hundred years. British railway stations have a great variance of architecture but there is little doubt that Miteside is unique in Britain. Its waiting shelter is the hull of an upturned boat, beneath which a small seat provides comfort for the station's few passengers. The original boat rotted away and the small fibreglass vessel standing on its end is the third to provide shelter for users of the Halt.

Miteside Halt

Eskdale.   Miteside Station.

Undated Photo of Miteside Showing Earlier Boat Waiting Shelter
(Tony & Nicky Harden)

Unlike Murthwaite there is a raised platform and a sign requested that passengers remain on this at all times, although as it measures only about two by four feet, raises the question as to what should happened if more than three people want to catch the train. Today there was just me, which is one more than usual. The station lies on a rare stretch of straight track so even if he didn't expect to have to halt there was plenty of time for the driver to see my signal. The guard told me he'd never stopped here before and was glad that as I already had a ticket he didn't have to issue one and delay the train.

The rain having decided that it definitely wanted to stop, I chose an open carriage and the full Ratty experience of wind in hair and smoke in face, although wasn't too upset to miss the smuts in eye. The locomotive was *Typhoon,* dating from 1926 and on loan from England's other major 15 inch railway, the Romney Hythe & Dymchurch.

By the time we reached Ravenglass the clouds were breaking up. I called in briefly at the Rosegarth, deposited waterproofs and rather pointlessly given the state of my walking shoes, replaced wet socks with dry ones, then returned to the station. This time the big railway – the Cumbrian Coast to Braystones as you will have read in the preceding chapter.

MAP 4 – WALES

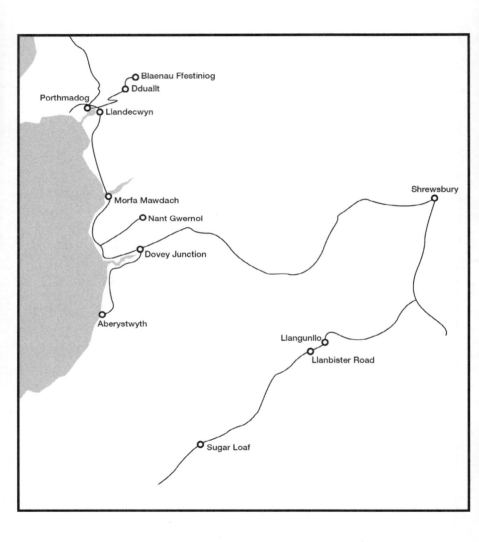

CHAPTER EIGHT

CAMBRIAN COAST LINE: DOVEY JUNCTION, MORFA MAWDDACH & LLANDECWYN

(And Bonus – TALYLLYN RAILWAY : NANT GWERNOL)

For a coastal town of 4,000 people Porthmadog has remarkable railway links. Visitors can arrive along the highly scenic Cambrian Coast Line, or on narrow gauge trains through the Snowdonian Mountains from either Caernarvon or Blaenau Ffestiniog. I'd been here twice in recent years, once when writing *No Boat Required* to visit Cei Ballast, a man-made tidal island outside the harbour and again when repeating childhood journeys for *The Next Station Stop*. Leaving a June heatwave in Essex, I returned for a three night stay, breaking the journey for lunch with my brother in Shrewsbury and enjoying a relaxing ride along the Cambrian railway. Porthmadog was to be an ideal base to explore some of the abundance of remote stations in North Wales.

It was raining when I got off the train. It didn't stop all evening. To fit in with seasonal running of the narrow gauge lines this was a trip out of sequence but I'd hoped for a bonus of summer sunshine. My last visit had been in winter and I'd stayed at the Royal Sportsman, Porthmadog's premier hotel, but for three nights this exceeded my budget. The Travelodge was cheaper and served its purpose, although hidden unsigned on an industrial estate it took a while to find.

My evening started with a rather modest dinner – a Chinese takeaway in my Travelodge room, eaten rather awkwardly as there was no knife provided and the plastic fork broke on its first venture into the duck. After removing from the carpet sufficient grains of rice to at least make the consumption of food less obvious, I ventured out into the rain. Porthmadog isn't at its best on a wet evening but I found welcome shelter in Spooner's, the Ffestiniog Railway's bar and restaurant. Disappointed that I hadn't discovered it earlier, I compensated with a large dish of rhubarb crumble. Rain was forecast for another two days, but although for most of the time it looked as if waterproofs would be required at any moment, after a night hanging to dry they were to spend the rest of the trip rolled up in the bottom of my rucksack.

With so many to choose from, selection of remote stations on the Cambrian Coast Line hadn't been easy. One however was an obvious choice as soon as I'd first contemplated these adventures. *"There's not much there you know"* isn't the expected response when asking to buy a ticket, but I doubt the guard sold many returns to Dovey Junction. As the junction between the Cambrian Main Line to Aberystwyth and the coast line to Pwllheli, it's fairly well used as an interchange but few people leave the platforms. There is no settlement of Dovey Junction and no road. Access to the station is along a half mile long path.

With a busy schedule for the day I had just over an hour to explore, half the time that a passenger on my train yesterday almost had to wait. He'd got off to wipe the window and was nearly left behind, the driver stopping again to let him back on. For ten minutes Dovey Junction was busy. Passengers crossed the platform for the Aberystwyth service, which arrived soon after the Birmingham train that was to join with mine at Machynlleth, the next stop towards Shrewsbury.

As the train disappeared towards the coast I was on my own. Sitting in the middle of Dyfi Nature Reserve, Dovey Junction was a peaceful spot to spend an hour. The river (Dyfi or Dovey depending on whether you prefer Welsh or English names for places in Wales) is close by and views are across reed beds and countryside to a panorama of hills.

The station is on its third set of buildings. The original Cambrian

Railways buildings were replaced by a flat-roofed structure in the 1970s, but this was far larger than needed and after falling into disrepair a 'bus shelter' replaced it. The glass and metal construction is quite unusual, having a domed roof, and seems rather oversized for its four seats. Another seat outside completed the station's rudimentary passenger facilities.

At the eastern end of the platform is one of our more unusual station signs.

Just down the line is a tall pole with a platform on top. On the platform is a nest – an osprey nest. The Montgomeryshire Wildlife Trust erected the platform in 2007 in response to increased sightings in the area and two years later set up the Dyfi Osprey Project to help support and conserve the osprey population in Wales. In 2009 the only nest was 30 miles north in the Glaslyn valley but after several years when just males visited, in 2011 a pair arrived and successfully raised three chicks, the first on the Dyfi for centuries. The project has been a huge success, with ospreys continuing to nest here, rearing young and catching fish to strengthen them for their migration to West Africa. Network Rail have played their part, providing electricity and a fibre optic connection to enable cameras to transmit a live feed through the internet. When I got home I looked it up. Three chicks were sitting in the nest. Now I knew for certain what the big bird with a hooked beak was that I'd glimpsed by the river as my train passed by yesterday.

After some time on the station I realised that I hadn't seen the way out. It wasn't signed. Not many people leave the station here. I found it at the western end of the Aberystwyth platform – a remarkably long platform. I paced it at 381 yards; almost a quarter of a mile for trains that are generally only two coaches. The reason is an unusual track layout, where trains travelling in both directions use the same platform. Passengers leaving the station have to cross the single track then follow a path over the Llyfnant River and for ½ mile alongside the railway. It was a pleasant walk with good views to the Dovey (Dyfi) River and the railway bridge which crosses it.

The path ends at the hamlet of Glandyfi on the A487 road, where the double arrow 'British Rail' sign must be one of the most remote from its actual station. There is a station house, now in private ownership, but this wasn't as it seems. Glandyfi once had its own station with a small goods yard and it was to this that the station house belonged. Since it closed in 1965 the settlement's few residents have had to walk to Dovey Junction to catch a train, but I wonder if there is anywhere else where a sign for one station has been placed adjacent to where the next stop down the line once was?

Dovey Junction

Undated Photo of Dovey Junction Showing the Waiting Shelter that Replaced the Original Victorian Building
(Tony & Nicky Harden)

Back at Dovey Junction, as I waited for the next flurry of activity a badger scurried across the track, seemingly oblivious of the lone rail passenger watching. He (or she) timed the journey well as soon a train arrived from Aberystwyth. I was no longer alone as four passengers alighted to change for the Pwllheli branch. We were soon crossing the Dyfi Bridge, leaving Dovey Junction station to the birds and badgers for another hour.

The Cambrian Coast Line is one of my favourite journeys. It's a wonderful ride by rivers and sea, with views to hills and mountains, and a railway that deserves to be better known. The line has more than its fair share of remote stations and choosing two was proving difficult. Eventually I decided that as Dovey Junction is also on the Cambrian Main Line, I could select two others. First however there was just enough time for a bonus trip.

Alighting at Tywyn, I walked the short distance to Tywyn Wharf station, home of the Talyllyn Railway. After a quick bacon sandwich I was aboard the 14.00 to Nant Gwernol. Feeling slightly guilty at having been given a 20% discount for arriving by train and a food voucher for signing up to Gift Aid, it seemed only fair to pay the two pound supplement for First Class.

One of the 'Great Little Trains of Wales', the Talyllyn is a remarkable story, and with many parallels to the Ravenglass & Eskdale. It too was originally built to take minerals from quarries to the sea, but here rather than iron ore, it was Welsh slate for Victorian rooftops that was desperately needed. As in Eskdale, pack horses were proving inadequate, so in 1865 a two feet three inch gauge railway was opened. Although built to serve the quarry at Bryn-Eglwys, the following year a passenger service was started, with the Board of Trade insisting on one unusual condition. The track had been built to a tight loading gauge, with very little clearance on bridges, so all doors on the south side of the trains had to be permanently locked. Fortunately all the platforms are on the north side!

In 1911 the railway was bought by Sir Henry Haydn Jones, the Liberal MP for Merionith, but the quarry was already declining. It closed in 1946 and two years later the remaining slate stocks had been moved, so the only traffic was passengers. The railway was in very poor condition with only one working locomotive and the track covered in weeds, but thanks to the support of Sir Haydn it managed to continue operating for a few days a week, even if the Ordnance Survey maps showed its stations as closed. When Sir Haydn died in 1950 it seemed that the Talyllyn would die too.

The author Tom Rolt had visited the railway during the Second World War (although on a day when no trains were running as an engineer was trying to repair the only serviceable locomotive) and often discussed it with fellow railway enthusiasts Bill Trinder and Jim Russell. On hearing of Sir Haydn's death the three men travelled to Tywyn and met with Edward Thomas, who had recently retired as Traffic Manager after 53 years working for the Talyllyn. Plans were drawn up for the Talyllyn Preservation Society and after publicity in *The Times* a meeting held at the Imperial Hotel in Birmingham.

The Society ran its first train in May 1951. They could operate for just two miles to Rhydyronen as the track beyond here was in too poor a condition, in many places being held in place only by the grass that grew around it. With no loop at Rhydyronen trains were turned round by the passengers themselves, shunting carriages by hand in the station's small siding.

Restoration of the railway was to require a huge amount of work on both the track and rolling stock. A pair of locomotives were purchased for £25 each from British Rail. These had run on the neighbouring Corris Railway and were renamed *Sir Haydn* and *Edward Thomas*, after the former owner and the longstanding manager of the railway. *Sir Haydn* was to become *Sir Handel* in the *Skarloey Railway* series by Rev. W. Awdry, a volunteer on the line and creator of *Thomas the Tank Engine*. An exercise by the Territorial Army improved the track and gradually the line was brought up to the high standards required by a modern tourist railway.

It was *Edward Thomas* who was to take me up the Afon Fathew valley. It's a beautiful ride into the hills and with more time I'd have stopped at Dolgoch to see the falls, but this was a bonus trip and my schedule allowed for just an up and back. Our stop at Abergynolwyn was extended for a little boy to use the toilet, although having delayed the train his father was rather cross that his urgent desire for a wee-wee evaporated as soon as the facility was available.

Passenger trains originally terminated here, the mile of track beyond used only by trains taking slate wagons to and from the quarry, or supplies to Abergynolwyn village which were lowered down an incline. In 1976 the Talyllyn extended the line along the mineral railway to the point where it had ended at an incline to the Bryn-Eglwys slate quarry. A new station was built at the terminus of Nant Gwernol.

Nant Gwernol

With no road access here, not only was I having a ride on this scenic and historic railway, but I could count another remote station. The single platform with a simple green shelter stands high above a gorge through which runs the fast flowing Nant Gwernol river. Although passengers can enjoy a network of walks through woodland and ravines, most spent just ten minutes at this lovely spot, while the engine ran round its train. With no facilities trains don't wait here, but instead pause at Abergynolwyn where there's a tea room. The guard was quite honest in telling us that the stop was to allow the railway to take more money from its passengers. Obviously I had to buy a cake and very nice it was too.

At Tywyn I spent the hour until the next Cambrian Coast train walking on the beach, unsuccessfully scanning the water for the dolphins. None were to be spotted today but I'd seen them from the train on my last trip here. The public address and information display were a bit over excited on the train north. The next stop would be Birmingham International it told us with an air of confidence, as we approached Tonfanau, a remote station which once served an army base but now has just a couple of houses nearby. The base was temporarily reopened in 1972 to house 3,000 Ugandan Asian refugees who arrived here by special trains that must have had to pull up several times at the short platform.

Now at least having us going in the right direction, but missing out nine intermediate stations, we were informed that the next calling point would be Harlech. The guard told us to ignore it and acknowledged my request to stop at my next remote station, Morfa Mawddach, but first I was to enjoy perhaps the most stunning part of this spectacular line. Approaching Fairbourne the train runs on a ledge cut high into the cliffs, with sweeping views across Barmouth Bay to the town nestling beneath hills. Waves crashed onto the beach far below and gulls nested in crevices on the cliffs. Not for the first time on these travels my notes said 'a wonderful railway'. The Cambrian Coast and its railway are less well known than their beauty deserve, but perhaps are all the better for it.

One of the quirks of the Cambrian Railway was its remote junctions – stations in the middle of nowhere which served as interchanges with branch lines but little in the way of local population. Dovey Junction was one. Moat Lane Junction, where the Newtown & Machynlleth Railway diverged from the Llanidloes & Newtown Railway, was another and I was about to arrive at a third.

Originally Barmouth Junction, Morfa Mawddach is a sorry shadow of its former self. With four platforms and a full array of station buildings, it once straddled a triangular junction with the line from Barmouth through Dolgellau to Ruabon, but is now reduced to just a single curved platform. The waiting room is a simple shelter, albeit adorned with an attractive frieze painted by children from Ysgol Friog School in Fairbourne. Standing on the platform looking across sand dunes to the sea it was hard to believe that this was once an important junction, which was staffed until 1968 and that so much had gone from the old photos. The tall signals that once proudly guarded the station approach are long gone, replaced by a green mast and whirring metal cabinet that operate the 'in cab' signalling.

Pwllheli-bound Train Departs Morfa Mawddach

Whilst no longer possible to change for the highly scenic line to Ruabon, the track bed to Dolgellau now forms the Mawddach Trail, a 9½ mile walking and cycle route. The station however has found another purpose and is used by visitors to Barmouth who park here and take the train over the bridge across the River Mawddach, avoiding a twenty mile road detour.

It opened in 1867 and was initially the line's terminus, as the wooden trestle bridge hadn't been approved for passenger use. For four months they had to alight here and continue their journey across the water by horse and carriage. The line to Dolgellau opened two years later and the triangular junction initially allowed trains to join it from both the south and north, but the former wasn't possible after the south signal cabin was removed in the early part of the 20th century. The track was however retained as a siding and used for turning steam locomotives until the early 1960s.

With a bit of exploring the old station layout can still be traced, although it took me some time to work it all out. The current platform is one edge of the original island, which had still been in place when we'd stayed at Barmouth in 1980, but is now overgrown with trees that hide any remains of the buildings. The opposite edge can be seen alongside the start of the Mawddach Way and the third side borders the car park which stands on part of the old track bed. It's all so far removed from the proud junction station that once stood at this remote spot by Welsh coast.

Old Platform Morfa Mawddach

Undated Photo of the then Barmouth Junction
(Tony & Nicky Harden)

I left Morfa Mawddach on foot to enjoy one of my favourite railway walks. A path runs beside the track into Barmouth, initially alongside sand dunes, then onto the Mawddach Bridge, affording fine views of the river and sea, the Rhinog Mountains to the north and the massive Cader Idris to the south. It's the sort of walk you could do every day and the view would never be quite the same, and one of the most beautiful stretches of railway in Britain.

The bridge had to be closed for six months in 1980 after damage caused to the wooden supports by teredo marine worms. Had this been ten years earlier it might have led to the line's closure but with the railway's value to the local community and tourism now fully appreciated, £2 million was found for repairs.

As Barmouth's rather dull station is a hundred yards from the beach I waited by the sea, the two coach train appearing on the cliffs south of Fairbourne a full thirteen minutes before arriving here. I wondered if there's any other station where one can spot a train so long before it arrives. I came up with Starcross in Devon, where you could arrive 45 minutes early and across the river see your train leave Exmouth en-route to Exeter, where it would reverse before eventually picking you up on its way to Paignton. We passed through Llandecwyn without stopping but I would return tomorrow to visit my final remote Cambrian Coast station.

Llandecwyn was just a ten minute run from Porthmadog and once again I was the only passenger to alight. As the train disappeared towards Harlech, on the platform a remote voice continued to announce its long procession of stops towards Birmingham.

There are no houses by the station but it serves the hamlet of Llandecwyn 1/3 of a mile away and gets an average of ten users a day. Amongst the short list of 'notable' residents Llandecwyn boasts Evan Evans, an 18th century poet, not the portly choirmaster of Grumbly and District Choral Society in which *Ivor the Engine* was first bass.

This was my third visit to Llandecwyn. In 1971 on a family holiday at Criccieth we'd walked from here to Llyn Tecwyn Isaf, an attractive small reservoir in the hills behind the station, and when writing *No Boat Required* I'd walked from Talsarnau, via the tidal island of Ynys Gifftan. In the few years since then the station has been completely renewed, making it the most modern of my forty remote stations.

A simple glass and metal shelter holds three seats, with three more perches should there be a rush of passengers. Access to the platform is by a ramp, with bright yellow hand rails, all suitably illuminated by seven tall lights. The bin is the standard anti-terrorist design of clear plastic with a polythene liner. Station furniture is limited – the bin, an electronic display board and the shelter, that's it. Llandecwyn is functional, minimalist and no doubt low maintenance, but for beauty one needs to look beyond.

The view from the station is one of the best. It stands on the Afon Dwyrwd estuary, with mountains to the right and Ynys Gifftan to the left. Across the water white houses in the Italianate village of Portmeirion nestle on the hillside and down the line Harlech Castle stands on a cliff. I could have sat for an hour on the plastic seat and enjoyed views from the glass shelter but I needed to explore.

When I came here from Ynys Gifftan I'd walked down to the river and as dusk fell watched a train cross Pont Briwet, a wooden trestle bridge over the Dwyrwd. I returned to the lovely spot on the sand, from where a path promises fine walks upstream and into the mountains.

Llandecwyn

*Undated (1960s or 1970s) Photo of Llandecwyn
(Tony & Nicky Harden)*

Studying Ordnance Survey maps opens the country to exploration, but doesn't help find the time for all the walks.

It is this bridge that explains the new station at Llandecwyn. The twenty one pier Victorian road and rail wooden bridge, which had been extensively rebuilt by GWR in 1932, is no more. Instead a functional but less interesting concrete structure takes trains and vehicles across the river. The old bridge was struggling. Trains were limited to 20mph and a two tonne weight limit meant that lorries, buses and even ambulances had to make an eight mile diversion via Maentwrong. In 2010 the Welsh Assembly Government announced plans for a new £20 million road and rail bridge. All however did not go to plan.

It was intended that the original crossing would remain open during construction but piling work for the adjacent new bridge was found to have damaged the timber viaduct, which was declared structurally unsafe and closed in December 2013. Vehicles had to follow the diversion and the railway closed. Trains terminated at Harlech with no service to Llandecwyn. Having planned for a closure of only four weeks while power cables were moved, the railway remained shut until the following September, during which time passengers had to use buses for the 22 miles to Pwllheli. Problems with cables and a water main meant that the road didn't open until the next summer. Sadly the Victorian bridge, which as a listed structure was intended to be converted to a pedestrian walkway, had to be demolished.

Southbound Train Crosses Pont Briwet as Dusk Falls (2010)

Pont Brewit (2017)

In the mid 1990s British Rail had sought permission to close Llandecwyn. The 1995/96 timetable showed just two northbound and three southbound trains stopping, with a note that the service may be withdrawn before 1ˢᵗ June 1996. Permission was refused and with every train now calling here (by request) passenger numbers have grown. Whilst the line was closed in 2014 the station was entirely rebuilt and usage now exceeds 2,000 passengers a year. The modern station in a lovely setting justifies the decision to keep it open. How many other stations around the country could have been similarly successful had a little more foresight been shown instead of the easy option to close?

No one joined me on the little platform as I waited for the train back to Porthmadog. It's yet another remote station that's in a lovely spot but where one wouldn't want a long wait on a windswept winter day.

Bus drivers can use indicator lights to let passengers know that they've seen their signal and intend to stop. Trains, going only where their tracks take them, don't need to indicate their intentions, so for a passenger boarding at a remote station there is a balance to be sought. How long do you keep the arm outstretched to ensure that the driver has seen you and knows you want to board, but whilst still appearing cool about the whole procedure? And if you also want to take a photo, when can you stop signalling and raise the camera? Once again I seemed to have got the balance right but not for the first time I wondered if drivers get a little pleasure from maintaining a touch of will it or won't it stop uncertainty in passengers' minds.

CHAPTER NINE

FFESTINIOG RAILWAY: DDUALLT

Tyndrum on the West Highland Line is the smallest place in the UK to have two National Rail stations. I wonder whether Porthmadog is the smallest place to have three stations and four railway lines? I'd finished my travels on the Cambrian Coast and now it was time to head into the mountains on the famous Ffestiniog Railway. Like the Talyllyn, this was originally built to carry slate and after closing to passengers in 1939 and freight in 1946, was purchased by Alan Pegler (former owner of *Flying Scotsman*) and has been restored by volunteers as a tourist railway, although it also provides a useful link across Wales, connecting with the Conwy Valley Line at Blaenau Ffestiniog. It runs through wilder country than the Talyllyn and passes through Dduallt, a truly remote station which played an important role in the line's restoration. Before boarding I found the guard and made my request to alight here.

We set off across The Cob, a stone embankment of almost a mile in length, which was built in 1811 by William Madocks to reclaim farm land in the Glaslyn estuary. Travellers paid a toll to cross, a practice that continued until the last five pence was paid at 3pm on 29th March 2003, after which the Welsh Assembly Government decreed that passage should be free. The embankment altered the course of the Glaslyn, which resulted in it scouring out a new natural harbour at what was then known as Port Madoc. Madocks built a port with the intention of it serving ferries to Dublin, but as Holyhead became the preferred sea port his family faced huge losses. They were however saved by growth in the Welsh slate industry.

Slate was being carried by pack-mule and sledge to wharves on the Dwyryd, from where small vessels took it downriver to a point near what is now Portmeirion. There it was transhipped to ocean-going vessels, but a more efficient method was needed. In 1832 an Act of Parliament gave powers to construct a railway from the mines around Blaenau Ffestiniog to the docks at Porthmadog. The line was built to a narrow gauge, with a 'ruling gradient', a constant descent which allowed trains to run downhill by gravity. Empty wagons were then hauled back uphill by horses.

By 1863 it was clear that the combination of gravity and horses couldn't keep pace with demand, so steam locomotives were introduced. As the demand for slate grew, longer trains were needed but the little engines struggled to pull them. The solution was found by Robert Fairlie, who designed an articulated engine which was effectively two locomotives back to back. It gave the power of two locomotives but with just one crew. Three 'Double Fairlies' still work the line and one of them, *Merddin Emrys*, built in 1879, was taking our train into the mountains.

As I enjoyed the views a lady further down the carriage provided entertainment. She was a lady with strong views. My notes say 'rude lady' so that's what I shall call her. Husband was kept firmly in place, daughter seemed relatively tolerant, while son-in-law stared resolutely out of the window, perhaps regretting coming on holiday with the in-laws. As we looked down the valley to Llandecwyn and Pont Briwet there was a crisis. A text arrived from their other daughter asking where the cat basket was. Pussy was assumed to be unwell but there was no further information. Rude lady wasn't happy. As we rounded a curve she spotted a steam engine ahead. Husband pointed out that it was pulling our train. Worried that we'd fall down the cliff to the river far below, rude lady suggested that they should be sitting on the other side of the carriage, for "*safety reasons*".

We stopped for a while at Tan y Bwlch, the main intermediate station. This reopened in 1958, the preservationists taking just three years to open the first seven miles of the line, but it would be another twenty four before the remaining six miles could be completed. To reach Blaenau Ffestiniog was to be a huge challenge as part of the track bed had been flooded by a hydroelectric scheme and an entirely new section of railway was needed.

As *Merddin Emrys* took on water a steward came through the train selling ice creams. Proudly announcing that he'd sold ten already, rude lady, now reassured by a text from the vets that pussy was going to be OK, was persuaded to make it eleven. After a delay while the points were changed manually (signal failure – they even happen here) we resumed our climb into the mountains.

Campbell's Platform, a tiny station, was passed without stopping. This is a private halt, serving Plas y Dduallt, a small manor house close by. The station was built in 1966 for its owner Colonel Andrew Campbell, who kept his own locomotive in a siding and was permitted running rights to Tan y Bwlch, where he parked his car. After returning, the Colonel would drive the engine back to his own station and send his shopping down to the house on an aerial hoist. He allowed railway volunteers to stay in one of the outbuildings and as a licensed explosives handler assisted with much of the rock blasting required for building the new route. On the platform of Dduallt station is a stone memorial to Colonel Andrew Campbell '*Friend of the Ffestiniog Railway*'.

Soon we passed under a railway bridge and slowed for Dduallt. From 1968 to 1976 this was the line's terminus but since then it has been just a request stop where few people alight. As was becoming the norm on my travels, the train stopped just for me. I watched as it puffed through the trees, then appeared behind me before crossing the bridge and heading off into the mountains. Once again I was on my own but what a wonderful place it was to be.

Nestled between a hill top and a small lake surrounded by marshes, with trees beyond and views to distant mountains, it must be one of the most beautiful railway stations in Britain. Thousands of people pass through but I was one of the privileged few to stop and take in the station's peace and beauty. Dduallt is however one of the better used of the railway's request halts, mainly with walkers going down the hill to Tan-y-Bwlch, or as I was to do, up to Tanygrisiau.

Adding to the scene, opposite the island platform is the attractive Rhoslyn Cottage. With a central door, two windows either side and a pair of chimneys, its symmetry, whitewashed walls and red shuttered windows gave the look of a toy house. Currently it is boarded up, so the only house that the station serves provides no potential passengers.

Dduallt

I climbed to a viewpoint at the top of the hill. What a view – mountains in all directions. Moelwyn Mawr at 2,527 feet was the most imposing peak. My father had wanted to climb it with me when we came to Dduallt on the Ffestiniog on holiday in 1971, but I was a bit scared of the brooding mountain.

A year earlier an alternative route had been agreed, taking the railway around Tanygrisiau Reservoir and linking with the original line into Blaenau Ffestiniog. It was to be a huge undertaking, requiring new embankments, cuttings, bridges and most ambitious of all, a new tunnel under the mountainside. The 'deviation' as it became known, was a mammoth project for a largely volunteer run railway but was boosted by a successful legal battle which secured £106,000 compensation for loss of profits resulting from the flooding of the original line. 'Deviationists' as volunteers were called, came from all over the country, giving up their time to work on this unique engineering project.

The new route was to run above the lake so height had to be gained. To do so the only spiral on a British railway was constructed, with Dduallt station sitting in the middle. From the spiral a deep cutting was dug, leading to the new Moelwyn Tunnel. As the extension progressed, in 1975 and 1976 a diesel hauled shuttle train ran from Dduallt around the loop towards the tunnel. We travelled on it in 1975, walking from Blaenau Ffestiniog on our family holiday at Llandudno. It was a busy station then, with a portable café providing refreshments for passengers.

With the help of three Cornish tin miners, in 1977 the tunnel was drilled and blasted out of solid rock. It emerged just above the reservoir but in order to pass behind the power station the line had to be built above the old route and new bridges constructed to pass over the water pipes. When it reached the old line at Tanygrisiau in 1978 the deviation was complete, but with money tight and a major rock fall to remove and stabilise, it wasn't until 1982 that Blaenau Ffestiniog was finally reached.

As I've visited remote railway stations I have researched information from a variety of sources but for Dduallt was fortunate get it first hand from the man who designed the station. Andy Savage, Executive Director of the Railway Heritage Trust, was a former director of the Ffestiniog Railway and ran a series of projects designing stone structures along the line. One of these was the station building at Dduallt, a solid structure well in keeping with its surroundings. It was designed to be of similar style to the long gone timber station building that stood here prior to the line's closure in 1939.

Most of the railway was restored by volunteers and it was mainly members of the Ffestiniog's Upper Thames Group who constructed Dduallt. This team was led by Nick Pearce who is now chairman of The Settle & Carlisle Properties Trust, which maintains stations on that line. The building is in two parts. One side is a passenger waiting shelter and the other used by permanent way workers as a store and place to make a brew. The solid building normally requires little maintenance but repairs had been necessary the previous winter when a tree was blown down onto the roof.

Andy told me that the Ffestiniog bought the then derelict Rhoslyn Cottage a few years ago. Previously it was owned by the local farmer, which caused a little difficulty when rock was being blasted out to construct the station and over enthusiasm with the explosives blew out all its windows. The Ffestiniog had to replace them.

For a few years after the line fully reopened Dduallt was used as a passing place, for which it was well suited with a long and fairly straight island platform. However, it was not worked automatically and having no road access was hard for staff to reach in event of problems, so Tanygrisiau took over. There is still track on both sides of the platform but the top end connection has been removed so what was the coast-bound line is now just a siding used for engineering trains.

As passengers look down from the spiral to Dduallt station and little lake beside it, few would imagine that swallowed up in the swamp is much of the stone that deviationists excavated from Moelwyn Tunnel. It is an attractive station in a wonderful setting. Andy said that it is not expected to change – I hope it doesn't.

A path from the top end of the station leads through trees to the old track bed. A piece of rail confirmed that I was heading the right way. Soon I was by the new line, stopping to photograph *Merddin Emrys* as she took my train back to Porthmadog. The tunnel entrance is just visible from above. Andy said that a future project will be to build stone portals at each end. The old tunnel is sealed so walkers have to climb over the hill, a view soon opening out to the reservoir and Blaenau Ffestiniog with its mountainous slate spoil heaps. The original track bed can be seen running into the water.

Porthmadog-bound Train on the Deviation Towards Dduallt

After walking the length of the reservoir I reached Tanygrisiau, a small village on the edge of Blaenau Ffestiniog, in good time for my train back to Porthmadog. Waiting on the station seat with a superb view down the lake I reflected how much the walk had added to my day. It's a great ride on the train but to get out and breathe the mountain air, hear the sounds, take in views far and near and get close to the railway's history, brings so much more to the experience.

I'd noticed a sign on the station at Dduallt, written in both English and Welsh, and found an identical one here.

THIS IS A REQUEST STOP
STAY AT END OF PLATFORM
AND SIGNAL FOR THE
TRAIN TO STOP.

AROSFAN AR GAIS YW HWN.
ARHOSWCH YM MHEN
DRAW'R PLATFFORM A
RHOWCH ARWYDD I
YRRWR Y TRÊN I AROS.

At first glance it seemed fine but then comes the question; which end? After careful consideration I compromised and waited in the middle. Avoiding the doubts I'd had at Llandecwyn, the driver of *Earl of Merioneth* waved to acknowledge my signal as he halted his long train just for me. There was no one at either end of Dduallt's platform as we passed through without stopping and with no rude lady the line's wonderful scenery could be enjoyed without distraction.

My travels in the Welsh mountains weren't yet over. After an excellent dinner at the Ffestiniog's Spooner's and a pleasant evening walk along the coast, next morning I was back at Porthmadog's busiest station. On the platform I met a couple whose travels were dwarfing my mere 40 remote stations. Geoff Marshall and Vicki Pipe were visiting 'All the Stations' a project that was to take them 3 months and through all 2,563 national rail stations in Britain. They wouldn't get out at every station but for it to count had to use a train that stopped. It was quite an undertaking and capturing media attention as they travelled round the country. They'd been along the Cambrian Coast the previous day and were using the Ffestiniog to reach the Conwy Valley Line before heading to Anglesey. I was travelling back, not by the Ffestiniog but by the more recently reopened Welsh Highland Railway. Running for 25 miles through Snowdonia to Caernarfon, the longest heritage railway in the UK is yet another impressive restoration project but one that has not been without its share of controversy.

Formed in 1922 as an amalgamation of three railways, the Welsh Highland was never a success. Slate production had peaked and the railway's outdated 1890s coaches were considered by many as too uncomfortable for such a long ride. With buses doing the journey in half the time, passengers were few and the company went into receivership. It was taken over by the Ffestiniog but despite their efforts to market the line for tourists couldn't be made to pay and the last passenger train ran in 1936.

Attempts began to reinstate the railway in the 1960s and in 1980 trains starting operating on a one mile section of track over what was known as Beddgelert Siding. Running from a terminus close to the

Cambrian Coast station at Porthmadog, this still operates as the Welsh Highland Heritage Railway. It is not to be confused with the Welsh Highland Railway which is owned by the Ffestiniog, who after a public inquiry successfully gained control of the original track bed from the receiver. Relations between the two groups have often been strained and as I'd found at Riccarton Junction, the politics of railway enthusiasts do not always run smoothly.

After serving for five years as chairman of the Welsh Highland Heritage Railway, in 2010 James Hewett was replaced at the society's annual meeting, the *Daily Post* reporting a claim that he'd been '*stabbed in the back*' and that '*people had transpired to get rid of him*'. Hewett had been vocal in criticising the Ffestiniog's refusal to allow access to a section of track, whilst the new regime preferred a more conciliatory approach with their neighbours. The whole dispute could easily fill a chapter or more but as far as I can see the outcome has been two very different railways who complement each other rather than compete.

The Welsh Highland's long trains and steep gradients require powerful engines and the articulated Beyer Garratt locomotives that were built in Manchester and operated on South African Railways appear far too large for the 1 foot 11½ inch track. Departing from Porthmadog is quite a spectacle with the train running down the middle of the road as it crosses Britannia Bridge. Stewards stop the traffic and passers-by wave as the train crosses the road and heads inland. Soon Cae Pawb, Britain's only mixed gauge flat crossing is negotiated, taking the line over the Cambrian Coast track. Charges for use of the crossing had been a source of discord between the original Welsh Highland and the Great Western and at one point the former had to escort their passengers over on foot.

Several stations on the Welsh Highland would class as remote but with all having road access I'd selected Dduallt instead, so could sit back and enjoy the full two hour run through the mountains. And what a run it is. The first highlight is the spectacular Aberglaslyn Pass where the train follows the river on a ledge cut into the rock. One of the most delightful stretches of railway in Britain, it was the cause of much controversy when the Ffestiniog proposed reopening the railway. The track bed had become a footpath and walkers were unhappy that this would be lost, however the Railway pointed out that another path, the Fisherman's Path ran alongside the river. It was then claimed that the danger from falling rocks would make the pass unsuitable for trains (although apparently not for walkers), but with remedial work carried out the line was allowed to proceed.

At Beddgelert we encountered a problem. The train pulled out of the station then came to a sudden stop, a mass of steam enveloping the locomotive. The guard came down the train with information. There was a problem with the locomotive. We'd run back into the station and review things there. It sounded bad. The chap sitting opposite told me that the railway was raising funds to buy a powerful diesel locomotive for such eventualities, but for now he didn't think they had anything to rescue us. Still Beddgelert is a lovely spot and there are worse places to be stuck. We ran back a few yards then stopped again. Could the engine not even get us back into the platform? Then without warning we started again – and this time forwards. Soon we were running through Beddgelert Forest, the locomotive seemingly right as rain. The guard came back with the explanation. It was *"top dead centre"*. Something technical to do with pistons stopping in the wrong place.

Welsh Highland at Beddgelert

It was a spectacular ride as the train loops through valleys and beside mountains. The line runs past the foot of Snowdon and paths run to the summit from both Snowdon Ranger and Rhyd Ddu stations. Either could merit inclusion in a list of remote stations, although on a sunny Saturday morning with walkers swarming around the car park as they prepared for the big ascent, the latter was certainly not quiet. Environmentalists had objected to the line, claiming that it would ruin one of the wildest parts of Britain, but were overruled. It is the cars not a narrow gauge steam train that seem out of place in the National Park and the railway now provides access without the need to drive.

With such spectacular scenery, remarkable steam locomotives and hot food served at passengers' seats, my first ride on the full length of the Welsh Highland Railway had been hugely enjoyable. I forgave the locomotive for its little steaming problem that meant a missed bus in Caernarvon and a £25 taxi ride to catch my train home from Bangor.

CHAPTER TEN

HEART OF WALES LINE: LLANGUNLLO, LLANBISTER ROAD & SUGAR LOAF

With 16 request stops on its 88 mile route through sparsely populated rural Wales, the Heart of Wales Line provides ample choice for travellers in search of remote stations. In fact there are so many that I decided to break my rule and visit three. It's far from fast, the full 121 mile run from Swansea to Shrewsbury takes around 4 hours, averaging about 30mph, but the slow pace gives plenty of opportunity for passengers to enjoy the scenery. After many hours deliberating over maps and timetables I decided to stay at Llandovery and make two trips further up the line in search of remote stations.

The single coach afternoon train set off from Swansea in pouring rain on its long journey north. I'd met the rain on emerging from the Severn Tunnel (it was sunny on the English side) and was not to see it go for almost 24 hours. The track curves sharply left as it climbs away from the station, the route a result of the closure of Swansea's Victoria station, the line's original terminus. The guard came round checking tickets and wrote passenger destinations on a scrap of paper. With doors to operate, fares to collect and request stop requirements to pass on to the driver, there's no time for guards to hide in the back cab on this line.

After reversing at Llanelli we were soon on the Heart of Wales Line proper, heading north to stop at stations serving small towns, villages, or almost nowhere at all. It's a surprise not that the line was on Beeching's list but that it survived this and another closure attempt a few years later. The several marginal parliamentary constituencies that it passed through may go some way to explaining why no government wanted to shut it down. Although the odd one has gone, thirty stations remain and perusing the timetable I noted that the longest run between them is just nine minutes, the sort of frequency one would expect for an urban line not a route through such thinly populated countryside.

After a while I became aware of drops of water falling on me. The train leaked. I moved back a couple of seats but soon found the same. I moved to a seat on the other side but water was coming in here too. This wasn't the best train to send on a four hour run through Wales, where I'd been told to expect rain every day, then be glad if sometimes it was dry.

As we headed north the scenery gradually became more interesting and the single track after the Swansea District Line departed at Pontarddulais more befitting of one of Britain's most rural railways. At Llandeilo the driver disappeared into a little hut to collect the signal token. The line is operated by a system known as *No Signalman Token Remote,* which enables it to be overseen by the signaller at Pantyffynnon and costs to be minimised. In 2008 the passing loop here had to be locked out of use for two years because spare parts were unavailable for the obsolete point machines.

The line runs close to the River Towy, crossing it on the Glanrhyd Bridge, scene of a tragedy in October 1987 when heavy flood waters caused it to collapse as the 5.27 from Swansea was crossing. A local farmer checking the floods in his fields had seen that part of the bridge was missing, but in these days before mobile phones was unable to pass on a warning in time. The driver and three passengers sadly drowned as the front coach broke away and was swept downstream.

Soon after the little station of Llanwrda we crossed the river once more then stopped at Llandovery, my base for the next two nights. Allan and Lynne made me very welcome at the Penygawse Guesthouse, a listed building dating from 1725. It had somewhat more character than the Travelodge in Porthmadog. The town too has character, with many buildings that are clearly old if not pretty and a pleasing selection of independent shops. After a delicious Welsh steak in the Kings Head I walked back to the station as the evening train to Shrewsbury pulled in. Just four passengers were on board as it headed into the hills.

After an excellent breakfast at the Penygawse I got to the station early next morning in order to visit the café, which is run by Friends of Llandovery Station. Here I met Glyn Evans, an ex school teacher, who enthused about the line. The café was set up by a local committee who took over the station building that had lain empty for some years after British Rail removed its staff. Glyn told me about the Heart of Wales Trail, a walking route that's being set up to link stations along the length of the route. Another book to write one day? I bought a book and a couple of photos from a large selection on the counter; one of each of the stations I was visiting today. How much will they have changed in 55 years? I asked about copyright and was told to talk to Tony Birdwood and after a couple of phone calls arranged to meet him in the café tomorrow morning. Finally I bought a cake, or at least tried to – they insisted I had it for free.

Just before the train was due a group of seven little children and three adult helpers arrived on the southbound platform. All dressed in brightly coloured raincoats, they sat on the seat, excited at a playgroup outing to watch a train. The 10.55 to Shrewsbury arrived on time but with barely a seat to spare. Most passengers were retired and taking advantage of the free winter travel provided by the Welsh Assembly. We returned the children's waves as our single coach train set off and were soon climbing into the hills.

At Cynghordy we slowed but didn't stop, no one wishing to board or alight at one of the line's most remote stations. There was once a passing loop here but only ever one platform. Just one derelict house stands close to the station and a short track runs to a lane which leads to the rather spread out little village. I very nearly chose it as one of my remote stations and had it been summer may have walked to Sugar Loaf, but instead chose to travel over more of the line and a shorter walk between stations. A good decision it turned out as rain was still falling.

I travelled on the Heart of Wales Line when writing *The Next Station Stop* (coincidentally it is chapter ten in that book too) and wrote of an interesting tale about Cynghordy. Whilst I don't like to repeat myself, I think this one bears retelling:

> *There's an interesting tale about the little halt of Cynghordy which we passed through without stopping. Many years ago a goat was due to be sent to Scotland to mate, but the station master couldn't sort out the right paperwork, so simply tethered the animal underneath the signal box. Her owner, who returned two weeks later to collect the goat, must have wondered why the trip had been unfruitful – and the goat was probably a bit disappointed too!*

The next section is the most spectacular on the line, passing over the 18 arches of Cynghordy Viaduct, 102 feet above Afon Bran, a tributary of the Twyi which the railway had roughly followed from Llandovery, then climbing to Sugar Loaf tunnel. No one requested the tiny Sugar Loaf station, but I would be doing so tomorrow.

Our first stop was at Llanwrtyd Wells, a well preserved station with passing loop, which serves the town that claims to be the smallest in Britain. A couple of passengers boarded here and more got on at three of the next four stops, Llangammarch, Garth and Builth Road. Only Cilmeri was passed without stopping, illustrating how the Heart of Wales Line is a vital link for local people and not just for tourists.

The spa town of Llandrindod Wells was established by the railway and remains its busiest intermediate station and favoured visitor destination. I'd expected the train to empty here but although quite a few got off, almost as many joined, mostly local people travelling to Shrewsbury. The guard at Llandovery hadn't been able to sell me a ticket as his machine had broken but train crew swapped here as we crossed a Swansea-bound train and the new one was able both to take my money and request to stop at Llangunllo. He also corrected my hopeless attempt at pronunciation – it's 'Llan – gunth – lo'.

The railway was far busier than I'd expected but I wasn't surprised to be the only passenger alighting. A mile from its small village, usage averages just under a thousand passengers a year. Many are walkers and passenger numbers are said to be reduced as some villagers prefer the longer but level walk to Llanbister Road to the climb up the hill to Llangunllo. As that too averages little more than a thousand users, it seems the walking preference of Llangunllo's villagers doesn't have a huge impact on the usage of their two local stations. I was to be walking from one to the other, so sharing my patronage equally.

Llangunllo / Llangynllo (2016)

Llangunllo is an attractive little station, its loneliness accentuated by the track curving away at either end. The adjacent former station house and railway cottage are the only buildings nearby and as the busy train left me on the platform I was pleased to be outside in remote Wales once more. I took out the photo that I'd bought in Llandovery but there was nothing recognisable. It was hard to believe that the

73025 in Charge of Down Passenger Service at Llangynllo (1963)
(HoWLTA)

picture of a steam locomotive with four coaches in the double-tracked station had been taken in my lifetime. The southbound platform is now overgrown although just visible, but all the wooden buildings have gone. The remaining platform has a raised section, a more solid version of the Harrington Hump, although as this is some way down the platform it resulted in a moment of alarm when I thought the driver wasn't stopping for me.

This is a fine illustration of how with some effort and a bit of money even a little station can be made homely and welcoming to use. An attractive brick-built shelter with a wooden canopy supported by three metal pillars now takes pride of place on the platform. The floor is tiled and a green slatted seat provides rest for the weary walker. Such a contrast from those bus shelters. Daffodils in pots bloomed proudly and a notice invited people to join the team maintaining the station gardens.

Just beyond the station is Llangunllo summit, which at 980 feet above sea level is the highest point on the line. I suspect that this makes Llangynllo the highest national rail station in Wales but I'm not going to be definite for fear of the emails if I'm wrong! Banking engines used to assist heavy trains up the gradient from Knucklas and were detached at the station. Just beyond the summit is the 647 yard Llangunllo Tunnel. The ghost of a former banking engine driver who left the railway in disgrace is reputed to appear above the north portal on misty mornings, haunting trains coming up the bank and causing them to slip on the wet rails by the tunnel mouth.

The station exit is through the gated driveway of the two houses and as I stopped to read the map a lady popped out to check I was OK. I wished afterwards that I'd asked her what it was like to live so close to the railway, the station house being just a few feet from the track. There was no signal box here and the bay window used to house the levers in a ground frame on the floor, while a large water tank stood in what is now the garden.

I had three hours to walk to Llanbister Road and had worked out a route across the hills using part of Glyndwr's Way, a 135 mile trail looping through central Wales from Knighton to Welshpool. Photographing and exploring Llangynllo station hadn't taken up much of the three hours and there seemed to be ample time for the walk. Muddy paths however made for slow progress and then I had to stop for a distressed lamb.

Not understanding that grass isn't always greener, it had managed to get under the fence so stood outside a field baaing pitifully, while its mother stood the other side, also baaing. The rest of the flock looked on as I squelched through the mud to try to reunite mother and baby, but baby wasn't cooperative. Every step I took towards him he took one away. After a few minutes I gave up and walked on a bit, negotiating a particularly difficult section of path where mud completely covered my boots. Then I thought of the lamb again. How long could he survive without his mother's milk? If I didn't rescue him would anyone else come this way? I turned back, squelched through the mud again and hung my rucksack on a gate. Lamb however didn't seem to understand that I was here to help him (or was it her?). Once again for every yard I moved towards the lamb it edged another yard away. It was looking an impossible task but then up the hill came a farmer on his tractor. There was no reply to my question as to whether these were his sheep, but spotting the lamb's plight he marched through the mud and arms outstretched grabbed the creature in an instant. Popping him back over the fence he turned back to his tractor and with not a word drove off. With mother and baby back together I started back up the hill, then looked at my watch. Delayed by mud and a lamb time was getting tight. The prospect of sitting on Llanbister Road station for four hours wasn't appealing. Not wishing to risk missing the train I curtailed the hill walk and completed the journey along lanes.

It was a most pleasant walk nonetheless, especially once the sun decided to shoo away the rain clouds and pop its head out. We often talk of sleepy country villages but the tiny settlement of Llanbister Road could be described as comatose. A handful of houses, most fairly new, but not anyone about. Not even a barking dog or an investigative cat. Just sheep baaing on the hills. Was everyone hidden inside or had they all caught the morning train? The settlement didn't exist before the railway came, the remote station 848 feet above sea level being

Llanbister Road (2016)

Llanbister Road (1964)
(HoWLTA)

built for railway reasons rather than to serve anywhere in particular. It was constructed because of the need to maintain fairly even distances between signal boxes and this specific point chosen because it was here that the line switched from single to double track. The suffix 'Road' was used on a number of stations to denote that they were in the vicinity of a town but in this case it's not even on the road to Llanbister, just a tiny lane which could perhaps be described as the road to the Llanbister Road. The town itself is five miles way.

Tony Birdwood's 1963 photograph showed two tracks, a siding and a signal box. A four coach steam hauled train stands at the northbound platform, having just passed under a stone bridge and the main station buildings are on the opposite platform. The bridge is still there but nothing remains of the signal box. The station house has been altered but was clearly recognisable from its roof and chimneys. Most of the southbound platform has been taken over as its garden.

Surrounded by countryside, the station with its brick-built house, garden, bridge and small shelter similar to that at Llangynllo, is one of the most attractive that I visited. Having arrived with plenty of time to spare I took a walk across the meadow behind the station, crossed a crystal clear stream and climbed up the hillside. The view from the top illustrated the remoteness of Llanbister Road, its station and few houses sitting amongst fields and between hills. It reminded me of Barrhill but at least that had a village.

Outside the shelter was a wooden block marked '*Linsey's step*'. It looked to have been here for some time and I wondered what its story was. Was it a precursor of the Harrington Hump and passengers brought their own steps to reach the train, much like fathers used to carry wooden crates for their sons to use on football terraces? I guessed that Linsey was a local child who used the block to step onto trains and wondered how old was she now?

Any hope of another passenger to ask ended when at the due time I was the only person on the platform, so the responsibility of hailing the train entirely mine. I got the only free seat, sitting next to a lady from Llandrindod Wells who'd been shopping in Shrewsbury. When she got out I moved to a table, sitting with three people from Aachen in Germany who had flown to Manchester and were travelling to Llangadog from where they'd get a taxi to a yoga centre. They said their relaxing weekend had started once they boarded the Heart of Wales train.

Swansea-bound Train Arrives at Llanbister Road

After a pleasant evening and walk by the river in Llandovery, next morning I met Tony at the station café. He'd brought in a laptop with a huge selection of railway photos. I perused them with several interruptions while he dealt with a little problem. Tomorrow was the day that local people had to move their livestock to the common but in their wisdom the council had removed the cattle grid during the winter and no sooner would the animals be left to graze than they'd we wandering off. Several phone calls seem to resolve it, meanwhile I'd found a photo of Sugar Loaf Halt in the 1970s, when it was used only for walkers' trains. Glyn had brought a selection of railway books to show me which could have occupied most of the morning, but once again I was boarding the 10.55 to Shrewsbury.

The least used station in Wales, Sugar Loaf is another request stop. The guard told me we'd use the rear door but after calling at Cynghordy to let another walker off, she came back and said we'd make it the front "*to avoid pootling about*". I was a bit disappointed not to see what the pootling would have entailed. The little station is in a deep cutting just after the 1,001 yard Sugar Loaf Tunnel. It serves nowhere at all.

Sugar Loaf

Originally named Sugar Loaf Summit, the halt opened in 1899 for railway workers who lived in four cottages at this remote spot. Their children used the trains to travel to school in Llanwrtyd Wells and on Fridays the wives travelled to Llandovery for the market. There was a signal box at the south end of the station and trains halted here to exchange tokens before they entered the single track tunnel. The cottages are long gone and with no one to use it the station closed in 1965, but reopened for public use in 1984, serving walkers' trains on summer Sundays. Ramblers still make up most of the station's passengers, but although all trains now stop by request, average usage is only around three passengers a week. Given that most of these are in the summer and many will be in groups of two or more, the vast majority of trains pass through without stopping. As I walked down the packed train to a series of surprised comments from other passengers I felt like a minor celebrity to be getting off here.

Sunday Recreation Rambler Departs Sugar Loaf (c. 1985)
(Tony Birdwood)

Corrour

Mallaig train crosses the bogs of Rannoch Moor north of Corrour

Rannoch

Highland Sleeper approaching Rannoch

Beasdale

Locheilside

Barrhill

Stranraer

Whitrope

Riccarton Junction

Ribblehead

Dent

Braystones

Nethertown

Murthwaite Halt

Miteside Halt

Dovey Junction

Nant Gwernol

Morfa Mawddach

Llandecwyn

Ddaullt

Ddaullt

Llangunllo

Llanbister Road

Sugar Loaf

Coombe Junction Halt

Causeland

The author at Causeland (1977)
(Photo - Michael Caton)

Site of King Tor Halt

Site of Ingra Tor Halt

Island Line Platform Smallbrook Junction

'Freshwater' waits at Smallbrook Junction

Southend Pier

Site of Tollesbury Pier Station

Site of Walberswick Station

Berney Arms

Berney Arms

Shippea Hill

Havenhouse

Teesside Airport

Breich

Cairngorm Mountain Railway

Duncraig

The lights of Duncraig Station viewed from the Plockton Hotel as dawn rises across Loch Carron

Achnashellach

Scotscalder

Altnabreac

Northbound train approaches Altnabreac

It's a tiny station, the platform shorter than even this one coach train and in the deep cutting seemed particularly isolated. With twenty three steep steps leading to a small white wooden gate, one can hardly imagine a station with worse access for less mobile passengers.

I had about 1½ hours until the return train and chose not to walk along the road to the Sugar Loaf summit, a spectacular conical hill that once formed the boundary between the territories of the Welsh Princes and Norman invaders from the south. Instead I crossed the stone bridge that takes a farm track over the railway. An aqueduct attached to the side carries a fast flowing stream off the hillside.

The bridge forms an excellent vantage point for photography, with the tunnel portal visible one way and the tiny station the other. A sign by the track just south of the station indicates Sugar Loaf Summit, 820 feet above sea level. Whilst my pictures would have been enhanced by a train, one of the problems with photographing most remote stations is the sparse service meaning that unless one is prepared to spend many hours waiting, it's often hard to take the best photos and catch a train.

It was a lovely walk along a track that gently climbs the hill with views opening up across central Wales. Looking down to the station showed just how remote it is. Just a farmhouse nearby and the nearest settlement Llanwrytd Wells, 2½ miles away down the valley.

A red kite soared above. Not many years ago the British population consisted of just a few pairs surviving in Wales but concerted conservation efforts helped numbers to grow and visitors used the Heart of Wales Line to see them. Now common, not only in Wales but in parts of England, notably the M4 / M40 corridor, it was still pleasing to see one of these majestic birds amongst the hills where they were saved.

I greeted a farmer who was coming down the hill on his quad bike. In the trailer was a ewe and a poorly lamb. His collie dog stood by, keeping one eye on the sheep and the other on me. We chatted briefly but soon I realised that I was talking and he was saying just yes or no. When he said "So *what do you want*" I realised it was time to go.

Exploring Sugar Loaf station didn't take long. By now I felt I was becoming a bit of an expert in railway station shelters and the basic metal and glass construction here was one of the less interesting. Daffodils added colour to the platform, which down in the cutting is quite dark unless the sun shines. It did come out a few minutes before the train was due and I rushed back to the bridge to retake my photos in better light. There is an electronic indicator screen here. Not that it worked. The train however was on time and this morning's crew having swapped at Llandrindod Wells, the driver made his second stop of the day at Sugar Loaf.

Swansea-bound Train Approaches Sugar Loaf

As we descended towards Cynghordy the guard announced that we'd go very slowly over the spectacular viaduct so that passengers could take photos. A few did but not having been visited by Harry Potter it attracted somewhat less interest than the excited tourists on the Mallaig train when that driver had stopped on Glenfinnan viaduct.

Perhaps that summed up the Heart of Wales Line. It is certainly a very scenic ride but doesn't have the majestic grandeur of the West Highland. It provides a vital service to locals and brings visitors to the area, but not running through any traditional tourist areas, numbers are limited. In fact the whole thing seems to be on a very small scale; tiny settlements, tiny stations and tiny trains. It is the remoteness of the route and of so many of its stations that make me want to come back again and what better way can there be to get to know a beautiful part of the country than by walking from one remote station to another.

Passenger Access to Sugar Loaf Station

MAP 5 – South West England

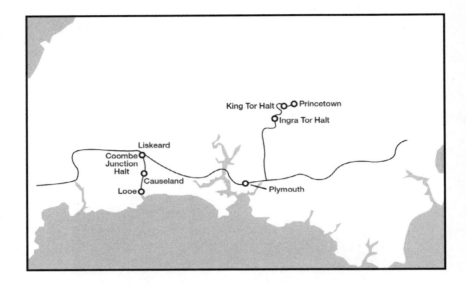

CHAPTER ELEVEN

LOOE BRANCH: COOMBE JUNCTION HALT & CAUSELAND

One of our more unusual railways, the 8¾ mile branch from Liskeard to Looe is also one of the most scenic. Its four intermediate stations could all qualify as remote but my first choice was easy. Coombe Junction serves nowhere in particular and can go weeks without seeing a passenger. Most trains don't even bother to run into its platform. My second choice was Causeland, the only intermediate station when the line opened in 1879.

I travelled to Liskeard in style, enjoying a superb brunch in the Pullman dining car on the *Cornish Riviera Express*. My parents joined at Reading and kindly footed the bill before departing at Exeter. We were to meet up again the next day for a family celebration in Devon. The restaurant was full and we shared a table with a pleasant lady travelling to Plymouth. Dining cars are sociable places and conversation was of children, books and food. Such a civilised way to travel but sadly a few weeks later Great Western announced that this brunch service was to be withdrawn.

The first oddity of the Looe line is that instead of the traditional bay for a branch, its platform is at right angles to the main line platform at Liskeard and faces completely the wrong way. Looe is south and Coombe Junction west, but the line heads north east. The explanation goes back to the railway's complex origins.

In the late 18th century Liskeard was a prosperous market town, surrounded by farms on which the acidic Cornish soil required liberal dressings of lime. Limestone deposits from the Plymouth area were burnt in a string of limekilns along the East Looe valley and the lime taken to the fields by packhorses. With four to five tonnes required for each acre, in the spreading season a stream of horses trudged to and fro, but it was slow and inefficient. Wagons and carts did not come into use in Cornwall until the turn of the 19th century, so water was an obvious alternative.

A 15 mile canal following the 300 feet contour and including two incline planes, was surveyed in 1777 but did not proceed. An alternative route, which would have taken the canal into the centre of Liskeard, was surveyed in 1795 but rejected due to the number of locks required to reach the town. In July 1823, Peter Glubb, a Liskeard solicitor, called a meeting to consider the improvement of communication with Looe and the surveyor James Green was engaged to advise on the possibilities of a turnpike road, canal or railroad. Had Green possessed greater liking for railroads, a railway along the East Looe valley could have been the only second in Cornwall (just the Portreath Tramway plateway was then in use), but his expertise was in canals and this was his recommendation. The Liskeard and Looe Union Canal fully opened in 1828, although its title was to some extent a misnomer, as Liskeard was bypassed and the canal terminated at Moorswater in the valley a mile to the west.

Traffic soon grew. 21,713 tons was carried in 1849 and 48,193 tonnes ten years later, which with boats taking eight hours to negotiate the seven miles and 24 locks to Looe harbour, was close to its maximum capacity. One day a year was however found for maintenance when the canal was drained. It is recorded that the Committee of Management took this opportunity for a little fishing, with two men holding regulation nets to catch salmon peel as the water receded. Many fish however were small enough to pass through the legal mesh, so another man went behind with a shrimping net. Thus it was ensured that there was sufficient for the Committee's lunch at the Bullers Arms Hotel at Sandplace.

Coal, copper and granite were the main cargoes but greater capacity was required to service the mines and quarries north of Liskeard and in 1857 a report showed that with just one locomotive a railway could carry 300 tons a day, almost double that of the canal's thirteen boats. Rail was the way forward and a year later the Liskeard & Looe Railway Act (1858) was passed. Five hundred tons of rails were ordered from the Rhymney Iron Company and granite blocks on which these were to be mounted, procured from Cheesewring Quarry on Bodmin Moor. The seven mile line followed the canal and was owned by the Canal Company. It was constructed at a cost of just £21,000, the price kept low as the Company already owned most of the land.

In an early precursor of John Major's railway privatisation arrangements, the Company had no money for rolling stock so hired this in. Trucks were rented from the Liskeard & Caradon Railway, a mineral line which brought copper and granite to the canal at Moorswater and a four wheel tank locomotive secured for three pounds a day from James Murphy of Newport. Named *Liskeard* this arrived on the main Cornwall railway and was taken down the road to Moorswater by 28 horses, albeit not without difficulty. There had been a heavy fall of snow and teams of men were required to hold it back on the descent, although several times all went flying on the slippery surface.

Official opening was on 27th December 1860 when twelve open trucks hauled by *Liskeard* left Moorswater to the cheers of spectators. On board were the Company's directors, several gentlemen of the neighbourhood and the band of the Liskeard Rifle Corps. The *Royal Cornwall Gazette* reported that '*at every little village and hamlet through which the train passed, the cottagers came out and cheered lustily*'. On arrival at Looe station on the town's quay '*everyone turned out and did his best to welcome the train*'. '*The streets were gaily decorated and arches of evergreens erected in great variety, with all kinds of appropriate mottoes*'. A public dinner was held in the afternoon and in the evening there was tea and a concert in aid of Looe Artillery Volunteers.

The stand-alone railway had no link to the main line at Liskeard and with a large height difference this would be neither cheap nor easy to achieve. The Cornwall Railway had plans for a link but had insufficient funds and lack of finance again thwarted a Bill to construct a connection in 1877. As a compromise, James Temple, a carrier, was appointed to convey goods between Liskeard station, the town and Moorswater, for which in 1884 he was paid two shillings and sixpence per journey. Passengers however had to walk up and down the hill, requests to the Cornwall Railway to subsidise a bus coming to nothing. The GWR, who took over the main line, showed the connection to Looe in their timetables as by horse-bus from Menheniot.

It took the ingenuity of local engineer Joseph Thomas to finally make progress on the link. Thomas had worked all round the world but returning to his boyhood roots put his mind to solving the problem. First he suggested taking the line up the valley to Liskeard with a substantial viaduct entering the GWR station, but this was too expensive. His next idea, a 1 in 7 rack railway would have been no less expensive and not compatible with the main line, so was also rejected. In 1892 Thomas submitted a third plan, this time for a conventional railway running under Moorswater viaduct, then reversing before climbing to Liskeard. This was rejected, as was his proposal to build a new line from Looe to Menheniot, but his fifth scheme was at last accepted.

Thomas's extension, a horseshoe curve crossing under the main line, descending steeply and eventually turning 360° to reach the original Looe line at Coombe Junction, opened in 1901. To accommodate the curve and descent the link left Liskeard heading in the opposite direction to Coombe, explaining the unusual station layout. Moorswater station was closed but Coombe Junction opened where the new line joined the old, and remains here to this day, an accident of railway geography.

With a poor connection from the *Cornish Riviera Express*, rather than wait fifty one minutes I walked down the lanes to Coombe Junction. It took fifteen minutes but would be rather more to ascend the steep hill that a sign indicated was 16% but means more to most of us if converted back to 1 in 6. Towards the bottom a brown sign with depiction of a person, the British Rail logo and a steam locomotive pointed to the Looe Valley Line. The person is significant – access to Coombe Junction Halt is possible only on foot (or bicycle).

Leaving the lane and following a path I soon reached a level crossing. Ahead was Coombe House, to the left the points where the Looe and Liskeard tracks diverge and 200 yards to the right, Coombe Junction Halt. It didn't take long to explore one of our least used railway stations, a station that isn't even sure what it should be called. Originally it was just Coombe Junction but the station sign now proudly displays Coombe Junction Halt in GWR chocolate and cream. It seems that 'Halt' was added by GWR, taken off by British Rail in 1974 but put back by Network Rail in 2008. In the intermediate period it was known as either Coombe Junction or simply Coombe. Only one other station on the whole national network retains the suffix 'Halt' and that's the next stop down the line.

A smart wooden shelter, also in GWR colours, affords protection from the elements for the station's few customers, the bench inside long enough to seat several months worth of users should they choose to all arrive at once. A modern solar powered help point allows them to make enquiries should one of the four trains a day not arrive, contrasting with the payphone in the shelter that looked to have been out of order for years.

Coombe Junction

Surrounded by trees and with the stream one side and canal the other, the well-kept platform with its little shelter is one of our most attractive remote stations. Rusting rails continuing through a narrow stone arch towards Moorswater, from where very occasional freight trains run to a cement terminal, add to the scene.

The train from Looe was due shortly, although it wasn't going to run the last 150 yards to the station, so I returned to the junction to observe what has become a time honoured procedure. Soon the train came round the bend and slowly approached the junction, coming to a halt by the points. The guard alighted, suitably attired in an orange hi-viz jacket and entered a little hut where a ground frame controls the points. The driver was waved forward and the train taken a few yards towards the station, before halting once more and the driver walking through the single coach to the opposite cab. The guard then changed the points and reboarded before the train departed, this time bearing left up the steep hill towards Liskeard.

It's a slow procedure but took longer in steam days when the locomotive had to run round its train on the loop at Coombe. The delay was however convenient for any Liskeard Grammar School pupils who missed the train at Liskeard but could sprint down the hill and get to Coombe before it was ready to head off towards Looe.

Back at the station I was unexpectedly joined by another passenger – a gentleman with a large suitcase bearing a label from Inverness Airport. On a platform that normally sees an average of less than one passenger a week, when two arrive at once it would be inconceivable for them not to talk. It transpired that the man had travelled on the same train as me from London and also enjoyed brunch in the dining car. Bored with waiting at Liskeard, he'd decided to make the pleasant walk down the hill and join the Looe train here. Worryingly he said he'd done it before and once the timetabled train didn't bother to come into the station.

Usage of the Looe branch has grown considerably in the 21st century, rising from 68,000 at the turn of the millennium to 131,000 in 2015, justifying the intervention of Minister for Transport Barbara

Castle who stepped in to reprieve it just two weeks before closure was planned in 1966.

Coombe Junction Halt however still attracts few passengers, the Office of Rail Regulator estimated figures showing just 26 recorded journeys in 2014/15 and 48 the following year. In 2016 one man decided to do something about it. Peter Murnaghan, a Liskeard resident and regional officer for the *Chartered Institute of Logistics and Transport*, together with his friend Brian Oldham of *Liskeard Walkers are Welcome*, organised a walk from Liskeard station to meet the 10.52 back from Coombe.

On 14th May 2016 no fewer than 108 people turned up, along with press and a local TV film crew. The train crew had been advised to expect a few extra passengers but must have been somewhat surprised to see the little platform packed. With a good number already on board the 75 seater single coach train it was quite a squash for the two mile ride back to Liskeard. The guard's ticket machine couldn't cope with demand and nor was there time to issue tickets but to travel for free would have negated the trip's aim. It was agreed that tickets would be purchased from the booking office at Liskeard on arrival but only after assurances that they would all be credited to Coombe Junction Halt and not the main line station. Figures for 2016/17 estimated that 212 passengers used Coombe Junction station – more than half of them were on that one train to Liskeard on a Saturday morning in May. The event had achieved its aim.

Coombe Junction Halt

As I chatted to Coombe Junction Halt's other passenger the single coach train appeared down the line. Any worries that the driver might not have thought it worthwhile running that extra 150 yards to the platform were soon thwarted as it sidled into the station. The driver changed ends then we made our way along the winding track beside the canal. The guard came round to check tickets. I suspect that my request for a single from Coombe to Causeland wasn't one he heard often.

We breezed through the first station, the delightfully named St Keyne Wishing Well Halt, without announcement. I wonder how often the train is asked to stop by newly married couples, ready to race to the well, legend saying that whoever drinks from it first will be master of the marriage. If only someone had told me that thirty five years ago!

The guard announced Causeland in plenty of time – just for me, for once again I was the only passenger alighting at a remote station. Although one of the line's original stations, there has never been a significant settlement close by and there seems to be no place named Causeland. As not every train calls here even by request – some rush back non-stop to Liskeard to make main line connections, I had the choice of staying 25 minutes or 2½ hours. In summer I might have walked the mile up a steep hill to Duloe, a pretty village with an unusual prehistoric stone circle, but today I just took a short wander along the lane, passing a few scattered houses and holiday cottages.

There was though still ample time to explore the station, attractively positioned between the babbling East Looe River and the narrow canal.

A wooden bridge crossed the latter, leading to a hillside but as access to the field had long since been fenced, it served only to provide a pleasant view of the station through a mass of wild flowers, which didn't restrict themselves to the verges but happily thrived between the rails. On the platform a wooden trough housed more cultivated blooms but I preferred the wild ones, brave enough to grow on the railway too remote for Network Rail's weed killing train to find.

Like Coombe, the stone shelter has been attractively painted in Great Western colours. The seating capacity was lower here, but rarely can it exceed demand. Surprisingly the payphone still worked, although unless Causeland's spiders are unusually active, the covering of cobwebs suggested no one had used it for some time.

This wasn't my first visit to Causeland. We'd come here on an early 1970s family day out from Devon, first walking from Liskeard to the now closed Dobwalls miniature railway, then to the nearest station, Coombe Junction, from where we'd travelled to Causeland and walked back to St Keyne, visiting the wishing well on the way. As anyone who has read *The Next Station Stop* may recall, this was a typical Caton family outing, an upbringing which probably explains my liking for remote walks and places. I can be grateful to my parents for introducing us to the wilds of Britain rather than spending our holidays around Mediterranean swimming pools.

Causeland

Undated Photo of Causeland
(Tony & Nicky Harden)

Soon my train appeared round the bend and stopped just for me. I boarded once more for the bendy ride along the East Looe valley, warmly greeted again by the guard. I doubt he sells many singles from Causeland to Torquay, my destination for tonight. At Coombe Junction driver and guard repeated the points process. We didn't run down to the station – Coombe Junction Halt had already received its four trains for the day and must have gone to bed happy to have had the rare excitement of two passengers using its facilities.

Wheels and engine squealed as we negotiated the sharp bends, climbing out the valley towards Liskeard. The gradient was a challenge for steam locomotives and on the very first day of operation a passenger train had faltered here. With the town now on the railway map there had been great celebrations in Looe, including a 2½ hour luncheon in a marquee on the quay and many passengers were returning on the 8.35pm train. Soon after reversing at Coombe Junction the locomotive ran out of steam and couldn't get up the steep bank on the new line. Assistance was obtained but by the time Liskeard was reached the last train for Plymouth had departed and a large party of visitors from Devon were stranded. Fortunately Horace Holbrook, who had been recruited from the Great Eastern by the Liskeard and Looe Railway to act as Traffic Manager, saved the day by paying for a special train to run to Plymouth.

On Friday 15th June 1906 the steep gradient led to a much more serious incident. The previous day an eleven coach special had run for Looe Wesleyan Sunday School and six ex-Mersey Railway carriages were being brought back to Liskeard by steam locomotive *Kilmar*. The guard, a Mr J. Horrill, had been unable to find vacuum coupling hoses for the carriages so continuous breaking was disconnected. Hence on arrival at Liskeard the carriages ran back on the gradient, pulling the couplings tight. To hold the train Horrace placed the largest stones he could find under four wheels but as *Kilmar* eased back to slacken the couplings so the carriages could be uncoupled, it pushed them over the stones.

Slowly at first, but with rapidly gathering speed, the carriages ran off towards Coombe, pursued by all available staff whose attempts to halt the runaway with stones under the wheels were to no avail. *Kilmar* too gave chase but the now speeding carriages could not be caught. Liskeard signalman Husband telephoned signalman Edward Marsh at Coombe Junction to warn him of the runaway train approaching and Marsh set the road for Moorswater, before rushing out to stop a passenger train from Looe which was already in sight. Such prompt action avoided disaster as the six coaches rushed by at an estimated 60mph, surely by a long way the fastest train ever to pass through Coombe. Soon there was a sound like thunder as the runaway careered into Moorswater carriage shed, demolishing the building and three coaches inside. It was fortunate that carpenters working here had finished early for the day, so with remarkable good fortune the whole incident passed without injury. With much local excitement at the runaway train the *Cornish Times* rushed out a special 'Railway Smash' edition and after due investigation guard Horrill was suspended and signalman Marsh commended. Perhaps I should be grateful that just a single coach with no need for couplings now plies up and down the eccentric Looe branch.

CHAPTER TWELVE

PRINCETOWN RAILWAY: KING TOR & INGRA TOR HALTS

If there was a competition to find England's most remote railway station King Tor and Ingra Tor Halts would fare well. In the wilds of Dartmoor, with no access by road, they were arguably the loneliest of all. Having struggled throughout its existence, the Princetown Railway closed in 1956 but the moorland track bed largely survives, now a walking and cycle route and probably better used than most of the trains.

Although the line closed before I was born, my father Michael Caton travelled on it a number of times and I am pleased to be able to record some of his reminiscences of this remarkable railway from more than sixty years ago.

In the mid 1950s I became interested in Dartmoor and began a lifelong interest in walking in this fascinating area of wild moorland. At that time Dartmoor was almost surrounded by railways and a number of stations gave direct access to the moor. Sadly most of these were closed in the next few years and the first to go was the line from Yelverton to Princetown.

I was fortunate in being able to travel on the line on four occasions. I first saw the train when walking on the slopes of North Hessary Tor west of Princetown, an excellent vantage point to see the railway in action. I saw the little one coach train ascending towards Princetown as it wound round the tors by its circuitous route and ran down the hillside to take a photograph with my Agfa Standard camera.

I'd travelled to the West Country on one of Britain's greatest trains – The Night Riviera – a sleeper service to Cornwall. Asleep before leaving Paddington, I awoke to sunrise over Truro cathedral, dressed in time to enjoy views to St Michael's Mount and was in Penzance before eight. I've said it before but will say it again. Is there a better way to travel than our wonderful sleeper trains?

First work had to be dealt with and a car hired. Next time I must remember to be smarter leaving the train as the hire office was busy with sleeper passengers who'd beaten me to it. My meeting completed by lunchtime, I headed for Plymouth and two nights in Roborough Travelodge. Lack of character was balanced by price and a Toby Carvery next door.

Sadly no longer well served by railways, Dartmoor is one of my favourite places and as well as remote halts I'd planned several walks checking routes for my father's forthcoming book, *Walks on Dartmoor Paths & Trackways*. I was glad to visit the carvery after the first, a rather wet and cold walk to prehistoric remains near Trowlesworthy Warren.

It was a mixed start to the next day. Sunshine greeting me on opening the curtains was good but the Toby Carvery buffet breakfast was most definitely bad. I'll be generous and suggest that the chef had cooked too much then left it all under the heat lamps this morning and not before he went home last night. Securing the only Cornish pasty at a café in Yelverton and wrapping it in layers of clothes to keep it warm for lunch on the moors was good, as was the drive across Dartmoor, passing the old Dousland railway station, now a private house. Misreading the car park sign at Princetown and buying a ticket at coach parking rate must rank as bad, but I'm not sure how to classify my use of the ladies toilet by mistake. Probably good in that no one else was in there.

Were this a book about remote towns I may also have come to Princetown, sitting in the middle of Dartmoor, 1,400 feet above sea level and dominated by its Victorian prison. Its situation, smell of coal fires and typical grey weather always reminds me of Blaenau Ffestiniog.

I set out to follow the well preserved track across the moors, starting at the site of the terminus east of the town's centre. The station master's house and railway cottages still stand but all that remains of the station is the GWR stable, dating from around 1909, which housed the horses who hauled carts of goods arriving by train around the town. Princetown was soon left behind as I walked along the railway track that hadn't seen a train for more than sixty years.

After a mile and a quarter of gentle curves the line veers to the right, below Foggintor and Swelltor Quarries. By a siding to the latter was the site of King Tor Halt. There's not much to see now. The wooden platform is long gone and just the concrete base of a shelter remains.

As I arrived at the station my good fortune with the weather ended. With freezing rain blowing directly into my face I diverted up the siding to Swelltor Quarry. The entrance was far too boggy to contemplate, so I climbed the hill, looking down into the deep excavation. One of the largest quarries on Dartmoor, its granite was used to construct the Thames Embankment in 1847 and to widen London Bridge in 1902. Up to ninety men were employed before the First World War and one would have thought some would have used King Tor Halt, however although the railway opened in 1883, the halt wasn't built until 1928. Stone had been taken by rail, but by the late 1930s both quarries had closed and for the next twenty years the halt's few remaining passengers were walkers.

The view from King Tor Halt presents an interesting perspective of railway geography. Ingra Tor can be seen just under a mile away, but the track heads off in completely the wrong direction towards the rocky outcrop of King Tor. It rounds the tor then reappears a few hundred yards below the halt, having completed a loop of 1¾ miles. A further loop around the side of the valley requires another mile to reach Ingra Tor Halt, meaning that in order for the railway to gain height at a workable gradient the distance between the halts is five times that a crow would cover, assuming of course that it wished to fly in its traditional manner.

View to Ingra Tor from King Tor Halt

One day in 1955 the geography of the line provided a challenge to three young National Servicemen who were travelling to Princetown. Jumping from the train at Ingra Tor Halt, they set out across the moor with the aim to re-join it at King Tor Halt. The Princetown train never hurried but as the three men tore down the valley the fireman saw what was happening and rose to the challenge. The fire was stoked and the driver managed to reach King Tor Halt four minutes quicker than usual. Even this wasn't fast enough to beat two of the servicemen who boarded the train to applause from fellow passengers. The third however would have had a lonely walk across the moor to reach Princetown.

Almost sixty years later, three men, including Michael Heaton, son of one of the servicemen, decided to repeat the challenge to raise money for charity. With the trains long gone, local farmer Barry Landick volunteered to drive his Land Rover along the track, matching the railway's average speed of 18mph. On 9th August 2014 the three men set out across the moor from Ingra Tor as the Land Rover started to negotiate the line's two loops. Whilst the railway had the advantage to the point where the path crosses its track, from here it is just a short run up the hill for those on foot, but a long detour around King Tor for the train. There cannot be many stations between which a train could be beaten on foot but on this occasion all three men arrived at the halt first.

So setting off in completely the wrong direction, I headed for Ingra Tor Halt, following the railway around King Tor. A mile to the north is Merrivale Quarry, to which a branch was partly constructed, but abandoned, granite instead taken to the railway at Tavistock in wagons drawn by teams of horses. It took about 45 minutes of very pleasant walking to reach a point only ¼ mile below King Tor Halt. With the sun now shining there were good views over the moor, across Devon and as far as Bodmin Moor in Cornwall. The Princetown railway was not only one of our remotest but also amongst the most scenic. I'd crossed several overbridges where the route went over streams or gulleys but at the top of the valley the line passes under a well preserved stone bridge, which appears to serve no purpose other than to allow livestock to get over the line. A little way beyond the bridge is Ingra Tor Halt.

Like King Tor Halt there is little to show that there was once a railway station on the moors. The concrete base of a wooden hut on a raised bank and a few bits of wood by the track bed are its only

Undated Photo of Ingra Tor Halt
(Tony & Nicky Harden)

remnants. The wooden platform is long gone, as is the sign that warned passengers to beware of snakes. The station was open for only 19 years, being built in 1937 when granite waste from the adjacent quarry was taken away for road dressing but then kept to serve walkers and a farm in the valley below.

Dark clouds which I'd been watching as they approached at a pace from the west, arrived at Ingra Tor just as I did, depositing freezing rain which the wind kindly blew into my face. Shelter was sought in the quarry where two circular stone structures intrigued. They were apparently crane supports. This was a day of several seasons within an hour, and as patches of blue sky appeared I emerged into sunshine, divested layers of wet clothes and took photos before the next rainstorm arrived.

Standing on an old railway track with a pile of granite one side, the sparse remains of a station the other and a lone tree ahead, it was strange to think that more than sixty years earlier my parents had alighted from a train here.

Site of Ingra Tor Halt (to left of fence)

Undated Photo of Yelverton Train Arriving at Ingra Tor Halt
(123tony-tony – Ebay)

In the summer of 1955, Margaret, my wife to be and I used the train to the remote Ingra Tor Halt. It really was in the middle of nowhere. It was built by the Great Western during a period in the 1930s when they were adding these simple halts with platforms made of railway sleepers to attract extra business to their lines.

We boarded the train at Princetown having arrived there by Devon General bus from Newton Abbot via Moretonhampstead, and alighted for our walk at Ingra Tor Halt. The train was quite busy with 34 passengers. The moor was covered with thick mist and when we stepped out on the little halt we could barely see one end of the platform from the other. I remember the guard getting out in the mist to collect our tickets then the train disappearing out of sight.

From Ingra Tor the railway continued along open moor before heading across fields then into the woods around Burrator Reservoir. Here was another station that whilst not as exposed, was certainly remote and like Coombe Junction, seemed unsure of its identity. It opened in 1924 as Burrator Platform, serving workmen employed on raising the reservoir dam and with only one train each way calling. A year later the station was opened to the public and the name changed to Burrator Halt, with all trains stopping in daylight hours. It was changed again, to Burrator and Sheepstor Halt in 1929, indicating that it served the hamlet of Sheepstor on the far side of the dam, although the 1954 timetable refers to it as simply Burrator Halt. Like Ingra Tor its traffic was almost entirely walkers, including on one occasion my father. He had travelled to Cornwood on a stopping train from Newton Abbot and walked across the moor to Sheepstor.

I concluded by walking to the Burrator Dam, which I crossed then ascended the short path to Burrator Halt. It was a delightful sight to see the little train emerge from the trees. I was the only person to board here but there were eleven passengers in the single coach. Interestingly, although the halt was named Burrator Halt in the timetable, the name on the station was Sheepstor and Burrator Platform.

The guard came round to collect my fare. I asked for a single to Cornwood to meet up with my outward journey but he could only book me to Plymouth. I changed onto the Tavistock line train at Yelverton and again at Plymouth for my return to Newton Abbot.

This was one of my most memorable Dartmoor walks not only because it had taken me to a part of the moor I particularly wanted to visit but for the experience of travelling on Dartmoor's own railway in winter when it was serving the local people as it had done for seventy years.

With the weather continuing to veer from very pleasant to quite horrible, my return route to Princetown took the short cut that missed the rounding of King Tor and enabled me to reach the Old Police Station Café in time for a cream tea. There was just time to check part of another of my father's book walks, getting back to the car as darkness fell, before returning to Roborough and another much appreciated Toby Carvery.

Dinner was good but nothing to the next day's lunch. After a final short but damp Dartmoor walk, I boarded the 12.56 from Plymouth to Paddington, soon taking my seat in the Pullman restaurant. Brunch on the way to Coombe Junction had been good, but lunch and dinner are fine dining. Silver service and a fillet steak to match the best restaurant, all cooked by chef in a tiny kitchen and enjoyed with an ever-changing view of English countryside. The meal cost more than my ticket had, but what a way to travel.

I shall leave the final word on the Princetown Railway to my father:

My third visit to the railway was three weeks before closure when the train was made up of three coaches to cater for the large number of passengers saying farewell. Lastly I travelled on the final day in March when there were as many as six coaches to accommodate the even greater number of people paying their last respects to this piece of Dartmoor and railway history. This was another misty day on the moor and Princetown was grey and dreary. Motorists on the nearby road sounded their horns which added atmosphere to the occasion. A sad day indeed.

My Father's Tickets from 1956
(Photo Kieron Caton)

CHAPTER THIRTEEN

THE ISLAND LINE: SMALLBROOK JUNCTION

At 8.15 on 16th June 1862 a steam train pulled out of Cowes bound for Newport. This was the first passenger train on the Isle of Wight but by 1900 there were 55 miles of railway on the island. Sadly, as superbly documented by R.E. Burroughs in *The Great Isle of Wight Train Robbery*, by means fair or foul the island has been robbed of most of its railways. An unexpected result of the closures was the opening of a unique remote station, from where I would be changing from pre-war London Underground stock, to a train of coaches at least 100 years old, hauled by *Freshwater*, a steam locomotive that had recently celebrated its 140th birthday. Trains on the Isle of Wight are a little different.

In 1951 the Island's railways carried three million passengers. A year later the attack started. Claiming they would save £16,000, a year the Railway Executive proposed closure of the Merston to Ventnor West line. Ventnor Council objected, sending a deputation to the Executive and a letter to the Transport Users Consultative Committee (to which no reply was received) but to no avail. The line closed on 13th September 1952.

Just a year later British Rail proposed closing three more lines – Newport to Freshwater, Brading to Bembridge and Newport to Sandown. It was claimed that they were losing £271,200 a year, although BR initially refused to provide details to the three day hearing. When they were eventually made available it was clear that the accounting was at best 'creative'. At a further hearing in London the Isle of Wight Council's representative described them as '*fictitious*'.

Amongst many examples he pointed out that the proportion of fares for passengers travelling from the mainland was not included and total season ticket revenue shown as less than the County Council paid the railway for school children. On the Freshwater Line BR said just £5, but the Council paid £53 for school season tickets and other users took the total to at least £98. It was similar on the Bembridge line where BR stated £42 but the Council alone paid £72 for season tickets. Costs for replacement locomotives and coaches were based on brand new equipment, yet the Island had never had any new stock of any kind. Despite the dubious figures and protests of Islanders, by 1956 all three lines had closed.

During the hearings an account of a meeting between BR and the National Union of Railwaymen came to light, in which the management had told the union that it was their intention to close all the railways on the Isle of Wight. All that stood in the way was '*the weekend traffic in summer and getting buses to the pier head*'. So the main obstacle to closure was the millions of passengers who wanted to use the railways!

It came as no surprise when in March 1963 the Beeching Report recommended closure of all the Island's railways. There were protest meetings but a year later BR announced that subject to objections the lines all would close on 12th October 1964. With no shortage of objections and a petition of 81,733 signatures, a hearing had to be held. The Isle of Wight Railway Retention Association submitted a memorandum to the Minister of Transport setting out its case:-

The I.O.W railway carries over 2,800,000 passengers a year; with improved efficiency, B.R. could easily make the railway viable.

The holiday industry is the life-blood of the Island. On Saturdays from June to September five trains an hour in each direction enable visitors with their prams, luggage etc., to travel to and from their destinations with minimum of discomfort. To replace trains 50 buses an hour both in and out of Ryde would be needed in addition to existing services – and buses have little room for holidaymakers' luggage.

The I.O.W. has no main trunk roads, and at least 25% of the cost of any road widening would fall on the ratepayers; also this would destroy much of the Isle of Wight's distinctive countryside beauty which attracts visitors from all over the world.

If holidaymakers did not wish to visit the Isle of Wight then ferry services would show a loss, and many mainline rail lines would suffer diminution of takings. In other words, the Isle of Wight earns money for other sections of British Rail by causing passengers to use the main-line railways to London, Southampton and Portsmouth and then the ferry services across the Solent. This earning capacity should be taken into account when considering the profitability of the I.O.W. railways.

Heading the objectors, Mr Baines, Clerk to the Isle of Wight Council, challenged BR's figures, claiming that 2,800,000 was actually 500,000 or 600,000 short of the true passenger numbers. A discrepancy in the number of level crossings remaining on the island was discovered. BR had said there were 58 but at that time there was just one manned crossing and about a dozen unmanned, mostly in country areas. Mr Baines then brought up the matter of broken pledges. Minutes from a meeting of the Joint Consultative Committee on I.O.W. Transport held in 1956 were quoted. These stated that should there ever be an intention to close the Ryde – Newport – Cowes Line BR would give at least five years' notice, and for the Ryde – Ventnor Line, about seven years. Furthermore, they stated that there would be no closure of the Ryde – Ventnor Line 'except in collaboration with the local authorities'.

Professor E.R. Hondelink, a transport consultant to the United Nations, appeared as a witness and explained that having made a close study he had found a way in which the Island's railways could be made to pay. He proposed increasing visitors' fares by 3d. to cover the mile from Ryde Pier Head to Ryde Esplanade, as this wasn't included in the charge from Waterloo to the Isle of Wight, running trains with just two coaches off season and a close study of possible modernisation.

It was clear that there was a very strong case to keep the Island's remaining railways open and after the lunch adjournment on the second day of the hearing the chairman made an announcement that, subject to anything the BR spokesman might say, they were unanimous that closure of the Ryde to Ventnor line would result in severe hardship. The announcement was greeted with wild applause, all present believing that the line was saved. The Island's MP spoke saying *"I am quite certain that the Minister will just have to rule that these lines must remain open"*, and suggested that as a mark of gratitude to the Chairman, unless further objectors had any new points to make they should refrain from speaking.

Many objectors who had their names down to speak did not do so and the I.O.W Railway Retention Association, which had spent many months of hard work preparing their case, deliberately omitted much of it. Efforts were to be focussed on saving the Cowes line of which the committee were not unanimous in their assessment of hardship.

Then came a bombshell. Mr F.P.B. Taylor, Line Manager of the South Western Division of the British Rail's Southern Region, put forward his proposal to terminate the Ryde to Ventnor line at Shanklin. People from Ventnor and the intermediate village of Wroxhall were shocked, but it was too late to object. The conduct of British Rail and the way in which the hearing was run were both highly questionable, but no more could be done to influence the report that would be sent to the Ministry of Transport. What was in the Consultative Committee's report remained a matter of mystery. It was considered confidential and even two years after the hearing a request to examine a copy was refused.

With a General Election and change of government the Isle of Wight had to wait some time for a decision, but on 23rd July 1965 the Minister for Transport notified the Railway Board and five days later the verdict was made public. The Ryde to Cowes line would close and the Ryde to Ventnor line terminate at Shanklin. The fight to save them however went on.

A copy of the document prepared by BR for the Minister for Transport, containing all the facts and figures on which they hoped to gain closure of the Island's railways, was mysteriously obtained. This proved conclusively what had been known for so long – British Rail were deliberately using false figures to support their case for closure. Perhaps most outrageous amongst the figures was the sum of £153,500 for a new bus depot at Ryde Esplanade – to be paid for by British Rail. Alternatively a depot at Ryde St John's Road at £100,000, plus an annual subsidy of £10,000, to be paid by BR to the bus company. So a railway is closed because it is allegedly losing money, but the railway company is expected to pay for a depot for the buses that replace it.

The document contained another bombshell – the Ryde to Shanklin section would be closed in 1975, ten years later. When this was leaked to the press and a reporter from a national newspaper phoned BR's Public Relations Department at Waterloo he received the reply, "*Oh, so you've found out all about that have you?*"

The steam tank engines in use on the Island dated back to 1889 and could run for little longer. Comparatively modern steam locomotives that could have been used were lying redundant on the mainland, but BR favoured modernisation of the line – then closing it ten years later. They proposed third rail electrification at £680,500 for 8½ miles of track and associated costs, including bringing in forty year old London Underground stock which had been sitting rusting in sidings for five years. Many considered this figure excessive and it was suggested that BR were inflating the figures to deter the Minister for Transport from seeking to electrify the Cowes Line or carry it through from Shanklin to Ventnor.

The combined usage of Ventnor and Wroxall stations was 250,000 passengers a year. Hardly an inconsiderable number and with many holidaymakers using the railway, businesses in Ventnor feared ruin if the line closed. The campaign to save the Shanklin to Ventnor section intensified.

At 3.30am on 10th March 1966 the Island's Member of Parliament rose in the House of Commons. His twenty minute speech deplored the proposed closure of the Shanklin to Ventnor section. He quoted figures showing that the additional cost to electrify the four miles to Ventnor was agreed to be £80,000 but that the Ministry of Transport's divisional road engineer had concurred with the County Council's highways survey that road improvements required in order to run buses along the steep twisty road into Ventnor would cost £100,000. The MP questioned whether it was in the national interest to abandon a section of railway and spend £20,000 more than leaving things as they were.

It transpired that British Rail had said that they were '*not reluctant to support modernisation of the whole line*' provided the first move was made by the County Council without direct support from the railway. Figures showed that the whole line could be run at a profit and the Council agreed.

In the light of these developments a telegram was sent to the Minister for Transport asking for her to receive a deputation to reconsider the closure to Ventnor. No reply was received. After a follow up also drew no response the Clerk to the County Council wrote to the Prime Minister asking him to request that the Minister accepted the delegation. The outcome was a letter to the Island's MP from the Minister for Transport, which stated that she '*had no power to withdraw consent to a closure once it had been* given'.

So, objectors were misled at the hearing, the Minister made the initial decision based on false figures, the railways expressed apparent willingness to electrify the whole line if the County Council made the first move, and when they did the Minister refused to talk. Finally, on being prodded by the Prime Minister, she said she had no power to reverse the original decision, despite this clearly having been made based on false information.

On 21st February 1966 the line from Ryde to Cowes closed. On the 17th April 1966 the last train pulled out of Ventnor station. All that was left of the Isle of Wight's 55 miles of railways was the 8½ miles from Ryde Pier to Shanklin. It seems that the plan to close this ten years later, a plan which was partly responsible for BR carrying out electrification on the cheap, was quietly forgotten and ancient tube trains continue to trundle across the Island to this day.

Steam came back to the Island in 1971, preservationists opening a 1½ mile section of the old Ryde to Newport line between Wooton and Haven Street. After considerable effort, twenty years later the line was extended four miles to meet the Island Line at Smallbrook Junction. On 20th July 1991 a new station was opened here by Chris Green, Director of British Rail's Network South East, who had funded it, allowing passengers to change between the two railways – a station where there was never one before and with no community of its own to serve. A remote station!

A 22 minute hydrofoil ride from Portsmouth took me to Ryde Pier and the Island Line station, where the spacious hall and long platforms remain from the days when thousands of summer visitors changed here for trains around the island. No writer describing the two coach train appearing at Ryde Esplanade station and slowly approaching along the pier could fail to use the word diminutive. It was strange travelling along a pier on a London Underground train dating from 1938 and as the guard came round to check tickets one could be forgiven for forgetting that this is a real train service, not a tourist railway.

Island Line Train on Ryde Pier

After pausing at Ryde Esplanade we entered a tunnel, which is the reason why discarded underground trains have operated the line since the switch from steam. The tunnel is prone to flooding on high tides and in 1966 the track bed was raised by about 25cm to reduce the number of occasions when it would have to be closed. With a reduced distance from rail to roof, 'normal' trains won't fit through, so the line makes do with ancient tube trains.

Floods still occur and sometimes the line has to shut, but on one occasion it wasn't really the sea to blame. High tides had flooded the cellars of the Royal Esplanade Hotel and the fire brigade were called. They kindly pumped it out, however rather than running their hoses back to the sea, emptied them onto the railway, from where the water flowed into the tunnel and closed the line!

After St John's Road, Ryde's third station, we were soon in the countryside and halting at Smallbrook Junction, where I was the sole passenger to alight or board. On the opposite platform was a steam train and leaning on the fence a welcoming committee – the driver, fireman, guard and station master, all watching the Island Line train and sharing banter with its guard. With just a two minute connection there was no time to explore, so after buying a ticket from the little wooden booking office I hurried down the platform and jumped into a compartment, joining a family whose young son gave a running commentary on the journey.

The line's headquarters is at Haven Street, so after running through pleasant countryside and reversing at Wooton, trains wait here to allow passengers to explore. I was just beaten to the café by an entire coach party but enjoyed the excellent museum and even a falconry display, before resuming my journey back to Smallbrook Junction. Here there was time to watch the locomotive run round, the guard change the points in a little wooden hut and the train depart once more for Wooton. What a sight it made as the ancient Southern Railway coaches hauled by *Freshwater*, an attractive little locomotive that was built in 1876, headed back across the island.

The station is in two parts linked by a sloping walkway. On the

Isle of Wight Railway Platform Smallbrook Junction

steam railway platform a traditional wooden building houses the booking office, toilet and waiting room. Both platforms are wooden, with wooden fences and with trees on one side and fields on the other, it is a pretty little station. Just an ugly glass and metal shelter adjacent to the Island Line spoils the effect.

I'd been to stations where there is no road access but at Smallbrook Junction there's not even any way out on foot. Uniquely in the UK it serves only as an interchange, so presumably anyone failing to board the last train of the day would have to spend the night here. Indeed the wait could be longer. The Island Line only calls here when the steam trains are operating, so someone missing the last train in October would be quite hungry by the time the Santa Specials start in December.

Each year around 12,000 passengers use Smallbrook Junction but its long term existence is in some doubt. The railway from Ryde to Shanklin opened in 1864 and it was not until eleven years later that the Ryde to Newport line opened. As now, they diverged at Smallbrook Junction, although initially there was no physical connection here. Both

'Freshwater' Hauls its Ancient Coaches Away From Smallbrook Junction

ran on single tracks from Ryde St John's, which parted at Smallbrook. Later the Southern Railway installed a scissors crossover and small signal box at Smallbrook, making the two single lines into double track. In summer this increased capacity on the busy route to Shanklin and Ventnor, but it wasn't needed in winter when the signal box was closed, signal arms removed and points clipped, the operation reverting to two single tracks.

The Isle of Wight Steam Railway now have ambitions to run their trains to Ryde St John's, which would become the interchange between the two lines. It's far from a fanciful hope. The current stock on the Island Line will be almost ninety years old before more potentially suitable replacement London Underground trains become available. These will be forty years old and require expensive conversion. Serious consideration is being given to converting the Island Line to trams, with passing points to allow a 15 minute frequency. Currently the rather odd configuration (double track only between Ryde St John's and Smallbrook, with a passing loop at Sandown) means that train intervals are 20 and 40 minutes. This would release one of the two tracks between Smallbrook and St John's, allowing steam trains to run into the town but meaning the only purpose for Smallbrook Junction station would be as the shortest route from Shanklin to Wooton. With

Ryde St John's just a mile down the line it would be hard to justify keeping Smallbrook, so the price of what looks to be a positive plan for both railways might be to lose a little station that is unique in the whole of Britain.

Island Line Train Calls at Smallbrook Junction

MAP 6 – East Anglia

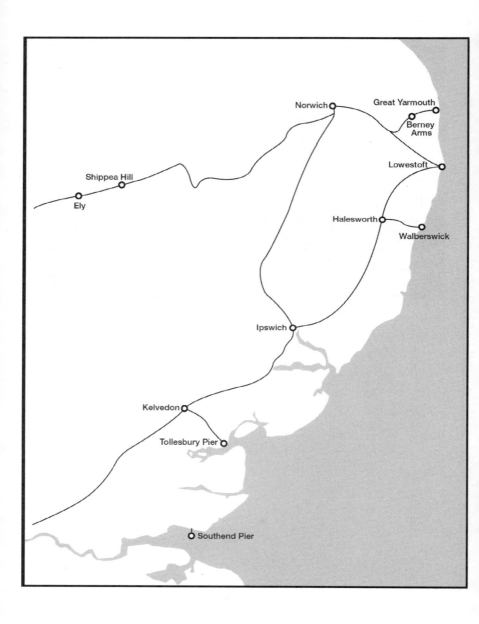

CHAPTER FOURTEEN

SOUTHEND PIER RAILWAY

A railway station 1½ miles from the shore, perched above the Thames Estuary, seemed to meet the definition of remote, so embarking on the simplest journey of all my travels I boarded a c2c train at Upminster for the 32 minute run to the Essex seaside.

Originally the south end of the village of Prittlewell, Southend started to grow as a seaside resort in the early 19th century, its recognition as a watering place resulting largely from a visit here by Princess Caroline of Wales. Before the railways opened Londoners came by boat, but with mudflats extending for over a mile at low tide, large steamers were unable to stop here. Many potential visitors passed by, travelling on to Margate or other resorts where docking facilities were easier. A campaign led by Sir William Heygate, a former Lord Mayor of London, resulted in Parliament passing an act giving authorisation for construction of a pier in 1829 and a year later the first pier opened. I don't suppose it crossed his mind that almost 200 years later a part-time author might travel behind a locomotive bearing his name on a railway to the end of the longest pleasure pier in the world.

Built entirely of wood, within five years it had been extended to half a mile in length but at low tide passengers still had to walk along a causeway of shingle, then be ferried across a channel to reach the 'Mount' a somewhat primitive structure of piles where the steamers could dock. This inconvenience was overcome in 1846 when the pier was lengthened to 1¼ miles, making it the longest in Europe.

It was on this pier that the first railway was laid, constructed from wooden rails. Initially trucks were pushed by hand to convey luggage to and from steamers but later a special truck fitted with a sail was employed when the wind was favourable. In 1875 new iron rails were laid, along which a tram was hauled by two horses in tandem. The line passed straight through the pier's entertainment pavilion, horses pulling the tram through the centre of the tent even while concerts were proceeding!

After just six years the tramway had to be closed due to the unsafe nature of the track. It had never been entirely satisfactory as the horses had a tendency to put their hooves through holes in the planking of the pier, a problem which one councillor suggested overcoming by obtaining an elephant.

The huge growth in the number of visitors after the London Tilbury & Southend Railway reached Southend in 1856 took a toll on the wooden structure and it was decided that a new pier should be built. This would be made from iron and incorporate what would be one of the world's first electric railways. Designed by James Brunlees, who had built the first iron pier at Southport, it was completed in 1889 and the ¾ mile 3 foot 6 inch gauge third rail electric railway opened a year later.

It was to prove an immediate success with 800 people travelling on the first afternoon and more than 3,000 on the following Monday, a Bank Holiday. Demand far exceeded the capacity of the railway's only vehicle, a small open sided car of 'toast rack' design, with six rows of cross-bench seats. In due course the pier received further extension and an upper deck, more cars were ordered for the railway and the line was extended to 1¼ miles.

By the mid 1920s annual usage was approaching 2 million and track work was carried out to increase capacity, including lengthening the mid-way loop. It was here that in September 1928 the railway's most serious accident occurred, when the last two coaches of a train travelling towards the shore were struck by the leading car of an outward train coming off the loop. The two cars were knocked off the track but fortunately towards the walkway and not into the sea. No one was seriously hurt but a number of elderly and infirm folk at the head of the pier remained stranded until bath chairs could be obtained to wheel them to the shore. The accident was found to have been caused by sudden illness of the driver. He was found employment elsewhere on the pier and in future all drivers received an annual medical examination.

A strange incident occurred one Saturday afternoon in the summer of 1937. A passenger rose from his seat while the train was in motion, lost his balance and fell over the railing. Fortunately the tide was out but as the train came to a halt passengers looking over the rail expected to see the man seriously injured. It was with much relief that he was sitting up and shaking sand from his hair, suffering only from shock and bruises.

The pier was closed to visitors during the Second World War but was renamed HMS Leigh and used as an assembly point for convoys, with anti-aircraft guns positioned on the pier head. The railway supplied ammunition and ferried casualties ashore from the ships, although masters of passing merchant ships complained that the trains set off acoustic aircraft early warning devices fitted to their vessels.

New trains were purchased in 1949 and the following year 4,713,082 passengers were conveyed, the only year in the line's history when the four million mark has been surpassed. In contrast, total visitors to the pier, including those who don't take the train, is now in the region of 300,000 a year.

At this point my detailed history of the pier came to an end. Jeremy at Swan Books had managed to get me a copy of the quite rare book *The Southend Pier Railway* by K.A. Frost, which at £25 for the 24 page booklet wasn't cheap, but is the most authoritative publication on the railway. It was however published in 1965, so ends on the positive notes that the 'new' trains were carrying two million passengers a year and had suffered no major breakdowns.

In October 1978 the railway closed. An inspection of the track showed it had deteriorated to a state where complete replacement was necessary but the cost was considered too high. Two years earlier a huge fire had destroyed virtually all the buildings at the pier head and with no railway, little to entertain visitors and a huge maintenance bill, Southend Council announced that the pier would close. There was an immediate public outcry and responding to protests they agreed that it could stay open until solution was found.

Three years later the Historic Buildings Committee gave a grant for repairs and not only was the pier to be saved, but the railway rebuilt. In 1986 Princess Anne opened the new three foot gauge railway, operated by the two seven coach diesel trains which are still taking visitors along the iconic pier. With a half hourly service, trains pass in a loop half way and whilst numbers are nothing like those in the pier's heyday, on a sunny summer's day often every seat is taken.

Before catching the train I visited the pier museum under the shore station. Here are kept three of the green and yellow coaches that ran from 1949 to 1978. These were the trains that we travelled on in childhood visits to Southend. Powered by third rail electric and with automatic doors, they always reminded me of the underground, although the views were somewhat better! Reversible seats meant that passengers could always face the front. The rolling stock had been scrapped in 1982 but these three coaches were rescued, one from a local scrapyard with a tree growing through the floor.

As I got my notebook out the lady from behind the counter asked if she could help. She told me that the trains had seven cars, three motorised and four trailers. There were four trains running a more intensive service than now. She pointed out the unusual circular windscreen wipers and the electric doors. Her enthusiasm for the old trains didn't extend to the current diesel ones. They'd *"ruined it"*. She said the diesel trains had been given a life of fifteen years, but have now run for more than double that with no sign of any replacements imminent.

After viewing a restored 1890 'toast rack' tram that had been rescued from use as a chicken shed, I made my way to the Tourist Information Centre that doubles as the pier railway's ticket office. Like many visitors, I bought a ticket to ride one way and walk the other. One train was out of use, berthed in the right hand platform. This was '*Sir John Betjeman*' named after the poet who famously wrote that '*The pier is Southend, Southend is the pier*'. The other arrived, disgorged its load of windswept passengers and soon I was heading out to sea behind '*Sir William Heygate*'. With the tide high the whole journey was over water. It takes just under ten minutes to reach one of our more unusually sited remote stations, along what must be the straightest railway in Britain.

Alighting onto the simple wooden island platform there is a sense of remoteness, although neither quiet nor solitude. Rarely does the wind fail to blow and in daytime the pier is never deserted. I imagine it would feel rather different if one managed to get locked in for a night.

The station is a simple affair with an attractive modern glass roof. It had to be rebuilt after a fire destroyed the pier head in 2005, one of many catastrophes it has survived. A fire in 1959 destroyed the pavilion at the shore end and another in 1976 burned down most of the pier head buildings. The bowling alley that had replaced the pavilion was itself destroyed by fire in 1995, but fortunately the shore station and pier museum were spared. The pier itself was severed in 1979 when the *MV Kingsabbey* inexplicitly sailed straight into it, destroying the lifeboat station and gentlemen's toilets. A man inside had a lucky escape.

Pier Head Station

The current station was opened by the Mayor of Southend on 16th September 2009 and replaced a temporary platform that had been in use since soon after the fire. The official opening however didn't go quite to plan. Mayor and Mayoress Brian and Lyn Smith were on board a train which was due to plough through a ribbon at the new station, but just past the half way point along the pier a loud clunk was heard and the train came to an abrupt stop. It was soon clear that the locomotive, *Sir John Betjeman*, had come off the track. The buggy used to transport lifeboat crew along the pier was summoned and after being photographed by the local paper pretending to lift the locomotive back onto the rails, the Mayor and his wife continued their journey by buggy. The other train was sent from the pier head to collect the rest of the guests and eventually to the accompaniment of a jazz band the station was declared officially open.

In recent years the pier head has been greatly improved. There's a new lifeboat station and RNLI shop, a pavilion with art space, a sun deck, plus of course somewhere to buy chips and ice creams. The new glass covered railway station is in keeping with the pier's modern buildings that have replaced those lost in the various fires.

Watching trains trundle by, listening to gulls overhead and licking an ice cream, I walked back to the shore, just as millions of visitors have done for generations. Like many families, we were taken here for a day out by our parents then brought our own children for a ride on the pier. The trains will need replacing and there will no doubt be more catastrophes to survive, but usage is increasing and now it's hard to imagine that the pier railway and its station over the waves will be allowed to close.

CHAPTER FIFTEEN

THE KELVEDON AND TOLLESBURY LIGHT RAILWAY: TOLLESBURY PIER

I started my day at a jam factory. No ordinary jam factory mind you – it's also a museum of jam making, perhaps rivalling the Keswick Pencil Museum and Southport Lawnmower Museum as our strangest, yet most British tourist attractions. I'd been past many times before on the way to walks on the Essex coast, but this time I called in. It's a jam factory whose history is intertwined with railways and without which the remote station of Tollesbury Pier may never have existed. Nor might it have existed if Prime Minister William Gladstone hadn't made a speech in which he commended the practice of fruit preserving.

When Gladstone made his unlikely speech Essex farmer Arthur Charles Wilkin had been growing fruit in the fertile fields around Tiptree for twenty years, much of which was taken three miles to Kelvedon station by horse and cart, then by train to London. The railway however wasn't particularly keen to carry the ripe strawberries, insisting on loading them into coal trucks under black tarpaulins, which caused them to ferment. They had no scheduled rate for soft fruit so charged the same as brittle furniture, 26 shillings and 8 pence per ton.

Inspired by the Prime Minister and disheartened by the railway's inefficiency in transporting his fruit, Wilkins decided to use the top quality produce to make jam. The Britannia Fruit Preserving Company was formed and within ten years 100 tonnes of fruit was being made into jam. This however needed to get to London, which still involved horses and carts over rutted tracks to the Great Eastern Railway's station at Kelvedon.

A railway was needed, not only to carry jam but for farm produce from the area, which had to be loaded onto carts and hauled behind shire horses to stations at Witham, Maldon or Kelvedon. The people of this isolated corner of Essex felt cut off and support for a railway quickly grew. Arthur Wilkin was a prime mover, offered his land for free and even threatened to move his factory to Dagenham if a line wasn't built.

It was proposed that the line be built under the Light Railways Act, which in order to encourage construction of branches into areas where traffic prospects were limited, permitted a lesser standard of equipment than the Board of Trade insisted on for main lines. This sparsely populated corner of Essex was such an area and the line was justified as much by its potential to carry freight as people.

An inquiry in 1898 received just two objections, one from Essex County Council who said it should be fenced throughout and the other from Maldon Rural District Council who wanted all the level crossings manned. A further inquiry arranged by the Board of Trade received just one objection, that being against the ruling that trains had to slow to 10mph within 300 yards of all level crossings. Authorisation under a Light Railway Order was made in January 1901 (with an amendment the following month that the 10mph limit should apply only within 200 yards of level crossings) and construction began in November 1902. The line was to run from Kelvedon, where a low level station was built below the GER line, through Tiptree with a siding to the jam factory, Tolleshunt D'Arcy and on to the coastal village of Tollesbury. An extension would follow across the marshes to the bank of the River Blackwater where Tollesbury Pier would become its terminus.

The first train ran on 1st October 1904, leaving Kelvedon at 11am in steady rain with a party of 120 guests on board. At Tiptree the jam factory workers turned out to applaud the new train and its arrival at Tollesbury was welcomed by a crowd of eager onlookers. The party followed the half-finished extension to the Blackwater Estuary, then returned for lunch at the Kings Head which had been decorated with bunting. The many Tollesbury villagers who later in the day enjoyed a first trip on their own little railway, taking the evening train to Tiptree, could not have imagined that it would last for just 47 years and that the pier extension survive for less than a third of this.

After perusing the jam museum, which I have to say was marginally more interesting than it sounds, mainly on account of containing a whole panel of information on the railway, I set off for Tollesbury and a remote Essex railway station that closed almost 100 years ago. First port of call was the Lighthouse Christian Cafe, where I met Eric Peacock who had a mention in *No Boat Required* as a rare person who'd once walked across the sands to the outermost of the Sandaig Islands south of Kyle of Lochalsh. He kindly gave me a copy of *Tollesbury to the Year 2000*, a most interesting book compiled by people of the village and containing a section on the railway.

Eric told me that having stood for many years in someone's garden, the platform of Tollesbury station had been removed to make more room for their horses. Like Kelvedon and Tiptree, Tollesbury was once an attractive station with a wooden waiting room, more permanent than three of the line's halts which used old railway coaches as buildings and Feering Halt where a converted single-decker bus served as both waiting room and parcels office.

It was a pleasant walk of about a mile along lanes then a rather muddy footpath to reach the remains of what locals named the Crab and Winkle Line, on account of the seafood it carried from Tollesbury, which in the early 20th century was a busy fishing village. It could just have easily been the Jam & Turnip. The extension route is fenced off but I didn't have to stray too far beyond a 'Private' sign (did I really just write that?) to reach a point where a farm track crossed it and I could look up the line towards Tollesbury and down to the river.

A six-sided brick building a couple of hundred yards inland was built in 1940 as a control tower for electrically controlled mines in the Blackwater. Although long closed, the extension's rails had not been taken up and the overgrown track was used by four locomotives to service mobile guns which were stationed along the estuary.

Site of Tollesbury Pier Station (Bradwell Power Station in the Background)

Undated Photo of the 'Crab & Winkle' Arriving at Tollesbury Pier Station (Tony & Nicky Harden)

A further half mile down the path (a legitimate one this time) took me to the riverside and Tollesbury Pier station, or rather, the site of Tollesbury Pier station. The station had been built with ambitious plans to bring wealth to the village. Houses were to be constructed at this lonely spot on the marshes, along with a pier and optimistic plans to develop it into a weekend yachting resort and continental packet station. An article by W. Parker in *The Railway Magazine* published soon after the line opened to Tollesbury talked of *'still greater things promised'*. *'Quite big boats will be able to tranship their contents into railway trucks'*. *'There is talk of a pier, whispers of prospective holiday visitors, and hints on many good things'*.

A timber pier was indeed constructed, extending one third of a mile into the river so shallow draught vessels could load and unload at all states of the tide and the railway's extension to Tollesbury Pier station opened on 15th May 1907. Three yards wide with wooden fencing either side, the pier made a pleasant walk and in good weather villagers would take the train to the terminus then walk home. Perhaps not surprisingly, the rest of the development on the often desolate salt marsh failed to proceed and plans for continental steamers were finally put to bed at the outbreak of the Great War. Four trains a day ran from Kelvedon to Tollesbury with most continuing to the pier, however passengers were few and just 14 years after it opened, the extension was closed in 1921.

Tollesbury Pier station had consisted of a small waiting hut and two old coach bodies. Like all the line's stations the platform was unusually low; just 15 inches above the rails. There were no staff based here and necessary duties were carried out by Jack Gallant, the station master at Tollesbury, who would ride down on the train. His deputy Arthur Lawrence was responsible for tending the navigation lights on the pier.

The site of the station is inside Tollesbury Wick Nature Reserve and a sign asks visitors to keep out in order not to disturb the many birds who live and nest here. Hence my exploration of Tollesbury Pier station was restricted to viewing across a fence by the sea wall. Not that there is much to see. The route of the railway can be seen heading

Undated Photo of Tollesbury Pier Station
(Tony & Nicky Harden)

across the marsh towards the WW2 control tower but all that remains of the station seems to be an earth embankment behind the reserve gate.

But what a site it must have been when the Crab and Winkle's little trains crawled across the marshes. Locomotives were 'Jubilee' 0-6-0 tanks, who worked the branch one at a time on a weekly roster. For some years they had their coupling rods removed to reduce wear and tear on the line's sharp curves, but eventually it was decided this was not a success and they were replaced. The coaches were most unusual, with four wheel compartment stock dating from 1877 to 1882, converted to meet the line's needs at Stratford Works. The normal 3ft 6½in wheels were replaced by ones of 2ft 9in diameter to provide a lower floor level in compensation for the low platforms. Compartment partitions were removed and gangways plus end doors with drop plates provided so the guard could walk through the train to issue tickets.

The practice of selling tickets en-route was a spectacle in itself. First the guard would walk the length of the train taking orders from passengers. Then he'd return to his van and make out the tickets which were of 'bus type' and printed at the GER works in Stratford.

Stages were printed down each side and the guard would punch them according to the boarding point of each passenger. The tickets would then be taken down the train and issued to passengers, who would watch in amusement at the acrobatic feats he performed in passing outside the train from coach to coach.

For many years the pier stood protruding into the Blackwater, a reminder of what might have been and the railway that ran across the marshes to serve it. A section close to the shore was blown up in 1940 as an anti-invasion measure but it wasn't demolished until the line was taken up in 1951. Most sources say that any remaining traces were washed away in the great floods of 1953, but in fact at low tide a line of timber posts can still be seen running into the river from a WW2 concrete pill box. I walked down to the shore, stepping gingerly on the mud, to photograph all that remains of an ambitious if unlikely plan from more than a hundred years ago. It may have been doomed to failure but it brought about one of our most unusual and remote railway stations.

I walked back to Tollesbury on the sea wall, a typical section of remote Essex coastline, looking across the marshes as the sun set and imagining a steam locomotive pulling its ancient coaches down to the lonely station by the river.

Whilst the remainder of the line survived until 1951, its demise was probably inevitable once improved roads were built and a bus

Remains of Tollesbury Pier

introduced following the same route, but terminating at Witham where there was a better train service to London. The bus of course could never have served Tollesbury Pier which was a mile from the nearest road. With little alternative transport the line had been well used in its early years. Sailing men travelled to Tollesbury to join yachts, while young women going into service joined trains at Essex villages to travel to London. In the First World War several hundred soldiers were transported to Tollesbury for training and exercises and in both wars servicemen travelled for free, being seen off for their duty at the station by their whole family. Safe returns were wished but not all came back.

Later people commuted to the capital for work, but it was a slow journey, the trains not being permitted to exceed 25mph and having to slow to 10mph at ungated crossings. Many were mixed passenger and freight, so time had to be allowed for shunting. Passenger trains took 30 minutes to Kelvedon whilst mixed ones were allowed 40, but with 24 minutes allocated for the short walk between stations at the junction, a journey from London might take 2½ hours. The train was an important part of Tollesbury life. It could be hailed almost anywhere along the line and would stop to pick up passengers who joined what was a very social affair. The later carriages had come from the Wisbech & Upwell Tramway, and had seats along the side with balconies at each end. Nearly everyone knew each other and it was a great place for exchanging gossip.

Up to 1,000 passengers a day had travelled in the line's early years but by 1947 this had dropped to an average of just 33 return journeys. With nationalisation in 1948 came pressure to cut costs and the loss-making Tollesbury branch was an easy target for British Rail. There was little opposition when closure plans were submitted and the final passenger train was to run on 7th May 1951. Once again the locals turned out in force. Most of them may not have used their railway but as with closures all over the country, they didn't really want to see it go and were keen to be here to watch the final train.

Thirty years after Tollesbury Pier station had closed without ceremony, 430 people crammed into three coaches for the final return journey from Kelvedon to Tollesbury. The local MP rode on the footplate as honorary fireman and the train was cheered on its way by bystanders with football rattles and fog-horns. A black coffin was placed on the platform at Tiptree, one of the wreaths covering it shaped in the letters 'BR'. On the engine's firebox was chalked *Born 1904 – Died 1951*' and on the bunker a solemn warning '*There may be many a poor soul have to walk*'.

The section from Kelvedon to Tiptree was kept open for freight, mainly to serve the jam factory, which now known as Wilkin and Sons was still owned by the Wilkin family. Traffic on the daily freight train dwindled and to save the £600 annual loss British Rail applied for closure. There were no objections and the last freight train ran in 1962. Many years later John Wilkin, grandson of Arthur Wilkin, agreed that it was sad after all the effort to build the railway in the first place, but said that they were really quite glad to see the back of it as so much jam was being stolen during the journey to Kelvedon.

The jam factory, without which one of our more remarkable railway lines may never have existed, continues to thrive. Produce is now delivered by road but just a few days after my visit I was pleased to find that Tiptree's apricot jam can still be found on a train, a little pot of it being supplied with my breakfast croissant on a Eurostar to Brussels. But how different things might have been. How much more romantic would have been a journey across the marshes on the Crab and Winkle, boarding a ship at Tollesbury Pier and steaming across the Channel to the Continent?

CHAPTER SIXTEEN

SOUTHWOLD RAILWAY: WALBERSWICK

On my first day as an author I'd caught the 10.00 from Liverpool Street to Norwich, enjoying breakfast in the restaurant car before setting off on my *Essex Coast Walk* from Manningtree. Today I caught the same service, still a proper Inter City train, hauled by a locomotive but sadly no longer offering walkers a breakfast to set them on their way. On a cold morning in Ipswich I was glad to change straight into a warm and comfortable two coach train for a ride along the East Suffolk Line, a journey I'd made for most of my *Suffolk Coast Walks*. Until reaching its destination at Lowestoft the line touches the coast (or at least tidal rivers) at only Ipswich and Woodbridge, so I was used to changing to buses to reach the sea.

From 1879 to 1929 passengers travelling to Southwold had no need for a bus, whether the horse drawn omnibus from Darsham that preceded the railway, or the motor coach from Halesworth that killed it off. For those fifty years visitors from afar would complete their journey to the newly discovered seaside resort with a ride along the eccentric little branch line. The three intermediate stations, Wenhaston, Blythburgh and Walberswick, provided villagers with convenient links to the terminus towns and outside world beyond. I'd walked part of the line as a chapter in *Suffolk Coast Walk* and noted then how Walberswick station must have been a lonely spot to leave the train.

The nine minute bus connection at Halesworth looked in doubt as we waited to cross a late running southbound train at Woodbridge. The bus wouldn't wait. Had the Southwold train still been running no doubt it would have done. With a little time made up we arrived two minutes before the 88A double-decker pulled in and I was soon bumping along Suffolk lanes to Blythburgh, a tiny village at the head of the Blyth Estuary, best known for its fine church.

The cold at Ipswich had given way to a sunny late morning and I was glad to find that Blythburgh now has a village shop, so duly stocked up with water and chocolate before setting out along the railway line. The whole route is walkable but the five miles from Blythburgh to Southwold is the most varied and scenic section. On my first visit I'd questioned whether I was on the right path, the narrow embankment beside the estuary seeming too small to have held a railway, but the discovery of a length of rail protruding from the mud confirmed this was the way. Three years later, and almost ninety years since the railway closed, the rail is still there, a reminder of the little trains that puffed along beside the water.

Track bed of Southwold Railway near Blythburgh

The railway was built to the unusual gauge of three feet, although with a wider loading gauge in case it was ever taken into the national system and converted. It wasn't fast, taking 37 minutes for the 8¾ mile run as drivers had to stick to a 16mph speed limit, the railway's rule book threatening two years' imprisonment should any exceed it. Trains were often mixed, carrying coal, fish and parcels, as well as passengers.

For such a small railway the company imposed a large number of rules on its staff. Rule 64 required the driver and fireman to frequently look back and *see that the whole train is following in a safe and proper manner*. On one occasion the guard took this duty one step further. Two schoolboys were travelling in the rear coach and as they looked through the back window noticed the coupling to a truck behind had come loose. The guard was informed and stepped out onto the coach's platform, leaned over the rail and held onto the truck until the train came to a halt at the next station.

Another occasion almost resulted in a far more serious incident. A locomotive hauling a busy evening train of six very full coaches from Southwold came to a halt on the gradient approaching Halesworth and was unable to reach the station. Three coaches were uncoupled and their brake applied, with the plan that the locomotive would return for them shortly. Unfortunately as the engine set off for Halesworth with the three front coaches, the three rear ones set off in the opposite direction. Either their brake was insufficient or the locomotive's parting jolt had sent them off down the incline. The coaches accelerated towards Southwold, which the local paper reported as causing *considerable consternation to the more timid passengers*, and couldn't be brought to a halt until the village of Blyford 2½ miles down the line. Fortunately no harm was caused and the locomotive soon arrived to take the rest of its train back to Halesworth.

Curving away from the estuary the route climbs into an area of tall pine trees known as The Heronry, a 1 in 88 gradient hard work for the little engines. Sometimes the train halted here for the driver to collect a hare from a snare that had been set on a previous journey. List's Cutting is traversed, named after the gamekeeper John List whose cottage can be seen through the trees, before the line emerges into classic Suffolk heathland. Half a mile of the track bed is inaccessible so walkers divert onto a path then the lane, before re-joining the railway on Walberswick Common, a national nature reserve.

Walberswick station is reached as the line emerges beside extensive reed beds just beyond a cattle creep, a small gap in the embankment to allow livestock to pass through. Sometimes however they preferred to walk on the track and there was one occasion when the train had to halt for a bull who simply refused to budge. The engine's boiler rake was employed in an attempt to drive him off, but the bull took the end in his mouth and much to the amusement of passengers a tug of war took place before he could be ushered away.

The station wasn't included in the original plan for the line. According to the company's minute book it opened on 2nd September 1881 but Board of Trade records state that approval was not given until 1st July 1882. Approval was granted despite toilet facilities consisting of only a urinal, anyone requiring other conveniences presumably being deemed capable of holding on until reaching Southwold or Halesworth. The original station building comprised of just a small hut but in 1902 this was replaced with a much larger timber-framed corrugated structure, incorporating a clerk's office, booking office and waiting room. Despite its isolated situation the station appears to have been reasonably well used and trains were often met by a pony and trap which carried passengers the mile into Walberswick village. Two sidings were provided for goods, with catch points to prevent wagons running out onto the main line.

All that remains of the station is a stone base on which a commemorative seat stands. An inscription advises that it was provided by contributions from members of the Southwold Railway Society and opened in 1996 by Mrs Margaret Chadd, a remarkable lady who devoted her life to healthcare and played a key role in the development of the hospice movement. On a sunny afternoon this was a most pleasant spot with views across the marshes to Southwold but like so many of my remote stations, must have been a desolate place to wait on a cold winter's evening. It would have been a wild walk into Walberswick when winds blew off the North Sea a mile to the east. In summer I might have made the walk myself and enjoyed a wander around the attractive village that has for many years been a popular haunt for artists. I might have been tempted by the particularly delicious cakes in the *Parish Lantern* but the little ferry that links Walberswick to Southwold doesn't run in winter, so I continued along the railway embankment, soon crossing a bridge over the Blyth.

Remains of Walberswick Station

Undated Photo of Walberswick
(Tony & Nicky Harden)

In order to allow navigation up the estuary the railway built a swing bridge, although in the event it was rarely opened. This was replaced in 1907 as part of a proposal to widen the line to standard gauge and remained in place until WW2 when the army blew it up in the interest of national security. The current Bailey bridge, a fixed crossing for walkers and cyclists, stands on the original plinths.

A branch on the right once served Southwold Harbour, while the main route continued across marshes then through a cutting bisecting the golf course (the club paid £50 to erect a footbridge largely constructed of old rails), then climbing into the town.

It was on this stretch of track where Arthur Wright, a guard on the line from the first train on 24th September 1879 until he retired in 1914, experienced his most embarrassing journey. One dark evening, while passing from one coach to the next he missed his footing and tumbled down the embankment. No one saw him fall so the driver continued unaware and Mr Wright came to his feet just in time to see the train's tail light disappear into Southwold Cutting. On arrival at the terminus it was found that the passengers were still locked in but there was no sign of the guard. A search party carrying lanterns set off down the track and met the fortunately unharmed Mr Wright trudging up the slope in pursuit of his train.

No signs of the terminus station remain, the land having been taken over by the fire station and later the police station, but the attractive station hotel opposite is still in business, now the Blyth Hotel. The line had closed in 1929 with the last train packed, a wreath on the engine's smokebox and a mix of sadness with celebration of the life of a unique railway. The track remained in place until 1942 when it was lifted as part of the war effort for recovery of scrap metal.

In the First World War the railway had played an important role moving troops who were stationed at Henham Park near Blythburgh. Special trains were run at night so the public wouldn't know of the military movements. The railway was called upon at very short notice when following the German bombardment of Scarborough, St Felix School in Southwold received a message from the War Office that their girls should be sent home at once. The next train was due to depart in just half an hour so Miss Daniel, the school's second mistress, went on ahead to warn the station master. On being told that all the spare carriages were kept at Halesworth as a war-time precaution Miss Daniel asked "*Have you any coal trucks*". "*Yes*" responded the station master, on which he was instructed to get them out. The girls packed into coaches and trucks, all reaching home that day, although some with their hands and faces black from coal dust.

I walked into the town then down to the sea, before returning to visit The Southwold Railway Shop. Soon after my visit this closed down and Southwold Railway Steamworks opened, not far from the original terminus. Here, as well as the shop and a café, a length of 3 foot track is being laid and a miniature railway constructed.

The Southwold Railway Trust is committed to restoring the line and is making moderate progress, although not without opposition. A replica of locomotive *No. 3 Blyth* is being constructed but the Trust's plans to lay track at Wenhaston were repeatedly thwarted by planning refusal. An initial short length has however been laid and five acres of land purchased. The people of Southwold may be unsure whether they want a railway bringing tourists to their genteel town and full restoration may be a long way off, but hopefully before too long the sound of steam will once more be heard beside the Blyth estuary.

CHAPTER SEVENTEEN

NORWICH – GREAT YARMOUTH LINE: BERNEY ARMS

Probably the most famous remote railway station in England, Berney Arms sits on the Norfolk marshes, surrounded by fields and water but very little else. There's a farmhouse 600 yards away, a windmill and a closed pub, but with no road access the thousand or so people who use it each year are mostly walkers. It's another station which asks the question, why was it built?

The answer is that like a number of our remote stations, it was part of a deal with the landowner to allow the railway to pass through their property. The more southerly of the two lines from Norwich to Great Yarmouth, it opened in May 1844, gaining the distinction of being the first railway in Norfolk. Thomas Trench Berney had sold the land to the Great Eastern Railway but few passengers used Berney Arms Halt, which they'd built to honour the agreement. Then the company realised that the deal was for a station and not for trains to actually call there, so they stopped serving the halt. A legal battle ensued which the company must have expected to lose, as in 1855 they started stopping trains here again, although the court didn't issue its findings until 1860. Agreement was then reached for one train each way to stop on Mondays, Wednesdays and Saturdays and for Mr Berney to be paid £200 in compensation, a not inconsiderable sum in those days.

Now on weekdays just one or two trains each way stop, although more call at weekends to cater for walkers. The first leaves Norwich in early morning, the other just before lunch, so it was this one I planned to catch. With only a nine minute connection off the recommended 9.30 from Liverpool Street I caught the 9.00, hence it didn't matter that we arrived 15 minutes late, as did the 9.30, although with commendable common sense the single coach Yarmouth train waited a few minutes for passengers to make the connection. Not that any were going to Berney Arms, where I was the sole traveller alighting. Initially the guard had said I'd need to use the front door but then decided that either would be OK and indeed both just fitted on the short platform. As the train disappeared into the distance on the straight track towards Yarmouth I was once again left alone on a remote station platform, this one three miles from the nearest road.

The closest house is Ashtree Farm 600 yards away but there was once a small community here whose access to the outside world was only by train, boat, or along a muddy track across the marshes. Sheila Hutchinson was brought up in one of the few cottages and lived at Berney Arms until 1963. She writes of her memories of life in this isolated settlement in *Berney Arms Remembered* and *Berney Arms Past & Present*.

Berney Arms

The railway was vital to the little community bringing groceries and water, and collecting milk churns from the farm, which were carried in the guards van. After the platform was cut back from 60 yards to a single carriage length, trains would pull up with the guards van in the platform and locals would use the adjacent carriage.

Post came by train and locals delivered it to the eleven dwellings of Berney Arms. After the two semi-detached station cottages were pulled down a postman was sent by train from Yarmouth three times a week and as recently as 1980 the *Yarmouth Herald* published a photo of Arthur Best on the station with his post bag and wellies, ready to deliver the mail. Until 1967 a room in one of the cottages acted as a Post Office as well as the railway ticket office and waiting room. With no electricity, a blazing coal fire kept users warm in winter. Rainwater was collected in barrels from the roof, then later brought from Yarmouth in churns. A bell on the station house wall was worked from Reedham signal box and rung to warn that a train was on its way. When it stopped working for a while the railway company sent a man to investigate. He soon found the cause of the problem – someone had jammed an old sock into it to stop the noise!

Surrounded by dead flat marshland and with long views along straight track in both directions, the remoteness of the tiny platform is apparent as soon as one leaves the train. With no hills or trees to block the view and no houses nearby, Berney Arms, which claims to be Britain's smallest station (as does Beauly in Scotland which has a shorter platform) is probably also the most remote in England. The platform boasts a station sign and a couple of notices but no shelter at all. The last one, a curious tall and narrow wooden structure that looked more like a sentry box, blew down in a storm, despite being constructed with holes in it to allow the wind through.

There was once a small signal box here which after closing in the early 1960s was bought by the Berney Arms pub and used as a store room. The switch gear box had been used by Kavan Hunt, one of the railway cottage residents, as a home for his ferrets. The signal box now resides at Mangapps Railway Museum in Burnham-on-Crouch. It

Berney Arms

was only used in the summer as with no loop here the sole purpose was to permit closely following trains, increasing the line's capacity to accommodate the many holiday specials arriving at Yarmouth from across the country. In winter the four signals were permanently fixed in the up position. This was not the original signal box, as Sheila Hutchinson writes that when her father moved to the station cottages in 1947, there was an old disused signal box in their back garden which had a copper inside for boiling clothes and was used as a wash house.

Berney Arms Station (1947)
(Courtesy of Sheila Hutchinson who was in the pram)

A short path leads to a crossing where the Wherryman's Way crosses the track. The path continues through a gate towards the river, passing a large station notice board. There was once a red phone box which was moved to the pub many years ago. Should anyone wish to call one of the taxi numbers listed on the station sign they now have to use a mobile to be told that with no road the taxi can't pick them up here anyway.

In winter months only one weekday Norwich-bound train calls here. A second stops by request at 17.54 from late March, but not in winter as the platform is unlit. I had the choice of a 3½ hour wait or walk to another station. Having no road there is no bus! Berney Arms is midway between Reedham and Yarmouth and my original plan had been to walk to the latter. It was only the night before that I'd decided on the more rural small town of Reedham, although I did wonder if I should change my mind again on reaching the river and finding I'd be walking all the way into a strong headwind.

Berney Arms Windmill

Just before the river is the impressive Berney Mill, one of the tallest in the country. It's owned by English Heritage but open only to pre-booked tours. The mill was built to grind clinker for the adjacent cement works which shut down about 1880, after which it was converted to work as a drainage mill until closure in 1948.

Before setting off upstream to Reedham I first turned left to visit the Berney Arms, until recently one of Britain's most remote pubs. Once the heart of this little community, a meeting place for fishermen, wherrymen, cement workers, wildfowlers and poachers, with the local population long gone it relied on passing trade from the river and walkers, but as boat traffic declined the pub closed in 2015. An application by the owner to turn it into a private house was refused and an attempt to buy it by selling community shares failed to raise enough funds.

I saw not one person on the five mile walk along the river. A large herd of cows showed a little too much interest in me, walking purposefully at cow pace towards the river wall. It's when they start running that you have to worry but I have to admit to being a little relieved to find they were separated from me by a channel of water. The only settlement on the way is Seven Mile House, an attractive building beside the river which would once have been home to the marshman in charge of the several drainage mills here. The railway isn't far from the river here but there was never a station, so with no road the residents had to walk 2½ miles to either Reedham or Berney Arms. This is isolated country.

With the cold wind blowing I didn't stop on the way, so arrived at Reedham with ample time to spare. There was time to take a ride down to Lowestoft, crossing the swing bridge over the Yare and following the River Waveney to the coast. This train was no single coach unit but a far more substantial affair – three coaches with a locomotive at each end. Like Northern Rail, Greater Anglia were short of rolling stock so had hired 1960s Class 37 locomotives to haul 1970s coaches, a most comfortable and nostalgic way to travel over the Norfolk marshes. The leading locomotive was none other than my friend from Ravenglass, 'Concrete Bob'.

'Concrete Bob' waits at Lowestoft

We called at Somerleyton, a fairly remote station serving a small village, then on the return stopped at the even more isolated Haddiscoe, whose village is a mile away. There were once two stations here, Haddiscoe High Level on the Yarmouth to Beccles route closing with the line in 1959. Even more remote is Buckenham, between Reedham and Norwich, where trains stop only at weekends and annual usage hovers around a hundred.

A few years ago I'd have taken dinner on the train back to London but in 2008 the popular and profitable Norwich restaurant cars were withdrawn, National Express saying that passengers wanted smaller meals served at seats. That these too were soon withdrawn appears to confirm that this was another case of a company telling its customers what they want. Instead I found a restaurant close to the station. I ordered duck. After a long wait the server brought lamb. If he'd offered a replacement rather than just asking "*Can you eat lamb?*", if the reply to my complaint email hadn't said that the dish was replaced to what was ordered and if the promised discount had been more than just a free drink, I might not have been telling you that the restaurant was Bella Italia.

CHAPTER EIGHTEEN

ELY – NORWICH LINE: SHIPPEA HILL

When I collected a copy of the Ely map and Jeremy at Swan Books commented that it hadn't used very much ink, a quote from *Black Adder Goes Forth* came to mind: Handed a map of the Western Front General Melchett utters, "*God it's a barren featureless landscape out there*", only to be corrected by his assistant Captain Darling – "*The other side Sir*". Whilst there's plenty of white space on the map, this part of the Cambridgeshire Fens isn't entirely featureless. There are some roads, lots of dykes, a few houses and a railway line, along which, sitting in the middle of nowhere, is what currently holds the title of Britain's least used station.

I say currently because it seems that this is an honour that is hard for any station to hold on to for long. In 2015/16 just twelve people were recorded as using the station, however in the few months before I visited I'd heard of several groups of people coming here just to travel on a train to our least used station. Such notoriety has already pushed Coombe Junction and Teesside Airport from their perch as Britain's least used station and is likely to do the same for Shippea Hill.

Mind you, Greater Anglia and East Midlands Trains are doing their best to make it a challenge. Although lots of trains pass through on their way between Norwich and Ely, on weekdays just one stops here all day (if requested), leaving Cambridge at 7.00, calling at Ely at 7.19,

Shippea Hill at 7.28 and continuing to Norwich. There is no return service for anyone wishing to either visit Shippea Hill (although there's not actually a place as such to visit), or returning here, perhaps after a day's shopping in Norwich. No trains at all stop on Sundays but on Saturdays there's a real service. Residents of the handful of houses scattered within a mile or so of the station can board a train at 7.28, spend a day in Norwich and arrive home at 19.27. The usage figures however suggest that few do. For those who may wish to travel from the east to visit Shippea Hill the Saturday trains allow a whole 11 hours and 59 minutes to explore its delights.

As the map didn't promise twelve hours of unbridled fun at Shippea Hill I chose to catch the early morning train at Ely and walk back. I arranged this trip for June, hoping for good weather for the 8½ mile walk to Ely. It was good, but perhaps too good. We were in the middle of a heatwave and after a ride on Great Northern's air conditioned train from Kings Cross, I was distinctly warm walking up into the beautiful city of Ely.

Perhaps I should have guessed that a hotel built as a 15th century coaching inn might not have had air conditioning. But perhaps on a day when temperatures were up to 30°C, the said hotel might have had thought to open the bedroom window and close the curtains to block the sun. It was like an oven, with the small fan that they had left running nicely circulating the hot air to assist with roasting of their guests.

After a look round the splendid cathedral, en-route to a walk along the river, I returned to the station to buy tomorrow's ticket. My request for a single to Shippea Hill elicited a look of shock – *"We don't sell many of these"*. With advice extending beyond purely railway matters, I was advised to wear a hat as *"it's very exposed out there"*. It seemed as if I was going into the wilds of Scotland, not just the Cambridgeshire Fens, but I confirmed that yes I would travel suitably equipped.

Heat and traffic noise meant I was awake in plenty of time for the 7.19 train. The hotel reception was not only closed but locked up, so leaving my key on a table I slipped out into the city. At 6.40am it seemed just the right temperature for walking but arriving at the station 15 minutes later I was already hot. As commuters hurried to catch trains to work in Cambridge and London I felt slightly out of place dressed for a hike across the countryside from the next stop down the line. Disappointed that nowhere on the station I could buy a bacon roll, I resorted to Tesco next door for a sandwich for breakfast and enough bottles of water to house a small shoal of fish.

As the 7.19 to Norwich pulled in I found the guard and asked to stop at Shippea Hill, a request which he acknowledged with a slightly disappointing lack of comment. Perhaps he considered that no words were necessary when dealing with a man who is travelling into deepest Cambridgeshire, simply so he can walk back – on the hottest day of the year. After six miles across flat countryside we duly slowed, then came to a halt so I could alight. As the train departed, leaving me alone on Shippea Hill's isolated platform, the guard asked if I had plenty of water. Too late now if I hadn't.

Like Berney Arms the station is on a long straight stretch of track, enhancing its remote feel and allowing a lingering view of the departing

Shippea Hill's only Train of the day Departs for Norwich

train. It wasn't going to take a lot of exploring but first it was time for breakfast. The driver of a passing train must have wondered if the man sitting in the station shelter eating a tuna sandwich knew that it would be 24 hours before the next one stopped here.

The station is somewhat sparse, although it is hard to argue that the facilities are not adequate for demand. Norwich-bound passengers have the bus stop style shelter but anyone waiting for the sole westbound train of the week has not even a seat on their platform. Three coloured plant pots on each platform held long dead plants, however on the overgrown eastern ends of both platforms a mass of poppies provided a wild flower display for passengers. One flower bed is still tended, so the station's single passenger a month can enjoy four lavender plants, and if like me they travel at the right time of year, their mass of purple flowers. Whether the cost of S.P. Landscapes & Tree Contractors Ltd supplying the plants and a large sign has been a financially beneficial venture must be open to doubt, but as they have been so kind as to help brighten up this remote station I shall tell you that they offer their customers 'a service that is high in quality, value and professionalism'.

A cornfield borders one side of the station, while a rather run down container yard is beside the other. There's no sign of the 'Hill'. An automatic barrier at the Norwich end of the platform controls traffic on the fairly quiet road that crosses the line here. Until 2012 wooden gates used to be open and shut by the signaller but after automatic barriers were installed the Victorian signal box was closed. Later that year the *Ely Standard* reported that it was to be demolished but five years later it still stands, although not quite upright. It leans a little and seems to be shored up by a rear extension. Its lower windows were bricked up to prevent possible bomb damage in WW2. Signs by the road indicate the platforms that passengers should use for '*Trains to Norwich*' and '*Trains to Ely*', although with just one a week to the latter the plural seems almost an exaggeration.

It's hard to believe it but Shippea Hill was once a busy station, with a ticket office and even porters. Hundreds of people used the station, including airmen from RAF Lakenheath, but it was freight that provided the main business. The fields of the Fens are some of the most fertile in England and the railway shipped vegetables around the country. Trucks were shunted in the yard and two freight trains a day departed with loads of produce. Trains with up to 35 trucks of cauliflowers could be seen trundling down the line but larger lorries and improved roads saw a switch away from rail. As I wandered around the station, lorries and huge tractors pulling trailers headed to and from the fields. Vegetables are still grown but none go by train.

The station opened in 1845 as Mildenhall Road, was changed in 1885 to Burnt Fen, reflecting the name of the area of this low lying agricultural land and again in around 1904 to Shippea Hill. The derivation is unknown. Not only is there no hill but most of the land here is below sea level and would flood if not constantly drained by pumps. The railway is slightly raised but is still no more than a few feet above sea level – some hill!

Nor is it known why Shippea Hill has escaped closure. The station at Prickwillow, a couple of miles down the line and where there is a real village, lasted just five years, closing in 1850, but other than this all the small stops on the 'Breckland Line' from Cambridge to Norwich have survived. Spooner Row has a fairly sparse service and only a few hundred passengers a year, as does Lakenheath, which is three miles from its village and has trains only stopping at weekends. Like Shippea Hill both are request stops.

It seems that its least used status, sparse service and remoteness are turning Shippea Hill into a minor celebrity station. On Christmas Eve 2016 BBC *Bake Off* contestant Ian Cumming offered a free mince pie to anyone disembarking here. Sixteen passengers arrived to take up the offer, perhaps tempted by the knowledge that some pies had a Viennese topping. Being a Saturday they had the choice of spending twelve hours in the Fens, or an eight mile walk or cycle ride back to Ely. I suspect however that more than a few took up his suggestion of finding *'a nice person'* to pick them up.

Several curious journalists have visited the station since its announcement as 'least used' and just a week after my visit more than

Shippea Hill

twenty people came to Shippea Hill to meet Geoff Marshall and Vicki Pipe, the couple I'd met in Porthmadog who were aiming to visit all 2,563 stations in 3 months. The event was even shown on BBC Breakfast TV.

My more low key visit ended with a splendid, if rather warm walk back to Ely. Turning right into a lane by the large station house, I immediately found a problem. A large sign indicated that the road was private and that '*Trespassers will be prosecuted*'. It would have been a long and hot diversion along the main road but as readers of my walking books will know, sometimes I just seem not to notice those private signs.

I carried on, keeping as much of a low profile as one can while walking along a dead straight lane, through dead flat countryside. In the huge fields people were busy picking and packing vegetables. Every so often an enormous tractor or lorry trundled by. Every time I feared it would stop and an irate farmer get out – probably wielding a shotgun, or if not accompanied by at least one vicious dog and quite likely two or three. But none stopped. Although it was still early the sun was already baking down. There's little shelter on the Fens. With eight miles to walk I began to wonder whether a ride back to Ely in a police car might be preferable.

The lane ended in two miles. Goodness me I exclaimed on seeing a private sign at the end. I'd reached the River Lark and now on a legal footpath sat down on the bank. What a lovely spot with birds singing, water lilies blooming and swans gliding by on the slow flowing river. With no shade I soon pressed on. Trees are few and far between round here and for the rest of the walk I stopped at almost every one to cool a little. I was glad to have taken the advice of railway staff to bring a hat and plenty of water.

There's a café at the pretty village of Prickwillow. It's in the Drainage Engine Museum. Thoughts of ice cold drinks and perhaps a cake (or two) were quickly dashed – both were shut. If the railway station hadn't closed more than 150 years ago perhaps I could have caught a train back to Ely. A lady coming out of her house agreed it was hot. She didn't like it. She was only putting some rubbish in a bin; I was walking 8½ miles. The next field provided some relief. A huge water spray was irrigating potatoes. I stood under it for a while. The farmer came by on his tractor. Was his cheery wave of sympathy or amusement?

A footbridge took me over the River Ouze and back to the railway. Several Gatwick Express trains sat in sidings. Were they lost? A couple of miles and a few trees later I was at Ely station once more. The train back to Kings Cross had no air conditioning. My visit to Shippea Hill had been as much of an adventure as those to the wilds of Wales or Scotland. Perhaps next time I'll go on a Saturday for the full 12 hour experience.

POST SCRIPT

As I suspected, the publicity gained by Shippea Hill for being our least used station boosted the number of people visiting it. Usage jumped from 12 in 2015/16 to 156 the following year, taking it right out of the bottom ten. The list of least used stations (in terms of tickets sold but not necessarily footfall) was now headed by Barry Links adjacent to Carnoustie golf course with Teesside Airport second and Breich third. With the British Open to be held at Carnoustie in 2018, Barry Links' hold on the title is however likely to last just a year.

Shippea Hill

CHAPTER NINETEEN

GRANTHAM – SKEGNESS: HAVENHOUSE

Each of the thirty two remote stations I'd visited so far stood out as remarkable in some way but it seemed there would be nothing special about the thirty third. Standing on flat fenland, the scenery around Havenhouse has similarities to Shippea Hill, but the station doesn't have notoriety as our least used. Nor is it on wild moors, beside a deserted beach, on an island, or over the sea and nor does it seem to have any particularly interesting history. It was only when I arrived at Havenhouse that I found something special – it has the most unusual waiting shelter that I found anywhere on my travels.

In more than fifty years of rail travel around the UK I've been to most places of any size but never to Skegness, so it was a bonus that a remote station on the Lincolnshire marshes gave me the opportunity to visit the East Coast resort. After a quick change at Grantham I was on a busy train heading through pleasant countryside and calling at a succession of small towns along the way. Between them just a few isolated houses stood by huge fields of corn and cabbages. The population density is low and whilst not spectacular moors or hills, this is very much rural England and good territory to find a remote railway station. In my many hours of perusing maps I'd spotted Havenhouse, a few miles from Skegness. With no village of Havenhouse, merely a farm of that name and a few other houses dotted about, just two trains each way calling here and used by only two or three passengers a week, I seemed to have found one.

My train was not one of the few to stop and we hurried through Havenhouse, soon arriving at the impressive Skegness station. Still busy in summer, it once received huge numbers of day trippers and holidaymakers, who arrived on scheduled and excursion trains to enjoy 'bracing' Skegness.

My wife was waiting for me at the station. She'd driven up by car the day before, visiting some of her own slightly obscure destinations – outdoor swimming pools. We were to spend a night by the sea and while she swam in the town's pool I was to visit Havenhouse. At least that was the plan but on arriving back at the station and seeing a long queue of passengers, many with bikes and suitcases, snaking across the concourse, there seemed some doubt as to whether we'd all fit into the two coach train.

On purchasing a single to Havenhouse I asked the booking clerk (I don't suppose they're called that now but having no idea what this year's correct title is I shall use the traditional railway name) whether it was a request stop. A traditional booking clerk would have known but like so many current day ticket office staff, knowledge was lacking. *"There's no such thing any more"* I was told. I didn't bother to put him right.

As the gate opened and passengers (I refuse to say customers by the way) made their way onto the platform it still looked touch and go as to whether I'd actually get onto the train. I didn't really want to arrive at a remote station by rail replacement taxi. The guard (or was he a train manager) did a good job of arranging bikes, cases and people and somehow we all squeezed in. I stayed by the door not wanting to fight my way off at Havenhouse. The lady next to me assured her friend that there would be more room when people get off at the next stop. I didn't like to tell her that the average number of people alighting here amounted to just 0.13 passengers per train. She was lucky that there was anyone getting off at all but as just I left the train she had a little more room to breathe.

Havenhouse was deserted. It's an attractive station with red-brick

Nottingham-bound Train Departs Havenhouse

buildings still in place on both platforms, although the signal box has gone. Part of the station house is lived in but the rooms adjoining the coast-bound platform were empty. The waiting room on the other platform was locked but the shelter for passengers awaiting Skegness trains is always open, on account of having no door. Optimistically signed as '*Waiting Room*' the concrete block construction was by some way the least attractive shelter I found in all my travels. With no window, an open doorway and a small bench seat on the back wall, it was neither aesthetically pleasing nor a remotely comfortable place to await a train. It has all the appearances of being a converted toilet but thankfully Havenhouse's passengers have refrained from treating it as such.

Surrounded by tall trees, Havenhouse is a pretty station and with the only road access being a dead end lane, it's very quiet, although hasn't always been this way. It opened in 1873 and was originally called Croft Bank, changing its name on 1st October 1900 after being enlarged with a new up platform and brick-built waiting shelter. A signal box and road crossing were operated by one of two porter-signalmen, one working 5.30am to 1.30pm and the other 1.30pm to close. The station

'Waiting Room' Havenhouse

doesn't appear to have ever served more than a few scattered houses but was well used by the local farms.

Worth Farms even ran their own two foot gauge light railway to bring produce from the fields to the main line. Three miles long, it crossed the River Steeping on a sixty foot span steel bridge then ran alongside the river to Havenhouse station. Corn, hay, straw and potatoes were transported to Havenhouse, with fertiliser and 200 tons a year of seed potatoes taken the other way. The little trucks were hauled by a petrol powered locomotive that in dry conditions could pull loads of up to 15 tons and was sold to a company in Skegness for use in brick pits when the line closed in 1968/69.

A very quiet lane leads from the A52 half a mile away and crosses the railway at the Skegness end of the station. It then becomes a private road from which tracks lead towards Skegness and Gibraltar Point with its bird sanctuary. On summer Bank Holidays Jack Measures, whose farm the road served, used to close the private road gates to stop day trippers using the short cut, which no doubt pleased the signalman who had no need to operate the crossing gates.

The following day we visited Gibraltar Point Nature Reserve a few miles south of Skegness and chatted to the warden. For three days a week he travels from Lincoln, catching the 6.17, one of the few trains to call at Havenhouse. He'd never known anyone get on or off. From Skegness he has an hour's walk to the reserve. Havenhouse is actually closer but lack of a convenient bridge over the river means that it's a longer walk, so denying the remote station a regular passenger who could roughly treble its annual usage.

In 1912 an unfortunate accident occurred near Havenhouse station. Six year old Jessie Caborn was sitting on a passenger's knee aboard an excursion train from Horncastle to Skegness when her attention was drawn to some cows in a field. She jumped down and ran to the carriage door, which flew open as she touched it. Jessie vanished but by good fortune the engine driver happened to be looking back and saw her fall. As the train halted passengers jumped out and Jessie was soon found on the other line, dazed and bruised but otherwise none the worse for her experience. It would have been a different outcome had a train been passing in the opposite direction. On arrival at Skegness she was examined by a doctor and pronounced well enough to go for a paddle in the sea.

Leaving the pretty station I set out down the lane to walk back to Skegness. It was a lovely and varied walk through a flat landscape not dissimilar to that around Shippea Hill. Once again it was hot and once again I had to assume that a private sign didn't apply to me (I hope it was just for vehicles), but this time instead of ending the walk beside a river to a cathedral city, it was along the beach to the rather brash but still endearing resort of Skegness. I doubt that any of the thousands of visitors had considered a train trip to a remote station and five mile walk back but I can thoroughly recommend it. 2016/17 figures showed that just 106 people used Havenhouse. If just one couple a week did as I'd done that would be doubled. With a bit of marketing usage of many remote stations could be increased but it seems that train operators prefer to keep them quiet, perhaps hoping that one day they'll be allowed to shut them down. What a shame.

CHAPTER TWENTY

DARLINGTON – MIDDLESBROUGH: TEESSIDE AIRPORT

Integrated public transport is an important provision if we are to reduce car usage and its impact on climate change, so a dedicated railway station serving an airport would seem to be an excellent idea. With the railway from Darlington to Middlesbrough running alongside Teesside Airport, in 1971 British Rail opened a station specifically to serve it. Trains called regularly but passengers were few. This example of 'integrated transport' had a crucial flaw – the airport terminal is 15 minutes' walk from the station. For a while a minibus was provided but few used it so the service was withdrawn, leaving travellers to carry their luggage on the long walk to the terminal. Not surprisingly hardly any did and with virtually no one using the station the number of trains calling here was gradually reduced. Whilst many trains hurry through, for some years only two have bothered to stop, one each way on a Sunday morning.

Northern Rail's timetable allows a convenient 80 minutes for any passengers wishing to visit the airport (they quite reasonably assume that no one will use it if flying), but the Sunday morning service meant I needed to stay overnight in the North East. Enduring a Saturday night in Middlesbrough, surely one of England's dullest large towns, was balanced by having enjoyed West Ham's fine win at The Riverside.

The 10.02 from Middlesbrough took me back to Darlington where a ticket had to be purchased. With recorded usage ranging from 8 to 30 per year and some of them assumed to be enthusiasts who buy tickets but don't travel, it must be a rare occasion at Darlington booking office when someone requests a return to Teesside Airport. However, no bells rang, no light flashed and there was no call to staff to gather round and observe the transaction. I was simply reminded that just the 11.07 calls there and that only one train returns, before being handed a ticket to one of England's least used railway stations.

Teesside Airport's Weekly Train Waits to Depart from Darlington's Impressive Station

The 11.07 to Hartlepool turned out to be the same two coach train that I'd caught from Middlesbrough. We were to join part of the Stockton to Darlington railway, the world's first public steam hauled railway.

On 25th September 1825 the very first train had set out from Shildon, hauled by *Locomotion No. 1* and driven by George Stephenson who had designed both the railway and locomotive. The train of 36 wagons plus one coach carried an estimated 600 passengers and was to reach speeds of up to 15mph. The most important of the invited dignitaries were allocated seats in the coach, while lesser guests joined ordinary passengers in four wheel trucks, some sitting on top of coal, as they set off behind a man on horseback with a flag.

The *Durham County Advertiser* published a full account of the momentous day but the *Newcastle Courant* carried just 136 words, its proprietor Edward Walker having *'deemed it prudent to give the ceremony a wide berth lest the iron horse do him some mischief'*. The steam locomotive had given rise to a mix of excitement, amazement and fear, some bystanders running away in fright as it let off steam believing that a horrible explosion was about to occur. A witness recalled how *'the happy faces of some, the vacant stares of others, and the alarm depicted on the countenances of not a few, gave variety to the picture'*.

The journey did not pass without incident. Company surveyors who were travelling in one wagon were concerned about its severe jolting and passed word up the train for the locomotive to halt. It was found to have come off the rails, so was hauled back again and the journey continued. Soon the surveyors complained again and once more the train was halted. Investigation found that the wagon had a faulty wheel (some reports say it dropped off), so the truck was shunted into a siding where it struck a bystander, John Davison of Aycliffe, who was badly shaken but fortunately not seriously injured.

Locomotion set off once more but soon lost power and came to a halt. Stephenson found the problem, rope in the feed pipe, and after a 35 minute delay the train continued on its way. Arriving at Darlington it was greeted by a crowd of 10,000 people. The 8½ mile journey had taken two hours, with one wagon abandoned on the way and one man badly bruised, but overall was judged as a resounding success.

Just one other passenger joined me on the 11.07, which a lone photographer watched depart. Northern Rail had done their best to honour the line's heritage, also providing a basic four wheeled vehicle that bumped along the track, but at least the Pacer had a roof and arrived possessing the same number of wheels with which it had departed. We called at Dinsdale, which originally served Dinsdale Spa and was later used by service personnel from RAF Middleton St George, a WW2 bomber command centre. Four minutes later the two coach train slowed for Teesside Airport, where of course I was the only passenger alighting. The guard asked if I'd be returning with them then signalled to his driver that they could depart, leaving me alone on another isolated railway platform.

The station was relatively sparse but well maintained and certainly adequate for its use – or should I say uselessness. There's a little shelter on the eastbound platform, with salt spread on the ground lest it should

Weekly Train to Hartlepool Departs Teesside Airport

freeze, but does anyone ever travel to the airport on a Sunday morning, walk to the station and board the train to Hartlepool, where they could spend 15 minutes (or 7 days and 15 minutes) before returning?

Of most interest was the station's footbridge or rather the signs positioned at each side of it.

Cross at Your Peril

Perhaps I shouldn't have had that second sausage for breakfast. Both ends of the bridge were supported with scaffolding but I crossed without initiating its collapse, despite (and don't tell anyone) stopping briefly part way to take a photo. There's no exit to the adjacent A67 so the bridge is crucial to the station's operation – without it passengers would be stuck on the eastbound platform for seven days until next week's train came to rescue them. Sitting between fields and an airport, but serving nowhere (owners of the farmhouse nearby can watch the weekly trains stop but with no access to the main road couldn't get to the platform should they fancy that 15 minute stay in Hartlepool), the station really is completely useless.

A sign indicated one platform for Darlington and the other for Hartlepool and Middlesbrough, although trains to the latter no longer call here. This is another station that's unsure of its identity. The timetable and my ticket said 'Tees-side Airport', but the station's signs omit the hyphen. Network Rail's website says 'Teesside Airport' but most train operators' sites don't even acknowledge that the station exists at all. All this however should be academic as the airport changed its name to Durham Tees Valley Airport in 2004!

The station duly explored I set off for the airport. The station exits onto a turning circle then a roadway that passes the air training school, fire service training building and sky diving centre, but all the time with the feel of a route that the public aren't supposed to use. Carrying a camera, I half expected a burly security man to appear and escort me from the area, possibly after a period of interrogation during which I would have to explain that whatever he may feel, it is actually perfectly normal behaviour to visit a remote railway station, just because it's there.

I'd read that the route into the airport was blocked by a closed gate, but whilst a gate across the road was shut, a smaller one beside allowed pedestrian entry. Soon, and without having been arrested even once, I was outside the terminal of Durham Tees Valley Airport.

The airport wasn't exactly what one would call bustling. In fact it was deserted as the railway station – but a great deal warmer. A plane had taken off just after I'd arrived at the station but the next flight wasn't for more than five hours. The station's two trains a week don't even connect with any flights. Voices could be heard from behind the screens but I was the only person sitting in the passenger side of the terminal. It's not the busiest of airports (passenger numbers have fallen to less than 20% of those in 2000), averaging about five flights a day and serving only Aberdeen and Amsterdam (plus Jersey in summer). The website however advertises over 200 destinations, although all but two need a change in Scotland or the Netherlands. By that criteria, the station serves numerous destinations from Penzance to Inverness, simply with a change at Darlington.

Nicely warmed after 20 minutes sitting in a deserted airport, I made my way back along the service road, passing one chap who far from challenging my presence concurred that the weather had improved and reaching the station in plenty of time for the 12.36 to Darlington. I was of course the only passenger, although the station is much busier than it used to be. In both years 2012/13 and 2013/14 a mere eight tickets were purchased, so that's just four people arriving and departing in a whole twelve months, however publicity seems to have increased usage. In May 2016 a trip organised by Alex Nelson, owner of the independent travel company Chester-le-Track, brought 28 people here, boosting the annual count by 56.

When it originally opened the airport entrance was slightly closer to the station, but it was still too far to realistically walk with luggage – hence the lack of usage leading to the current minimal service. It is another station which is only kept open to save the cost of closure and served only by the minimum number of trains required to meet the franchise commitment. Things might change – there's been talk of moving it 500 yards down the line but that's probably still too far from the terminal to attract passengers and unless the airport regains its former business or the rumoured new houses are built here, the station seems destined to stay where it is and cater solely for those of us who enjoy visiting unusual places.

My outlook for Teesside Airport station may have been too optimistic. Usage for 2016/17 was down to 30 journeys, making it the second least used station in the UK. Assuming that everyone travelled both ways that's 15 people using the station in 12 months – including me! I was 6.67% of the station's passengers for the whole year.

But worse than that, citing costs of £6 million for maintenance, Northern Rail announced that the airport had agreed to removal of the footbridge and one platform, so it would only be served by trains running one way from Hartlepool to Darlington. The station wouldn't close as that would require support from regional stakeholders and rail authorities, so instead it was to be made even more useless.

The figure of £6 million over 3 years sounds highly inflated but based on current usage figures it seems hard to argue that the stop is worth the wear and tear on train brakes let alone repairing the footbridge. However, if more trains were to stop here and connect with a shuttle bus and flights, it might attract a few more users and new housing might justify it being moved. A station with one platform and one train a week may seem useless but as long as it remains open there is potential for growth. If it wasn't already, Teesside Airport station is destined to become our most useless railway station but maybe like Ribblehead and Llandecwyn one day it will rise again.

CHAPTER TWENTY-ONE

EDINBURGH – GLASGOW
(Shotts Line): BREICH

My first glimpse of Breich station came the same way as most railway passengers – through the window of a passing train. Only two trains a day stop but more than sixty pass through on the busy Shotts Line between Edinburgh and Glasgow. I'd done the same a few weeks earlier when the Glasgow sleeper was diverted to the East Coast Main Line, but still being asleep missed an early morning view of one of our least used stations. A 1960s Class 47 locomotive had hauled us from Edinburgh to Glasgow and one chap had travelled all the way from London just to ride behind it. Today I'd travelled all the way from Essex just to visit Breich station.

It had been on my 'possibles' list since the start but having set a limit of forty, some remote stations would have to be missed. In the end it came down to a choice between going back to Norfolk one Saturday and walking to Buckenham, or a trip to central Scotland. When I heard that Network Rail wanted to close Breich the decision was made and a few weeks later I was on a Virgin train heading north.

The Shotts Line was being electrified, a task that required huge expenditure in related infrastructure, including raising the footbridge and rebuilding the platforms at Breich station. The need to do this would of course have been known at the outset, so one would assume it had been included in the overall £160 million budget, however

Network Rail chose to press ahead with the electrification, then part way through announce its plan to close Breich. A £49 million contract had been awarded to Carillion Powerlines Ltd for erecting stanchions and stringing the wires, but although a major part of the remaining cost was to cover raising bridges, Breich's footbridge had been missed out – or given the timing was it initially in there but a chance seen to save some money?

Having boarded at Edinburgh, I alighted at Fauldhouse and walked back to Breich to catch the one Glasgow-bound train of the day. It was a pleasant walk, mostly along the track bed of the long closed Wilsingtown, Morningside and Coltness railway, which was built mainly for mineral traffic, carrying coal and iron ore, plus a sporadic passenger service. This was once a busy industrial area and it was the collieries, iron and lime works which had provided most of the passengers for Breich station. My walk was completed along the A706, finding the station adjacent to a busy road junction but no houses nearby.

With platforms resembling a wild flower garden one could forgive a passing passenger for thinking that Breich is already closed. The station has an abandoned feel about it, not least the footbridge where rust permeated not only the structure but the walkway, in a manner which would have caused any safety officer to have kittens. Anti-slip chicken wire had long rusted away from much of the floor, leaving just a brown imprint, but the sections of rusty wire which remained protruded as a trip hazard ready to catch an unwary passenger. It was quite a shock to see such neglect on our modern railway and something that could have been put right in an afternoon's work.

Passengers on the Edinburgh-bound platform have the luxury of a shelter which provides a perch but no seat for waiting passengers, whilst those heading towards Glasgow have just a seat. A loud announcement that smoking was not permitted caused me to jump, but at least confirmed that the remotely operated public address system was in good working order. These, plus a help point, are the total of passenger facilities at Breich.

With a while to wait I settled on the seat and was half way through a tuna sandwich when something started ringing. Looking round I realised it was the help point. It's supposed to be for passengers to seek help or information, so why were they calling the station? Intrigued I got up to answer but found no facility to do so. Perhaps I should have pressed the help button and in hindsight I wished I had but after a while the ringing stopped. If someone had wanted to talk to Breich's only passenger they'd missed him.

Still with a while to wait I took another walk round the station, managing to cross the footbridge for a second time without injuring myself in any way. I wondered what the person who had put up the no standing sign on Teesside Airport station bridge would have made of this one. Access to the station is by a short roadway from the busy A71, so everyone who takes the train towards Edinburgh has to cross the footbridge. Just west of the station is a newly raised bridge which takes the A706 over the line. As I surveyed the selection of grasses and wild flowers on the platform an idea struck me. It's only about 70 yards from the end of the station to the road. Rather than erect a new bridge why not just make a path to the A706, saving money and partly negating the justification for closure?

Another loud announcement advised that the 18.38 to Glasgow would soon be arriving. This was a matter of some relief as I'd started to wonder whether the call to the help point was to tell any passengers that it wasn't coming today. To facilitate electrification work buses were replacing trains from 20.30 and I had just a little concern that they might have decided to start early tonight. It was a very big step up to the train yet not even a set of steps were provided. Breich does seem to have been abandoned, visited only by the occasional passenger and the man who pinned up the closure notice.

Breich Looking Towards Glasgow (2017)

Undated Photo of Breich
(Tony & Nicky Harden)

But should it close? This was a matter that I gave a fair bit of thought to over the coming weeks. Network Rail claimed that the cost of work to bring it up to safety and accessibility standards following electrification could not be justified by the very low usage, so the money would be better spent elsewhere on the railways. At first sight this seems reasonable but were they telling us everything. A little research suggested they weren't. Of course usage is low if only two trains stop. Funding for the work must have already been included in the electrification budget and what about my idea for a path instead of the bridge? There was one issue however that was my overriding concern.

As a result of governments implementing most of Beeching's recommendations more than 5,000 miles of railway and 2,000 stations closed. Some were justified, but with hindsight many should have been kept. As population increases and with the measures to reduce car use essential to limit climate change, the trend now is for rail reopening and new stations. No railway station had been closed in Scotland since Balloch Pier in 1986.

As I've talked to people about my travels to remote stations I'm often asked why they remain open. A key factor is that it costs less to retain them than to close them. The closure process is complex and expensive. Extensive documentation must be produced and all interested parties consulted. My concern is that if Network Rail succeed in closing Breich they may try to do the same at some of the other lightly used stations around the country. Breich could be a test that shows they can get away with closures, and where will that leave the likes of Shippea Hill or Altnabreac. Every objection has to be considered so adds to the cost of closure. Whilst it can be argued that the money might be better used elsewhere, I believe that there is a case to oppose Breich's closure, so here's my objection.

Dear Sirs
I wish to submit a formal objection to the closure of Breich station.
Whilst living in Essex, I travel regularly to Scotland and enjoy

walking in all parts of the country. I used Breich station on 6th July this year, enjoying the pleasant walk through countryside from Fauldhouse station. If Breich received a more regular service I would be likely to use it more often.

My reasons for objecting to the proposed closure are as follows:

Justification Based on Low Passenger Numbers but no Attempt to Boost Usage

The usage figures quoted by Network Rail are based on the very limited service of one train per day in each direction. Unless one walks to or from another station, or uses another form of transport, the service is only practical for travelling for the day from Breich to Edinburgh (or intermediate stations). It is not practical for use when travelling in the Glasgow direction, or for shorter periods to stations towards Edinburgh. It is therefore not surprising that the usage is low. There has been no attempt to boost usage at Breich by providing a more regular service (possibly as a request stop), or to market the station in any other way, for example for ramblers. There has been no attempt to provide car parking facilities, which along with provision of a more regular train service, would make Breich a far more attractive proposition to potential passengers.

Potential users and future users should be considered in the closure process. It is not reasonable to justify closure of a station based on low usage when the service has been cut back to the point that it is barely usable. It could be argued that this is an attempt to achieve 'closure by stealth'. It should be noted that patronage of Breich station is increasing, the 138 users in 2015/16 being the highest number since 2008/9. Network Rail's Public Consultation Document makes no projection for the increased usage that would be expected to result from a more frequent service at Breich.

Failure to Adequately Consider Proposed New Housing Developments

Breich is the closest station to both the villages of Breich and

Longridge, whose populations are approximately 400 and 850 respectively. The West Lothian Local Plan and the Local Development Plan have identified areas of housing development within these two settlements, proposing a total of 198 new properties, with the number of households in Breich increasing by 80%. Network Rail have not accounted for this significant potential growth in population in the area served by Breich station. It cannot be dismissed based on the existing minimal level of service. The potential for increased usage from future new housing development should be considered, taking account of both increased population and provision of a more frequent train service for Breich station.

Excessive Cost Quoted to Upgrade

Network Rail are justifying closure on the basis of low usage and the cost of replacing the station footbridge, platforms and other work which would be required to accommodate electrification of the railway, including upgrading the station to 'modern standards'. Network Rail quote £1.4 million, which seems to be a high price for this work. There appears to be no breakdown of this cost in the closure document. It should be noted that Network Rail state a cost of £241,000 to cover demolition of the station if it were to be closed.

I believe that Network Rail have inflated the costs of running and upgrading Breich station, a tactic that was frequently used by British Rail to justify closures. For example, ScotRail state a cost of £15,000 per year for one of their staff to visit Breich station five days a week, which appears to be rather high for the time this would require, and given the low usage and frequency, an expense that could be reduced. If an employee cost was say £60,000 per year this would imply that they are spending 25% of their time checking on Breich station, which seems barely credible. Have other costs been similarly exaggerated? Whilst Network Rail quote their figures to support closure, railways should exist to provide a service and in some cases financial support is necessary to ensure this service to passengers.

Network Rail Costs Include Unnecessary Upgrades

Whilst electrification would require replacement of the footbridge and work on platforms, some of the additional upgrades to the station which Network Rail have included in their costs are not essential. Given the low usage of the station some proposed additional upgrades, whilst desirable, are by no means essential. There are many lightly used stations on the network with very basic facilities and were it not for electrification and the subsequent desire to close the station, it is highly questionable whether Network Rail would have made these improvements at Breich, yet they now add to its closure case.

Alternative Access Negating Need For Footbridge Has Not Been Considered

It is clear that the footbridge needs repair, replacement or removal, and in any case this would be necessary to permit electrification. However, Network Rail's closure proposal documents make no mention of a lower cost alternative, which would be to provide access to the Edinburgh-bound platform by means of a path from the A706 road to the west end of this platform. There are other stations on the network (e.g. Seascale) where separate access means there is no link between platforms within or immediately adjacent to the station. The path would need to be about 75 yards long and to construct this, plus access to the road, would be far cheaper than renewal of the footbridge. Failure to consider this option totally undermines Network Rail's justification for closure.

Timing of Announcement – Funds Already Allocated to Breich

A rolling programme of electrification expected to include the Shotts Line was announced by the Scottish Government in June

2012. *Advanced work to clear the route, raise bridges (including the road bridge adjacent to Breich station), re-deck platforms and demolish structures, was due for completion by December 2016. The contract to erect stanchions and string wiring was awarded to Carillion Powerlines Ltd in January 2017. Network Rail's application to close Breich station was not announced until June 2017.*

Given that it would have been clear from an early stage that the footbridge at Breich station would need to be raised and that some work would have been necessary on the platforms, one would assume that these costs had been included in the budget for the line. As there was no mention in the electrification plan that Breich station would be closed, it would seem to be a reasonable assumption that the cost of modifications to the station were included in the overall electrification budget. I therefore consider that the application to close Breich station is opportunist and that Network Rail have seen it as a way to reduce costs on the project. If closure of Breich station was to be proposed this should have been included and justified in the original electrification plan.

Precedent
There are many railway stations around the UK which although lightly used, provide an important service to local people and visitors. Closure of Breich station may prompt Network Rail to consider closing other stations, so having a knock on effect that would cause inconvenience and hardship beyond the users of Breich.

Summary
In summary, I believe that Network Rail have inflated the cost of retaining Breich station, have not considered all options, in particular a path from the A706 to the eastbound platform, and that neither Network Rail nor ScotRail have made any effort to grow usage, or consider the effects of proposed new housing, an

improved service and car park. The proposed closure is opportunistic
and should not be approved.
Yours sincerely
Peter Caton

What had started as a token objection grew as I learned more about Breich. From thinking it would be a shame to close, now I really didn't want it to go. West Lothian Council had submitted an objection and local MSP Neil Findlay had posted a page on his website asking people to send comments to him which he'd pass on to Network Rail. I contacted Geoff Marshall from *All the Stations* and we agreed that I'd start a petition which he would publicise.

Under the heading 'Save Breich Station' it was worded:

Network Rail have applied to close Breich station on the 'Shotts Line' from Glasgow to Edinburgh. Their case for closure is that the cost of work on the station and replacement of the footbridge which are required due to electrification of the route, is not justified by the small number of passengers using the station. It's not surprising that few passengers use Breich – only one train in each direction stops here. Network Rail have not considered the potential for increased usage if more trains stopped, if parking facilities were provided and if proposed housing developments nearby go ahead. Nor do they appear to have considered building a path from the eastbound platform to the A706, so negating the need for a footbridge. Closure of Breich station was not part of the electrification plan for which the budget would have included funds for the required work. Railways should be to provide a service, not for profit. The proposed closure is an opportunistic attempt at cost saving and has not considered all options, so permission should not be granted.

Gaining signatures to save a station 400 miles from home with the number of annual individual users in single figures wasn't easy, but in six weeks I had 283 names and it went with my objection to Network

Rail. Now the fate of Breich lay with Transport Scotland and ultimately the Scottish Government.

Breich raises another issue. Whilst the statutory process to close a station is rightly rigorous and expensive, there is no such procedure required to permit a reduction in service. Hence, as at Breich, train operators can cut the service to a point where it's barely usable, then cite the lack of passengers as justification for closure. This 'closure by stealth' was a common British Rail tactic leading to the shutting down of branch lines in the 1960s. I was contacted by Olga who as part of the campaign for Pilning station had started another petition – 'Stop Closing Railway Stations by Stealth'.

Pilning is an interesting case. The last English station before the Severn Tunnel, it has been neglected and unwanted by the railway for years. Before December 2006 one train each way stopped every weekday but this was cut to just one train in each direction on Saturdays only. Then electrification came along and in 2016 the footbridge was removed, so only one platform could be used. Two trains still called each Saturday, but both running in the same direction, so a return journey is only possible via Wales! Anyone taking the morning train to Bristol can only get back by travelling through Pilning, through the Severn Tunnel, getting off at Severn Tunnel Junction and taking the afternoon train back to Pilning. Such has been the publicity from the campaign to get the footbridge reinstated that despite the inconvenience of the service, usage has increased five-fold. In 2015/16 there were just 46 users but for 2016/17 usage had risen to 230.

Six weeks after the deadline for objections there was an announcement from the Scottish Government.

Passengers at Breich station will welcome news it is to remain open and could benefit from enhanced services in the future.

Use of the station was reviewed as part of the Scottish Government's investment into the Shotts Electrification project, with a consultation undertaken by Network Rail on behalf of

Transport Scotland to consider its long term viability given low patronage.

The 12-week consultation considered the views of relevant transport stakeholders, the local authority, trade unions plus the local community and their elected representatives.

Transport Minister Humza Yousaf said:

"The overwhelming response to the consultation was in favour of keeping Breich Station open. Not only that, many respondents wished to see more services calling at Breich Station to increase patronage."

"Having taken on board the strong support for Breich Station, I have made the decision it should remain open. My officials are working with the ScotRail Alliance to see how we can increase calls at Breich to make it a more viable station which encourages greater use of rail."

Any additional calls at Breich will be included in the May 2019 timetable change following completion of the Shotts electrification project which is expected to reach completion early 2019.

Breich had been saved! If Network Rail had announced their intention earlier and perhaps arranged with ScotRail to stop more trains there to test the market, maybe the case for closure would have been stronger, but clearly they underestimated the strength of opinion that people do not want to see our railway stations close.

A few weeks after the reprieve the latest station usage figures were announced – just 48 passengers had been recorded at Breich. It will cost a lot of money to rebuild. The station was saved for largely political reasons. Whether it was justified remains to be seen but the outcome must be good news for our other lesser used stations. The consultation process cost Network Rail a considerable sum and one suspects in future they may be more wary of trying to make such a closure.

I look forward to going back to Breich one day, alighting from a train at a convenient time, enjoying a walk, then being able to get on another train and return to where I'd started.

MAP 7 – North Scotland

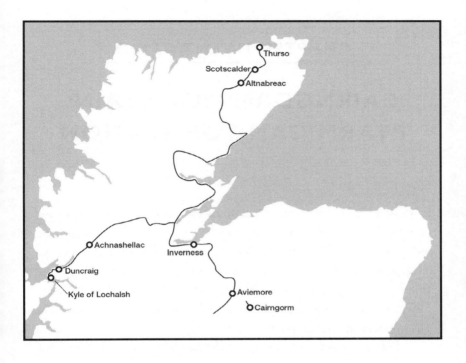

CHAPTER TWENTY-TWO

CAIRNGORM MOUNTAIN: PTARMIGAN TOP STATION

It is not an everyday journey that starts by waiting in a queue for the number 31 bus with a man carrying an ice axe, but Ptarmigan is no ordinary station. Nine miles from Aviemore and 3,600 feet above sea level, it stands 500 feet below the summit of Cairngorm Mountain, Britain's sixth highest peak. Scotland's only funicular railway, which as I was to find, offers a very different experience in winter than summer, was my destination for today.

I'd travelled up from Glasgow the day before, meeting an interesting lady on the train to Perth. As a child she used to be taken to London on the *Flying Scotsman*. They used to go to the dining car for afternoon tea, the only meal her family could afford and as steam trains were so dirty her mother would take clean socks for them to put on before relatives met them at Kings Cross.

It was a spectacular run through the Highlands to Aviemore, although I always feel that ScotRail's little three coach trains are inadequate for such a majestic main line and was pleased to hear that discarded HSTs will be introduced soon. There was no snow in Perth but at Pitlochy the mountain tops were white. By Dalwhinnie it was several inches deep on the platform and just the shiny steel rails protruded on the track bed. I'd travelled this way many times but rarely in the depths of winter with a scene reminiscent of Alpine journeys. Meanwhile on-train entertainment was provided by a lady across the aisle who quite spectacularly spilled her coffee into the bag of the passenger opposite. Apologies were profuse.

After a comfortable night as the only guest at Dunroamin B&B I joined the axeman, several passengers with skis, a man with a snowboard and a couple carrying no winter sports equipment at all, as we waited outside Aviemore railway station for the Cairngorm bus. It was 20 minutes late. The driver blamed traffic in Inverness where he'd done a school run. In half an hour we were at the large car park on the lower Cairngorm slopes. Perhaps I should have realised then that the many coaches parked indicated that the mountain wasn't going to be as quiet as expected.

Before 2001 anyone wishing to ascend the mountain had either to walk or take the two section White Lady Chairlift. If it was windy the only option was to walk, as the lift couldn't operate in wind speeds over 30mph, so had to shut on up to 40% of winter days. Forty years to the day after the opening of the chairlift Britain's highest railway opened, increasing speed, capacity, comfort and allowing operation in winds up to 75mph.

It was a controversial plan, with conservationists concerned at damage to the mountain from both construction of the railway and the increased visitors it would bring. Approval was given only subject to many environmental conditions, including a legally binding visitor plan in conjunction with Scottish National Heritage. Hence, in order to protect the fauna and flora in this most sensitive environment, other than very limited numbers for guided walks, summer visitors are not allowed onto the mountain from the top station, although walkers who have climbed the mountain may use the train to descend.

Entering the lower station I was quite taken aback at the activity. There were only a couple of people buying tickets but a constant stream of skiers coming off the runs and joining a queue for the train. When I'd visited a few years ago in summer it had been a relaxed experience designed for tourists. In winter however it's a slick operation with the aim to get as many skiers up the mountain as quickly as possible. Trains run at twice the summer speed and up to 120 passengers are crammed in. The four minute run was like a busy tube train but with almost everyone carrying skis.

There are two trains operating as a pair, with electric motors at the top station hauling one up by its cable, assisted by the weight of the descending carriage. Assuming an even distribution of pie eaters, when the upper car holds more passengers than the lower, the drive motor becomes a generator and electricity can be returned to the grid, although at a seventh the price it is purchased. For those interested in statistics a board in the station gives plenty of figures:

Line Length	: 1960 metres
Capacity	: 1200 / hour (each way)
Maximum Speed	: 10 metres / second (22.5 mph)
Maximum Gradient	: 42.8 %
Rail Gauge	: 2 metres
Cable Diameter	: 39 mm
Carriage Weight	: 14.9 tonnes

In the loop halfway up we passed the almost empty descending carriage. There's a middle station here that's only open in winter, however when the railway is busy trains don't stop. Brightly coloured skiers rushed by on either side but views were limited by cloud, although few passengers were bothered. To the skiers the railway is just a quick way to get back up the mountain. The final 250 metres really is like the tube, running in a tunnel before emerging into the concrete complex of Ptarmigan station.

A few yards from the train I was in a different world – a world of whiteness where the only colour came from skis and skiers. Attempting to walk in normal footwear was hazardous to say the least. There were no paths, just snow everywhere. If I didn't slip on the slopes, I'd be knocked down by skiers. What's more it was cold, bloody cold. To attempt a walk would have been foolhardy.

Ptarmigan Station Cairngorm

In February this is a mountain top for winter sports but I was taken aback by just how many participants were here. Not only adults but children – hundreds of them rushing about on skis on the snow and taking over the building. If I wanted my remote station to be quiet I'd come on the wrong day. On Thursdays local children come here for PE lessons and today there were more for special races. Almost every inch of floor in the exhibition room was taken with children eating packed lunches. With more skiers filling the restaurant I retreated to the terrace outside, joining a very cold looking Chinese gentleman who seemed to be the only other 'tourist' on the mountain.

A few years earlier and just before he reached teenage cynicism, I'd brought my youngest son here on a trip to introduce him to the pleasures of sleeper trains, mountains and the beauty of Scotland. On an August morning the sky was so clear that we could see Ben Nevis, ninety miles away. A kind gentleman let us look through his telescope at a ptarmigan, a privilege to spot an iconic bird that live only in the Arctic landscape on the highest Scottish mountains. Today I could see 100 yards at best. A picnic table and chairs was covered with snow. This wasn't a place to linger.

Surprisingly, even in the depths of winter wildlife can be seen here. Far from being scared off by skiers, mountain hares and ptarmigan chose to stay close by. Despite their white winter colouring, a hungry golden eagle may spot them in the snow and swoop down for a tasty meal. The shy eagles however avoid humans so don't like coming close to ski slopes, which hence provide a degree of safety for their prey.

I spent another half hour walking around the building, but after three forays onto the snow and back to the terrace, slightly warmed each time by a couple of minutes 'browsing' in the shop, decided that sufficient time had been spent here to justify my visit.

Not a Place to Picnic Today

Light snow was falling as the train descended, topping up the slopes on what was proving to be a good ski season. It's an ongoing operation to keep the railway and slopes open, and staff arrive well before dawn to prepare for arrival of the public. The more the wind blows the more difficult their task.

The winter of 2010 was the worst in Scotland for twenty years. After three weeks of blizzards and temperatures down to -15°C, Inverness was cut off from the south by road and its airport repeatedly closed by snow on the runway. On the Highland Line snow and ice got into the brake mechanism of a freight locomotive, causing the driver to lose control as it descended the 1 in 60 gradient from Slochd Summit. It derailed on catchpoints outside Carrbridge station, blocking the main line from Edinburgh, but this was nothing to conditions on Cairngorm Mountain. Here parts of the track disappeared under 7 metres of snow and drifts were so high around Ptarmigan Top Station that you could walk straight onto the roof. It took many hours' work using modern snow clearing machines and the more traditional shovels before the railway and slopes could be opened for business.

High up a mountain and covered in snow, I knew that Ptarmigan would be very different to all my other remote stations. It is a remarkable place in all conditions but as I found, to get the full experience one needs to visit in both summer and winter. My winter visit however very nearly lasted longer than planned.

Over lunch in the marginally less crowded lower café I deliberated as to whether to get the 14.05 bus back or to spend an hour walking in the snow. It seemed a shame to leave the mountain but I wasn't adequately attired for snowy walks. Eventually deciding that it was just too cold I hurried across to the bus, boarding with a minute to spare. It was a good decision. Whereas train timetables show services that don't run every day in italics or with a wavy line, buses rely on tiny footnotes. Not for the first time I'd missed these and the driver informed me that after this run he was off to do school buses. The next one back from the mountain would be 17.05 by which time it would have been dark for an hour. In good weather Cairngorm Mountain is a place to spend all day but in sub-zero temperatures with snow falling, another three hours riding Scotland's highest railway might not have been the most enjoyable way to spend an afternoon. My train journey on to Inverness, walk by the river and sleeper back to London made for a far more satisfactory end to the trip.

Strange Sign for a Summit Station

Passengers' Downhill Transport Outside the Station

REMOTE STATIONS

CHAPTER TWENTY-THREE

KYLE OF LOCHALSH LINE: DUNCRAIG & ACHNASHELLACH

'Storm Doris is likely to cause travel disruption, damage buildings and send debris flying.'

'Up to 15cm of snow could fall across parts of Scotland in treacherous, blizzard-like conditions.'

'Commuters warned not to travel.'

'The Army confirmed it would be on hand.'

My visit to the Kyle of Lochalsh line, one of the world's great railway journeys, promised to be an eventful trip.

After a morning of meetings in Glasgow, a wet and windy walk around Stirling and a relaxing ride on the *Highland Chieftain* as it completed its long run from Kings Cross, I spent a night in Inverness. Next morning was wild. Sun one minute, rain the next, but constant wind. The Far North Line was running but only as far as Ardgay, from where a bus would carry passengers to Wick and Thurso – provided the driver considered it safe to proceed. I was assured that the Kyle of Lochalsh Line was running normally and on the dot of 11.00 my two coach train set off to cross from the east to west coast of Scotland.

This is a line whose construction was improbable and its survival even more so. After branching off the Far North Line at Dingwall it runs for 51 miles through remote moorland, mountain passes, beside rivers, lochs and sea, stopping at nowhere of any size. The most logical route through the spa town of Strathpeffer, which would have been the largest place on the line, couldn't be taken because landowners refused to allow access for the railway. The terminus at Kyle of Lochalsh, then just a few houses, wasn't reached until 27 years after the line opened and has since lost its ferries, first to Stornoway and more recently to Skye. Two closure attempts, the first under Beeching and the second in 1970, were survived, as were several blockages along the route which might have led to its demise.

Most of the original stops remain open, providing a rich selection of remote stations. I was heading for the village of Plockton, two stops from the terminus and from where I'd walk to Duncraig, but my second remote station was yet to be chosen. The plan was to look at them from the train on the outward journey then decide which to visit on the return.

Immediately curving left, we soon reached the River Ness, the second fastest flowing river in Scotland. It was here that the line had its most recent threat. For 127 years a stone viaduct took the railway over the river but at 8.10 on the morning of 7th February 1989 flood waters washed away the central buttress, leaving track suspended above the river. A freight train had crossed just ten minutes before and passenger trains to Wick and Kyle of Lochalsh had passed over earlier in the morning. By the next night four spans had collapsed but a disaster had been narrowly missed. It could have been a fatal blow for the two lines but John Ellis, General Manager of ScotRail, immediately gave a categorical assurance that the bridge would be rebuilt. Additional trains were moved north by road and until the new bridge opened 15 months later, buses linked Inverness and Dingwall.

After slowing to cross the swing bridge over the Caledonian Canal we were on the banks of Beauly Firth. Snow lay on distant mountains. Five minutes out of Inverness and the beauty of the Kyle line was already becoming evident. Just one door was opened for the tiny station at Beauly, a full car park testament to its successful reopening. Muir of Ord, home to a temporary depot for the stranded rolling stock when the Ness Bridge was washed away, was an earlier reopening and now part of the Invernet commuter network.

We curved left at Dingwall, the largest town on the route, leaving the Far North Line to wend its way to Wick and Thurso. A rainbow arched over snowy hills as we headed for the west coast, soon climbing through forest towards Raven Rock, an arduous route forced on the railway builders by having to avoid Strathpeffer. In 1897 the steep ascent contributed to what could very easily have been a serious accident, when the mixed evening train from Dingwall ground to a halt just short of the summit. A coupling failed and the coaches at the rear of the train ran back down the hill. Despite reaching what must have been quite a considerable speed they remained upright and came to a halt just before the Far North Line junction. The only damage was to a set of level crossing gates which were demolished by the speeding coaches.

Tall pine and twisted oak trees gave way to water and mountainside as we passed Loch Garve. The station at Garve provides an illustration of the optimism of the 19th century railway pioneers who built this improbable route across Scotland. It was envisaged that fishing boats would be carried on specially adapted wagons, saving their skippers the treacherous journey around Cape Wrath, so passing loops were built with extra distance between the lines. In the event the boats were never carried but the platforms at Garve remain unusually far apart.

Lochluichart, the next loch, has its own remote station serving just a couple of houses and a power station. The station site was moved to here in 1954 when the hydroelectric scheme raised the level of the loch and the railway had to make a two mile deviation. We didn't stop but I might come back tomorrow.

Now on wild moorland, the scenery similar to much of the West Highland Line, we paused to let a rare passenger alight at Achanalt, the least used station on the line. A sign by the road confirmed that it is a village but with just a few houses, a tiny cemetery but no church, it was another possibility for a remote stop tomorrow.

The next section is possibly my favourite of all, as the railway runs through a wide U shaped valley alongside the River Bran. It's wild country with no paths for walking. As rain beat hard on the train windows a ruined croft across the river oozed atmosphere and history. Achnasheen, the next stop, was once a far grander affair, with a station hotel whose dining room looked out onto the platform. Sadly the hotel burned down in the 1980s but with another passing loop here and a few scattered houses, unlike most on the line this remote station is considered worthy of a call by all trains, not just on request.

With pouring rain very little could be seen through the windows as we climbed to Luib Summit, at 646 feet the highest point on the line, then started to descend along the River Carron. There was once a very lonely station on this section, Glencarron Platform, which was another to have been built to secure agreement to pass through private land, but closed in 1966. It was reached by a narrow track, as is Achnashellach a few miles down the line. With no road access and no village, this was a definite possibility for tomorrow.

Strathcarron is another station where all trains stop and today we waited a few minutes to pass an Inverness-bound service. We were now at the head of Loch Carron and had reached the sea. The tiny and definitely remote station of Attadale sits beside the loch and serves Attadale House whose gardens are open to visitors in summer. With money tight, early plans for the railway were for this to be its initial terminus. A hotel and harbour would be built but it was decided to push forward another five miles to Strome, although constructing the line between sheer cliffs and the loch caused much difficulty.

In 1870 Strome Ferry as it was then called, became the terminus of the newly built railway. There wasn't enough money to take it on to the Kyle of Lochalsh. The owners had however succeeded in their aim to reach the west coast and steamers took passengers on to Portree and Stornoway. Until the A890 was built south of the loch in 1970, Stromeferry's connection to the outside world relied on the railway and a ferry to Strome North. Rockfalls have occasionally blocked the new road, resulting in a 140 mile detour via Inverness for road users and in 2012 a temporary reintroduction of the ferry service. The geography of this part of Scotland and the difficulty in providing replacement bus services is a major reason why the railway avoided closure.

The railway was however responsible for an unfortunate incident in Stromeferry's history. With steamers to Skye, Lewis and mainland villages meeting the trains, the village was a hive of activity and soon it became a railhead for freight. Fish, cattle and mail were carried and to meet demand the company decided to run Sunday trains. Observance of the Sabbath was however strong in the Highlands and locals would not accept such work being carried out on a Sunday. Such was the strength of feeling that on 3rd June 1883 two hundred fishermen took control of the pier, preventing fish being unloaded onto trains. The Chief Constable of Ross-shire arrived from Dingwall with six officers, all the force could muster, and together with railway employees charged at the fishermen. The riot even made the news in New Zealand, the *Otago Daily Times* reporting that *'sticks were freely used by the fisherman and the chief constable himself and two of his officers got some hard knocks'*. At midnight the men allowed the fish to be loaded and it reached London a day later, being sold at a reduced price due to its deteriorated condition. The following week 160 police were deployed and a detachment of soldiers sent from Edinburgh Castle to stand by at Fort George in Inverness, but conflict was averted by the efforts of Reverend Macdonald of Applecross. Ten men were imprisoned after police arrested the ringleaders, although not without difficulty when they were driven back by a body of men armed with spades, then by women who had filled their aprons with stones with which they pelted the officers so vigorously that they had to retreat.

Even when funds were finally secured to take the line on to Kyle of Lochalsh it was to be no easy task to construct. Huge quantities of rock had to be blasted away as the railway was threaded between loch and mountainside. The resulting route is so spectacular that passengers can be glad of the low speed limits. The rain had stopped and I could enjoy the views once more, the mountains of Skye now visible beyond the loch.

Approaching Duncraig the line runs through one of many steep rock cuttings, before emerging under a bridge to the little station beside the loch. We didn't stop. My intention was to check in at my hotel, walk to Duncraig, then catch the next train back to Plockton. I had no reason to expect that things might not go quite to plan.

It's a half mile walk from Plockton's well preserved Victorian station to the little village, one of the most attractive in Scotland, with its line of painted cottages facing onto Loch Carron. Sheltered by the hillside, palm trees line the main street and a small tidal island sits just off the shore. The view from my bedroom at The Plockton Hotel rivalled the Rhossili and Kyle of Lochalsh hotels for the best I'd ever experienced. Across the loch Duncraig Castle nestles in the hillside, its railway station close by beside the water.

Duncraig & Loch Carron

Duncraig was built as a private station to serve the castle which was constructed in 1866 by Sir Alexander Matheson, who according to more generous sources made his immense fortune 'trading with the Far East' and to those who prefer greater accuracy 'selling opium to the Chinese'. Being a drug dealer was however no bar to career progression in the upper echelons of 19th century society and after retiring at the age of thirty six Matheson went on to become a Member of Parliament and to be created a baronet. Naturally he needed a grand country house for entertaining summer guests, so built the castle above the shores of Loch Carron. Matheson had played a key role in building the railway and insisted that a station be provided to serve his castle. After use as a private home, it served as a military hospital in World War Two, following which the castle was donated to the local council who ran a boarding school for girls here until 1989. A somewhat chaotic bed and breakfast venture which was the subject of a BBC TV series *The Dobson's of Duncraig* eventually failed and for a while the castle stood empty.

Unsure how easy the walk would be I left exploring Plockton until later and set off for Duncraig. A path just before Plockton station runs down to the loch then alongside the railway, before crossing under it through a delightful little stone bridge. A sign warned *Beware Falling Rocks* but of course being aware of the risk and being able to do anything about tumbling rocks are entirely different matters. Taking a branch to the left I followed the path (or was it a stream) as it descended through woodland, rounded a pretty tidal inlet and reached the track that links the castle and station. Turning left I was soon on the platform of what is quite possibly the most magnificent setting for a railway station in Britain.

Sitting right beside the loch, with a wooded islet just off the shore, views to the white houses of Plockton and the hills and mountains beyond, Duncraig could hardly have a more idyllic setting. Not many people however get to enjoy it. With the only access a two mile walk from Plockton, or the private track to the castle, only around 500 people a year use the station. Had Beeching got his way no one would be able to use it and the castle would have lost its station but the not so good doctor reckoned without the will of Scottish train drivers. Although the station closed on 7th December 1964, the line's drivers refused to accept it and continued to stop here whenever passengers requested. After eleven years of 'closure' the station was reopened and Duncraig put back in the timetable as an official request stop.

The platform itself is unremarkable, containing the usual facilities of a remote railway station. A seat with capacity for three travellers of normal girth allows those waiting for trains to sit while they take in the spectacular view. Two signs instruct that passengers must not cross the line, while a third provides information on onward travel – or rather advises that there is none. Neither buses nor taxis venture here. There's a bin with a notice indicating that where possible ScotRail will separate recyclables and what seems to be obligatory on Scottish stations – a bronze tidy station award.

Just behind the platform is one of our most unusual and attractive station waiting rooms. The beautifully preserved little hexagonal wooden building with pointed tiled roof was built by Matheson to copy one of the rooms in his castle. With seats all around the wall it provides sufficient capacity to cater for a couple of weeks' worth of station users, should they all arrive at once.

The arched stone bridge at the end of the platform adds to the station's aesthetic appeal. Guessing that this would be a good spot for a photo I followed the track which crosses the bridge, leading to a gateway to a lone house by the loch. A short flat-topped section of drystone wall made an excellent vantage point and slabs of stone protruding either side formed a stile leading to the wooded area by the loch. Looking down from the wall it was a fair drop ahead. I remember thinking that I wouldn't fancy falling down there. Photo taken, I stepped backwards from the wall. Seconds later I was lying on the ground, my left hand in the air holding the camera and my right hand under me. I must have slipped or missed the step down. The camera was fine, my right hand wasn't. Beneath the blood it was clear I'd done something nasty to the index finger. A big bulge and the joint not moving suggested dislocation.

Remote stations have a tendency to be, well, remote. When someone injures themselves at Kings Cross or Euston a well-practiced procedure rolls into action. Announcements are made, first aiders arrive, the patient is moved to a quiet room and bandages are applied. Duncraig doesn't offer quite the same facilities. There is a phone in the shelter but my injury didn't seem to justify 'emergency', so I'd have to wait an hour for the next train to Kyle. The small amount of water in my bottle didn't make much impression on the blood and I was about to walk down to the loch to wash it when I thought of the castle. There may not be anyone there but hopefully I could find an outdoor tap.

Approaching the grand castle I spotted a man working by an outbuilding. Seeing my plight he gave me a hose to clean up then took me into the castle. It was strange walking into a historic building, paintings hanging on the wall but mess and dust everywhere, and trying not to drip blood onto the floor. Matthew and his wife were living there, doing the place up for the owner to make it into what will one day be a wonderfully situated B&B. What a view there is over the loch from their kitchen – where the first aid kit is kept. We all agreed that the finger didn't look good and that medical attention was required. A phone call to the medical centre at Kyle of Lochalsh told me that they couldn't deal with it; I'd need to go to hospital. The nearest was 16 miles away, on the Isle of Skye. Matthew insisted on driving me there. What a kind chap he is.

Broadford Hospital is probably unique. It's 100 miles and two to three hours drive from the nearest large hospital so has to deal with all sorts of emergencies, which are stabilised before transferring to Inverness, Fort William, Aberdeen or Glasgow. They are used to dealing with major injuries to climbers who have fallen down mountains, so my finger from falling off a wall was run of the mill. The staff were superb. I was assessed, cleaned up, x-rayed and the dislocation confirmed. The next bit wasn't so pleasant but with plenty of injections to numb the pain and a good deal of brute force, the young Irish doctor managed to pull the bone back into place. After being taken into A&E (just the one bed) to apply stitches, another x-ray to confirm all was well and a

£30 taxi ride, I was back at The Plockton Hotel just in time for dinner. It could have been worse. I'd visited a remote railway station although not boarded a train there, but should I ever want to write a book about remote hospitals, one was ticked off the list.

Duncraig – Photo Taken From Wall by the Bridge – Not Recommended!

Undated Photo of Duncraig
(Tony & Nicky Harden)

I woke early the next morning and from the warmth of my bed watched dawn arrive over Loch Carron. The lights of Duncraig station shone brightly across the water. Silhouettes of mountains ringed the loch, rocky details emerging as the blueish light brightened. The water was still, dead still. Away from this idyll of serenity Breakfast TV promised chaos across the country. Storm Doris was unleashing her fury. The worst of the winds would be further south but heavy snow was expected in Scotland. Severe transport disruption was inevitable. With a painful finger and conscious that the railway passes over high ground where there's little protection from drifting, I considered taking the first train back to Inverness.

Fortified by an excellent breakfast I felt more positive. I'd take the train to Kyle of Lochalsh and provided snow wasn't falling, on the way back to Inverness get off at Achnashellach, which after much consideration I'd chosen as my second remote station on account of it not being served by a road. However, as a connoisseur of tidal islands I couldn't leave Plockton without first walking to Eilean nan Gamhainn. Too small to get more than a mention in *No Boat Required*, it was just a short walk but with slippery seaweed, rocks and mud, one which I took with far greater care than usual. Much as the Isle of Skye is beautiful, I didn't really want to have to present myself to the doctor at Broadford and admit to repeating the dislocation.

Confidence gained by the successful tidal island visit, I thought once more of Duncraig. Although I'd visited the station I hadn't boarded or alighted from a train. Should I repeat the walk and catch the Kyle train from there? Light rain was falling and it would be slippery. Yesterday the path had been very wet and several times I'd had to duck low beneath overhanging trees. A heavier rucksack wouldn't help with balance. A slip and instinctive putting down of my hand would be likely to send me back to Broadford. But would the book be complete if I didn't catch a train. Checking out of the hotel I told the story of yesterday's accident and said I was about to walk back to Duncraig. *"No need to do that. We'll give you a lift."* I've stayed at hotels who offer a lift to the local station but never to the next one down the line.

Courtesy of Alan from the hotel I was soon back at Duncraig station. First port of call was the bridge to look at the scene of yesterday's little accident. The result of my informal investigation was that the fall was due either to my right foot slipping on the stone step, or to overbalancing because the step was lower down the wall than one would expect. Either way I realised how fortunate it was that only my finger had been hurt. A more serious injury and I could still have been lying there. It was certainly a lesson to take more care in remote places and I vowed that in future I'll carry a first aid kit.

The run into Kyle of Lochalsh is possibly the most scenic part of the whole route as the train hugs the sea shore, passing rocky promontories and tiny wooded islands. Kyle itself has suffered from being bypassed as most travellers to Skye go straight over the bridge. Once busy with cars and foot passengers, it is now somewhat rundown, although I was pleased to see that the old railway hotel is still open. The station, which retains its original chalet style buildings remains one of the most spectacular on our network, standing by the pier with views across the water to Skye.

As the train had arrived at Duncraig without a covering of snow I was hopeful that all would be well for my planned visit to Achnashellach. I'd have 1½ hours there but would change the plan if at Strathcarron we didn't pass what would become my return service to Inverness this afternoon. Achnashellach wasn't a place to be waiting for hours in freezing temperatures if trains were delayed by heavy snow.

The guard issued my ticket but refused to take for my fare from Duncraig to Kyle. He hadn't come round during the journey and didn't want the money when I'd tried to pay at Kyle. I'm not sure that his explanation is company policy but it suited me – *"If the cat doesn't catch the mouse by the end of the day then the mouse has got away"*.

A couple of minutes after we stopped at Strathcarron the westbound train duly pulled up alongside and with no sign of having driven through snowdrifts. If Storm Doris was bringing her blizzards they hadn't reached this far north. Achnashellach would be my next remote station.

The guard told me that he didn't get many passengers for Achnashellach. Sometimes campers get off here in summer but they come back covered in bites as it's a terrible place for midges. The station was built to serve Achnashellach Lodge, a shooting lodge by Loch Dughaill dating from 1870 and once owned by His Highness the Maharajah of Gaekwar.

Achnashellach

I walked down the ¼ mile track that runs through woods to the road, nodding to forestry workers who stopped their sawing to allow me to pass. A sign at the bottom indicates that the station track is private and for foot passengers only. I'd hoped to walk down to the loch but soon gave up when I couldn't find a path, returning to the station and taking the track that climbs into the hills. What a good decision. In milky sunshine rather than the expected blizzards it was a brilliant walk towards Fuar Tholl, a rocky mountain of almost 3,000 feet. The track is the start of a spectacular ten mile route to Torridon and Achnashellach station provides superb access to the mountains for walkers and climbers who make up a good proportion of its users, the few scattered houses nearby providing rather limited custom.

Surrounded by trees with mountain tops peeping above them, the station certainly felt remote as I sat in the tiny shelter. A loop here was taken out in 1966 and the bridge and attractive wooden station buildings removed in the early 1970s. The remains of the second platform can still be seen where undergrowth has been cleared back. The current small shelter is formed of white painted stone blocks and whilst more interesting than the bus shelters that proliferate across the network, lacks a door and the snugness of Duncraig's.

The former station master's house still stands, a little way to the west, although when Achnashellach first opened his accommodation was not so grand. It was a summer only stop and with funds tight the company expected the station master to sleep in the booking office. A fine cottage costing well over £100 was promised but when the Laird of Achnashellach decided against making his expected contribution a rather more modest wooden building was put up.

While researching stations I've read of many accidents and having written about several instances of runaway trains vowed to include no more until I read of a bizarre incident at Achnashellach. On 14th October 1892 a mixed train was being shunted, the operation involving hauling trucks with a rope. Somehow the locomotive and its train parted company and the passenger coaches and wagons trundled off into the darkness at ever increasing speed. Naturally the distraught engine driver set off in pursuit of his escaped train and after a while made contact with it. However the train had been halted by an adverse incline, so after stopping momentarily had set off back down the hill towards Achnashellach, hence the meeting with its locomotive was somewhat violent. It is fortunate that the trucks were at the rear so the collision between the locomotive and its own train resulted in only a few bruises to passengers.

Other than the forestry workers I'd seen no one at Achnashellach and it was quite a surprise just as the train was due to see an orange clad figure rushing alongside the track pushing a bicycle. I could hear the train approaching and it was touch and go as to who would get to the station first. Would the cyclist get a telling off or is trespass on the

Achnashellach Station Signs – No Cars!

railway viewed more leniently here? I would never know. Just as the train rounded the corner by the station house the cyclist reached the foot crossing, but rather than climb up to the platform he turned right and disappeared down the hill. Yet again a train stopped just for me.

Back in Inverness I checked on the trains south. It wasn't looking good – snow, wires down, trees on track – delays and cancellations. The northbound *Highland Chieftain* was running more than four hours late but the sleeper would run. It might be delayed but yes it was expected to leave on time. And so it did. There was snow on the platform at Aviemore and deep snow at Dalwhinnie but we trundled south, picking up cold passengers on the way. I was asleep before Pitlochry, stirred briefly with the shunting at Edinburgh, then woke at 4am. We were at Preston and seemed to be stopped for ages. Displays showed that the first trains of the day had been cancelled and buses arranged. A late arrival in London seemed inevitable (if we were to arrive at all) so I cancelled my alarm and returned to the land of nod. I woke again as the train slowed. It was five to eight. I pulled up the blind – Euston! We were only 15 minutes late. The attendant said we'd waited at Preston because part of the station roof had been blown off but we'd "*flown down from Crewe*". With the other passengers gone he'd leave a door unlocked for me, trusting it seems that I'd soon be on my way and not taken to the carriage sheds for the day.

Storm Doris survived, first port of call on the way home was to take a letter from Broadford to my GP. Stitches were soon removed but having not originally attended my local hospital getting an appointment at the trauma clinic was problematical. I was seriously considering returning once more to Broadford to get my finger examined, so when an appointment letter finally arrived (or more precisely two identical letters in different envelopes) it was with a tinge of disappointment that I wasn't going to get another ride on the wonderful railway to Kyle of Lochalsh.

CHAPTER TWENTY-FOUR

FAR NORTH LINE: SCOTSCALDER & ALTNABREAC

My final trip started as the first, boarding the Caledonian sleeper at Euston and arriving in Scotland next morning. This time I was in the Inverness portion and a Highland breakfast was enjoyed in the lounge car as morning dawned over the Cairngorms. I'll have to say it again – is there a better way to travel?

My visit to Inverness was brief and I was soon aboard the 10.40 to Wick, embarking on another of Britain's great railway journeys. The Far North Line is less celebrated than the West Highland and Kyle routes, however its scenery is more varied but often as spectacular and its remoteness perhaps even greater. It was to be a four hour run to Thurso on Britain's longest rural railway, passing sea, rivers, lochs, mountains and huge expanses of peat bogs. This is a journey where the view from the window provides an ever changing vista of wild Scotland; a Scotland missed by tourists who visit Edinburgh and think they've seen the country. I would be experiencing more than just remote stations, for this is a remote railway, and a line that merits description from end to end.

The first section along the picturesque Beauly Firth I'd covered en-route to Plockton. At Dingwall we parted from the Kyle Line and hurried along beside Cromarty Firth, a 19 mile finger of sea which forms one of the safest anchorages in the north of Scotland. This large safe haven was used by the Royal Navy in both world wars but more recently has seen much activity as a base for construction and repair of oil rigs. Approaching Invergordon several huge rigs stood in the water, a strange sight against the natural beauty of the Scottish coast.

The Dornoch Firth is reached at Tain, from where I once walked across an RAF bombing range to the tidal island of Innis Mhor. Here the railway heads on a long loop inland, whereas since 1991 the A9 road has crossed on a bridge, shortening the route by 26 miles and helping buses get to Wick in not much more than half the time the train takes. There was an unsuccessful campaign to have the railway diverted over the bridge but although the road is quicker, train passengers get the better views.

It was a lovely run alongside the water to Ardgay, the clickety click of wheels on rare jointed track so evocative of rail journeys past. The next two stations are just 750 yards apart and one of the closest pairs in the UK. Culrain serves a handful of homes on the south bank of the Kyle of Sutherland, while across the Shin Viaduct, Invershin has just a hotel and even fewer houses. This time it is rail passengers who get the shorter route, as by road it's an eight mile journey via the next bridge.

Heading north again we climbed to Lairg, where a single passenger carrying a huge rucksack left us to board the minibus to Durness, the closest village to Cape Wrath. I wondered what adventure he was going on in the remote north western corner of Scotland. Turning east we were soon running downhill along the broad Strath Fleet, slowing for a level crossing at Rogart but not halting at the station that easily qualifies as remote. Three railway carriages here offer budget accommodation with a discount for guests arriving by train. Another for my 'one day' list. By an isolated cottage a black and white Shetland pony watched the train, then after due consideration decided that perhaps it ought to be scared and lolloped off across the paddock.

Back by the sea at Loch Fleet we passed The Mound, a closed station and once junction for the Dornoch Light Railway, which in its final years had been operated by two Great Western panier tank engines that had been steamed all the way up here from the West Country. The Mound served little other purpose and closed on the same day as the branch in 1960. At Golspie we were back by the open sea and soon stopping at Dunrobin Castle, one of our more unusual railway stations.

Originally a private station for the Duke of Sutherland, who owned much of northern Scotland and was largely responsible for building of the railway through Forsinard, it is now open for public use. It is however one of the very few stations on the main network that is open seasonally, closing in the winter when the castle is shut to visitors. Falls of Cruachan on the Oban Line and Okehampton and Sampford Courtenay in Devon are the only others I can think of that don't stay open all year. The attractive Swiss chalet style building has been perfectly restored and the station houses a small railway museum, plus a toilet that was opened by Michael Portillo when he came here filming *Great British Railway Journeys*.

From here to Brora, then Helmsdale the railway hugs the wild North Sea coast. It would make a great walk but there's no path. People here are rarer than wildlife. Birdlife abounds and last time I travelled here I saw otters on the beach. This time a seal poked his head out the water to watch the train go by. This is real wild Scotland.

From Helmsdale we headed inland once more, the railway making another huge loop, further reason why from Inverness to Wick the road is 58 miles shorter. The more direct coastal route has to negotiate the Muir of Caithness, a granite mass with hills ending sharply at the sea, and whilst the road achieves this with twisting bends, it was extremely difficult terrain for a railway. It was considered easier to take the line inland through valleys, hills and moors, and some sources suggest a secondary aim, which was for the railway to open up development of this sparsely populated area of northern Scotland. It hasn't!

The line runs along a U shaped valley, following the meandering River Helmsdale, with hardly a house to be seen. This is lovely scenery but the remotest was yet to come. Approaching Kildonan the river narrows and cascades over rocks, the waterfalls and pretty valley worthy of exploring 'one day'. With just a handful of houses Kildonan is the least used station on the line and has the fewest passengers of any non-request stop in the whole of the UK.

It's quiet here now but in 1868 the valley was the centre of a gold rush. Within six months of the announcement that gold had been found six hundred hopeful prospectors had arrived, with two shanty towns growing up in the glen. At the time the railway had been built only as far as Golspie, so adventurers had to hike the last thirty miles on foot. As the price dropped and finds were less than hoped, the rush soon subsided, but flecks and the occasional nugget are still found and panning equipment can be hired in Helmsdale.

Climbing out of the valley we were soon in a different world – The Flow Country. Covering much of Caithness in Scotland's far north east, this ancient environment is the largest area of blanket bog in Europe and one of the biggest in the world. Dating from the last ice age, the huge expanse of peat bog has formed as layers of sphagnum moss slowly rot, forming a landscape that is unsuitable for farming and hence has been largely preserved from human development. Other than some injudicious conifer planting in the 1980s, much of which is now being felled and attempts made to restore the bog, it has changed little for thousands of years. It is an incredible landscape when viewed from the train and even more so when the world of tiny pools, streams, flowers and birds is experienced close up. It is a place that we are privileged to have in our country and even more so that despite Beeching's wishes, one that can still be reached by train.

From the very remote station at Kinbrace we headed north across the peat bogs, an environment that is as inhospitable for a railway as it is exciting for its passengers. There are similarities to Rannoch Moor but it is perhaps an even greater wilderness and for me the highlight of this remarkable journey to the very north of Scotland.

We paused at the little settlement of Forsinard to await a southbound train. One of our more interesting stations, the waiting room is an RSPB visitor centre, part of a huge nature reserve protecting the rare birds and wildlife that inhabit the peat bogs. A new lookout tower gives unique views across the pool system on the Dubh Lochan Trail, a mile long route across flagstones that takes visitors into the heart of this remarkable landscape. I came to Forsinard when writing *The Next Station Stop* and this short walk was one of the most amazing I've ever experienced. Sadly the Forsinard Hotel where I'd stayed is now closed and up for sale. It was a real experience to stay at the remote hotel that had been built by the Duke of Sutherland for his men to lodge when travelling to collect rents.

At Forsinard we left the little road that had accompanied the line from Helmsdale and headed north east on what rivals Rannoch Moor as the most remote stretch of railway in Britain. Mountains poked their heads over distant ridges but just old snow fences rose above the expanse of peat. The only sign of human activity was the railway and other than distant patches of conifers, nothing else seemed to have changed for centuries.

Soon we slowed for Altnabreac, six miles from a road and possibly the most remote station of all. We didn't stop but I'd be back tomorrow. Leaving the plantations that surround the station we were soon out on the open peatland where the only animals to be seen were deer. It was here that a train famously got stuck in the snow, however not in steam days as in most such stories, but as recently as 1978. *The Next Station Stop* describes how the 17.15 from Inverness to Wick became lost in a blizzard, a locomotive sent to find it had to turn back after getting stuck in a drift and the seventy passengers were eventually rescued by helicopter 24 hours after they'd left Inverness.

As the line descends approaching Scotscalder the land gradually changed from brown to green and the first fields for many miles could be seen through the window. I would be back at this attractive and remote station in a few hours time.

Georgemas Junction, the station that's so good they stop here twice. Locomotive hauled trains used to divide here, with the rear coaches taken north to Thurso, while the remainder continued east to Wick. When Class 156 DMUs replaced them in the early 1990s these too were divided but the '158's that currently operate the line work as single sets, so the train goes to Thurso and back before completing its journey to Wick. Fortunately an easement to ticket restrictions in the National Routing Guide allows Wick passengers to remain on the train without being charged for their ride to Thurso and back. This too is a remote station, with no settlement of its own, however serving the village of Halkirk 1½ miles away. It has played an important role as a rail-head for freight, notably nuclear waste from Dounreay to Sellafield for which a large crane sits astride a siding where the southbound platform originally stood.

After reversing, the final six miles of the ride was completed alongside the fast flowing River Thurso. It had been a thoroughly enjoyable four hour journey on this remarkable railway line to Britain's most northerly station. After a warm welcome from Sheila at Thurso House, my friendly B&B accommodation for the next two days, and a quick walk down to the sea, in less than two hours I was back at Thurso station. This time I would be travelling for just eighteen minutes; to Scotscalder.

It was the same train I'd travelled up on and as soon as it pulled in with a handful of passengers from Wick I found the guard. Writing my request in a note book he confirmed it would be no problem to stop at Scotscalder. I was his only request to alight and no one was waiting to board at what is one of our least used stations. Beautifully cared for, with a well preserved station house, old style name board and an arched stone bridge at the northern end of the platform, it is however one of our more attractive stations.

Undated Photo of Scotscalder
(Tony & Nicky Harden)

REMOTE STATIONS

Scotscalder

I was used to being alone on remote stations and as I wandered up and down the platform taking photos a sudden voice made me jump. The house is occupied and Celine, one of the owners, had come out to say hello. She lives here with Mark and their basset hound Abby and it seemed was glad of a visitor to their little station. They'd been here for 13½ years and love it.

The station house is one of the few to survive on the northern part of the line and was sold by British Railways Board in 1988 as a private residence. It was sold again and renovated as a holiday home, for which it won a 1993 Ian Allan Railway Heritage Award that is commemorated by a plaque on the building. Mark and Celine bought the house and surrounding land in 2004, carried out further renovation and have lived here since. It's certainly convenient for the trains and their journeys to Inverness and Thurso probably contribute a significant proportion of the station's annual 300 or so users.

There are a few houses dotted around the station but no village as such. Celine said that like them, most of the occupants come from England, attracted to this remote spot on the edge of Scotland's Flow Country. In my forty minutes here I counted just five cars passing on the lane. With the sun shining we agreed that I'd been lucky with the weather and keen for a short walk I bade farewell to Celine.

With more time I'd have climbed the hill of Ben Dorrery a couple of miles away but today there was just time to walk down the lane to the ancient Sithean Harraig cairn with views to Loch Olginey. Yet again I returned to a remote station feeling I wanted to come back and explore further.

A brisk walk back gave me a few more minutes to enjoy the station. It is a fine example of what can be achieved if buildings are preserved and used, rather than standing empty and boarded up, or replaced with bus shelters. A little shelter at the end of the platform, with room for four passengers on its bench seat, and a help point, are just about the only modern additions to a station that could easily belong to a bygone era or a heritage railway. There's even a proper clock with Roman numerals on the wall, although this is not quite what it seems.

In the centre of the dial is written '*Scotscalder 1874*', a reference to the date the station opened. It is however not the original clock. That was cosmetically restored in 2006 by Chris Edwards of Aberdeen at the request of ScotRail but the movement found to be missing. A new electronic movement could have been installed but this required a continuous electrical supply and the only one operated by ScotRail was a timed system for the station lights that was some distance from the clock. It was considered too expensive to install a suitable supply so the clock was left as a static heritage piece. When Mr Edwards passed through Scotscalder some years later he was dismayed to find that the original clock had gone and in its place was the current modern timepiece. Whether historical authenticity should take precedence over provision of a working clock for passengers is a matter of opinion, but as he points out, surely the better option would have been to install the electric movement into the original clock.

And so to Altnabreac. It was a distinctly nippy morning in Thurso as I waited for the 8.34 train south. Above the station's all-over timber roof a rainbow stretched between sunny blue sky and brooding dark clouds. It seemed that I was set for the four seasons in a day that Celine at Scotscalder had told me to expect here in the very north of Scotland.

The helpful guard said he'd tell the driver to stop at Altnabreac and printed out times of return trains for me. We agreed that with four hour gaps between trains I'd be hungry if I missed it. He said that in summer Altnabreac is relatively busy *"considering where it is"* but that few use it in winter. As we reversed at Georgemas Junction an American gentleman expressed dismay that their journey to Inverness was going to take four hours and the train would stop 23 times on the way. Perhaps he didn't realise how big Scotland is. Inverness isn't the top – there's another 100 miles of fabulous and often remote country before you reach there and of course the islands beyond.

As we slowed to allow me to alight at my final remote station the guard warned me to take care as the platform is low. We concurred this wouldn't be the best place to break a leg. I didn't tell him of my little mishap at Duncraig or he might not have trusted in my abilities to look after myself on the railway. The train hurried on south, taking its grumpy American who perhaps should have been asked to alight here too in order to understand what Scotland is really like. Not that I wanted company. I'd expected solitude but found that since my visit for *The Next Station Stop* the station house has become occupied. No one was about but a car parked outside and the steady hum of a generator indicated that there was life at Altnabreac.

The station's origin has been a matter of much debate – well at least in the circles of people who like to debate such things. A commonly held view is that it was built to serve Lochdhu Lodge, a hunting lodge a mile to the south, which operated as a hotel until 1975 and is now a private house. Altnabreac station however opened in 1874, twenty one years before the lodge was built, so although the railway brought travellers to stay here and most of the materials used to build it, Lochdhu was not the reason why a station was opened here.

The answer as to why a station should have been built in such a remote spot where it appeared to serve no one at all, is that it was simply for railway operational reasons. A passing loop and facility for steam locomotives to take on water were needed on the long run north. A station was built on the loop and like Whitrope and Sugar Loaf, a tiny community of railway workers lived here. A single–teacher school was set up for their children and a handful of others who came by train from surrounding settlements. The lodge provided regular passengers but Altnabreac was never busy. With around 300 passengers a year it is one of our least used stations, although one may wonder why even that many come here. Perhaps some words from Wikipedia give the answer: '*One of Britain's most isolated stations, it is a request stop used almost solely by walkers and those who enjoy visiting obscure locations.*' That's me then on both counts.

The passing loop continued to operate until 1986 and remains of what was the northbound platform can still be seen. The signal box has gone but the stone based water tank still stands at the end of the old platform. Passenger facilities are rudimentary; a brown wooden shelter, a seat, cycle rack and a help point. A sign indicates the taxi drop off and pick up point, but another advises that the nearest taxi rank is at Halkirk, eleven miles away as the crow flies and longer by roads and the gravel forest tracks that are the only non-rail link to the outside world.

Stacks of wooden sleepers and rails at both ends of the platform looked to have been here for some time and I wondered if anyone would bother to take them away. With trees on both sides the station

Water Tank Altnabreac

REMOTE STATIONS

Undated Photo of Altnabreac
(Tony & Nicky Harden)

is less open and hence perhaps less remote feeling than before conifers were planted but looking down the track towards Forsinard gives a fine view over the Flow Country. Was this the most remote I'd felt? I wasn't sure. Altnabreac rivals Corrour for isolation, both being in wild country miles from the nearest public road, but at neither was I alone. When I'd come here in 2012 the station house was empty and I had to confess to being a little disappointed that today I didn't have Altnabreac to myself.

The front of the platform is gravel covered, with grass behind it and to exit a grassy path leads through a gate. I followed the path past the station cottage and the old school where a sign announces '*Altnabreac DC twinned with Washington DC*'. On my previous visit I'd walked through the conifers and past the lodge which stands opposite Loch Dubh. I had thought then that the grey stone building with its mysterious turret looked a little foreboding. When later I read Dixe Will's account of his encounter here when he wrote *Tiny Stations* I was glad I hadn't lingered. It's worth a read!

Instead I turned left, following a forestry track parallel with the railway to Loch Caise. What a beautiful spot this is. Clouds reflected in the still water, its surface punctured only by little fishes rising to view a rare visitor. Dense conifers sheltered two banks, distant mountains rising behind them, while peat bogs extended from the others. Forsinard Fly Fishers' Club describe it well; *'this is one of the most delightful pieces of water an angler could visit'.* I sat for a while by a little wooden jetty, privileged to be able to walk to such a delightful spot, reached from what must be one of my favourite railway stations.

Northbound Train Pauses at Altnabreac

As I walked back to the station, I reflected on my travels and the two questions I knew I'd be asked; what is the most remote station and what was my favourite?

I would have to sit on the proverbial fence. The answer to the first question depends on definition, but I'd have to choose one of the four national rail stations with no tarred road access. Corrour and Altnabreac are obvious contenders, but Berney Arms and Dovey Junction felt just as remote, although roads are not so far away. If I'm to include closed stations, King Tor Halt on the wilds of Dartmoor and Tollesbury Pier on the Essex marshes should be considered. Riccarton Junction too cannot be discarded, as a whole village that once relied on only the railway for communication with the outside world and if I extend to heritage railways Ddualt is certainly a contender.

Perhaps I should make the choice based on where I felt the most remote. Cars (well a car) were parked at both Altnabreac and Corrour, so although they are not public roads I knew I could be rescued should the need arise. From Berney Arms and Dovey Junction I could see inhabited houses and here as Ddualt where the only house was deserted, I felt truly alone. Remoteness is of course subjective, but on balance I think it's fair to say that in wild country miles from a public road, Corrour and Altnabreac can share claim to being Britain's most remote railway station.

As for my favourite, well that's even more subjective. My first thought was that Rannoch and Duncraig might win based on the attractiveness of both their stations and settings. If I had to choose between the two I might be swayed by my unfortunate experience at Duncraig compared to the delights of the Moor of Rannoch Hotel. Then I looked back at my photos and decided that surrounded by wild moorland and snow topped mountains, with a restaurant but no road, perhaps Corrour was best of all.

All those I've mentioned as being potentially the most remote were special and I should add to these Breich, which would have been one of the less significant until my small part in its reprieve. Maybe I should decide based on which of the forty stations I'd choose if permitted to return to just one. After much reflection one became two. I'd take the sleeper to Rannoch, stay for a few days in the wonderful hotel, meet the deer, enjoy a cake in the station buffet, and one morning take the train to Corrour and walk eleven miles back on the mountainsides.

Back at Altnabreac I stood at the platform end looking down the track as it descends across an expanse of peat bogs. 10.29 came and went with no sign of the train. There's no information display at Altnabreac. If I went to the help point might it pass through while I was waiting for news from a faraway office. The next one wasn't due for another four hours and as I'd agreed with the guard this morning, I'd be hungry by then, so I stood enjoying the sun and view. Then the little train appeared. It was going at quite a lick, the driver making up time and probably hoping not to have to call at request stops. I held my arm out, brakes were applied and for the final time the train stopped – just for me.

BIBLIOGRAPHY

The West Highland Railway, John Thomas, House of Lochar 1998

Tales of the Glasgow & South Western Railway, David L. Smith, Ian Allan 1970

The Trains Now Departed, Michael Williams, Preface 2015

The Railways, Simon Bradley, Profile Books 2015

Ribblehead Re-born, W.R. Mitchell, Castleberg 1992

Ticket to Dent, Robin Hughes, Book Law Publications 2017

Abroad, Eric Robson, Arena 2014

Cumbrian Coast Railways, David Joy, Dalesman 1968

The Visitors Guide – Ravenglass & Eskdale Railway 2012

Talyllyn Railway Guide Book 2016, Talyllyn Railway

Ffestiniog Railway A Traveller's Guide, Ffestiniog Railway Company 2013

Welsh Highland Railway Your Traveller's Guide, Ffestiniog Railway Company 2012

Remote Britain, David St John Thomas, Frances Lincoln 2010

The Illustrated Heart of Wales Line, Rob Gittins & Dorian Spencer Davies, Gomer 1985

Heart of Wales Line Guide, HoWLTA & Kittiwake 2004

Great Walks From The Heart of Wales Railway, David Perrott & Les Lumsden, Kittiwake

The Heart of Wales Line Travellers Companion, David Edwards

Heart of Wales Line Forum 2013

Caradon and Looe, The Canal, Railways and Mines, Michael Messenger Twelveheads 1978

The Great Isle of Wight Train Robbery, R.E. Burroughs, The Railway Invigoration Society 1968

The Southend Pier Railway, K.A. Frost, Peter R. Davis 1965

The Kelvedon and Tollesbury Light Railway, N.J. Stapleton, Town & Country Press 1968

Tollesbury to the Year 2000, Tollesbury Millennium Publication Group 1999

The Southwold Railway & Blyth Valley Walk, Southwold Railway Trust 2012

Memories of the Southwold Railway A. Barret Jenkin's, Southwold Press 1973

Branch Line to Southwold, Vic Mitchell & Keith Smith, Middleton Press 1984

East Anglia Railways Remembered, Leslie Oppitz Countryside Books 1989

Berney Arms Past & Present, Sheila Hutchinson 2000

Berney Arms Remembered, Sheila Hutchinson 2003

Branch Lines East of Norwich, Richard Adderson & Graham Kenworthy, Middleton Press 2010

Railways to Skegness, A.J. Ludlam, Oakwood Press 1997

The Kyle Line in Pictures, Northern Books 2005

The Kyle of Lochalsh Line, Ewan Crawford, Amberley 2014

Highland Survivor: The Story of the Far North Line, David Spaven Kessock Books 2016

ALSO BY PETER CATON

THE NEXT STATION STOP

A 10,000 mile tour of Britain, discovering what it's like to travel on our modern railways and comparing experiences with train journeys made over the last fifty years.

Inspired by finding a childhood notebook, the author revisits locations of family holidays, looking at how the journeys and places have changed, and wondering why his parents chose such unlikely destinations.

His travels take him to some of the most beautiful and remote parts of the country and on trains so eccentric that sometimes he wonders if Thomas the Tank Engine is round the corner. Sampling a selection of Inter City routes, he questions whether the pursuit of speed and efficiency has taken away some of the enjoyment of travelling by train, but on sleepers to Cornwall and Scotland finds the romance of rail travel is still alive. He ends with a journey to Italy, with a diversion up a snowy mountain, comparing European train travel with British railways.

We read of the author's experiences of missed connections, inflexible computers, waving to Marjory and upsetting a machine gun carrying policeman. He writes of his frustrations with 'health & safety' and ridiculous announcements, and how these combine to give the book its title.

Illustrated with sixty colour photographs covering the steam, diesel and electric eras of the last 50 years, The Next Station Stop will appeal to anyone who travels on Britain's trains.

£9.99 260pp ISBN 978-1-78306-050-4 **Published by Matador**

ALSO BY PETER CATON

NO BOAT REQUIRED
EXPLORING TIDAL ISLANDS

When is an island not an island?
Peter Caton takes us to all four corners of England, Scotland and Wales to find out.

Sharing our nation's fascination with islands, Peter sets out to be the first person to visit all 43 tidal islands which can be walked to from the UK mainland. Along the way he faces many challenges: precipitous cliffs, vicious dogs, disappearing footpaths, lost bus drivers, fast tides, quicksand and enormous quantities of mud, but also experiences wonderfully scenic journeys by road, rail and on foot. He contrasts the friendly welcome from most islanders and owners with the reluctance of others to permit visits, and tells how he was thrown off one secret island.

An entertaining narrative illustrated with colour photographs, No Boat Required contains a wealth of information as the author unearths many little-known facts and stories. It tells of the solitude of the many remote islands and the difficulties of balancing the needs of people and wildlife. We learn of the islands' varied histories – stories of pirates, smugglers, murder and ghosts, of battles with Vikings, an island claimed by punks and another with its own king. He writes of the beauty of the islands and our coast, and reflects on how these may be affected by climate change.

In No Boat Required Peter Caton takes us to explore islands, some familiar but most which few of us know exist and even fewer have visited. He finds that our tidal islands are special places, many with fascinating and amusing stories and each one of them different. It adds up to a unique journey around Britain.

£12.99 344pp ISBN 9781848767010 **Published by Matador**

ALSO BY PETER CATON

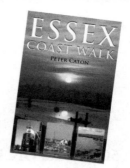

ESSEX COAST WALK

When Peter Caton set out to walk the Essex coast he had no idea of the beauty, wildlife and stories that he would find on the way. He takes the reader up and down the many creeks and estuaries of the longest coastline of any English county, through nature reserves, seaside resorts, unspoilt villages, sailing centres and alongside industry past and present. On the way we read of tales of witchcraft, ghosts, smuggling, bigamy and incest. We learn of the county's varied history – stories of battles with Vikings, of invading Romans bringing elephants, a fort where the only casualty occurred in a cricket match, burning Zeppelins and of Jack the Ripper.

Whilst an entertaining narrative, not a guidebook, Essex Coast Walk contains a wealth of information, including many little-known facts and stories. With gentle humour to match the coastline's gentle beauty, and illustrated with photographs and maps, the book makes for easy reading.

The book highlights how climate change may alter our coast and looks at new methods of coping with rising sea levels. It tells us how tiny settlements grew into large holiday resorts and how other villages have remained as unspoilt and isolated communities. The author's thought provoking final reflections consider how the coast has changed over the centuries and what its future may be.

Written in an accessible style, Essex Coast Walk has been enjoyed not only by those living in the county, but by others who have been surprised to read of the beauty and history of this little-known part of our coast.

£9.99 376 PAGES ISBN 9781848761162 **Published by Matador,** reprinted & updated 2016

ALSO BY PETER CATON

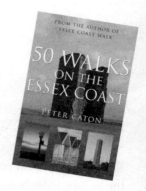

50 WALKS ON THE
ESSEX COAST

A walking guide describing 50 walks along the Essex coast, the longest coastline of any English county. Peter Caton discovered the wonderful Essex coastline as he narrated his journey along its whole length, writing ESSEX COAST WALK.

He now describes walks covering the entire publicly accessible coast, helping others to follow in his footsteps. Detailed route instructions are provided, along with high-quality maps, while background information and colour photos add context and interest. Following rivers, creeks and open sea, on paths, tracks and promenades, often with circuits completed across countryside, the walking and views are varied. There is much history and wildlife to be seen as the walker discovers picturesque villages, smugglers' haunts, nature reserves and little-known gems along the coast.

Walks range from 2 to 15 miles, with most having different length options, plus the possibility of linking adjoining routes. Produced in full colour, 50 WALKS ON THE ESSEX COAST is an invitation for serious ramblers, or those looking for just an afternoon stroll, to discover the hidden magic of the Essex coast.

£9.99 200pp ISBN 9781785892578 **Published by Matador**

ALSO BY PETER CATON

SUFFOLK COAST WALK

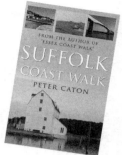

Combining travel writing with a walking guide,
Suffolk Coast Walk provides a wonderful insight into this fascinating
county and is the companion book to Essex Coast Walk by the same author.

Peter Caton explores all 162 miles of Suffolk's unique coastline, describing the route for fellow walkers, with an engaging narrative that tells of the beauty, history and wildlife of this mysterious and varied coast.

The reader is taken up and down Suffolk's remote creeks and rivers, past sandy beaches and huge expanses of shingle, through nature reserves, seaside resorts and tiny villages. We learn of the county's abundant wildlife, not just through its famous bird populations but also of equally interesting and less celebrated creatures, and how habitats are managed to balance the needs of nature and mankind.

Throughout his journey, Peter uncovers many mysteries and considers the stories behind legends of Anne Boleyn, invading Germans, a half-man half-fish character, UFOs, Crazy Mary and bells tolling beneath the sea. He visits Suffolk's only island and takes a boat trip to investigate the secret world of Orford Ness.

More than 100 colour and black & white photos illustrate the story of the walk and the beauty and atmosphere of the county's remarkable coast. With maps at the start of each chapter, this is a book for those who enjoy a short stroll, a longer ramble or simply wish to follow the coast from the comfort of an armchair.

£9.99 272pp ISBN 9781784620967 **Published by Matador**

ALSO BY PETER CATON

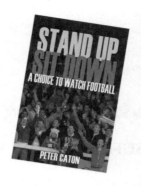

STAND UP SIT DOWN
A CHOICE TO WATCH
FOOTBALL

For a hundred years most supporters watched football from terraces, a culture that was an integral part of the game. By the 1980s though, neglected stadia, hooliganism and a lack of concern for safety meant that football had to change, and after 96 Liverpool fans tragically died at Hillsborough, Lord Taylor's report recommended that our grounds should be all-seated. Many people however believe that something of the soul has been taken away from watching football and that standing is the natural way to feel part of the game.

In Stand Up Sit Down Peter Caton considers the arguments for and against the choice to stand to watch football. He visits the 23 English grounds that still have terraces, seeking the views of clubs and supporters, travels to Yorkshire to watch rugby league and to Germany to stand on a convertible terrace.

With extensively researched background, the author analyses the disasters and hooliganism that led to all-seating, and the many changes that have occurred in the game. He considers various solutions proposed to allow standing, and highlights obstacles facing those backing the choice to stand. His own experiences of watching football at all levels add insight and interest. The book ends by asking its own questions and with a whiff of conspiracy.

Illustrated with colour photographs, Stand Up Sit Down is a fascinating read, which unearths some surprising facts and raises many controversial issues relevant to all who love football.

£9.99 320pp ISBN 9781780881775 **Published by Matador**